Human Resource Leadership for Effective Schools, Fifth Edition

by JOHN SEYFARTH

QUICK GUIDE TO THE TEXT

Emphasizing the relationship of school human resource management to positive outcomes for student learning, this book is driven by recent research and offers real applications throughout.

UNIQUE FEATURES

- Clearly connects human resource management decisions to student learning and achievement to illustrate how critical this function is to schools.

- Contains case studies to give students a detailed picture of various personnel problems. **Thirty new case studies** on topics such as No Child Left Behind, teacher recruitment and selection, reductions in force, professional development, and teacher dismissal focus on recent developments in the field.

- Describes alternative forms of collective bargaining used in school districts to avoid the adversarial approach of the industrial model of collective bargaining.

- **Suggested Activities** near the ends of chapters provide opportunities for students to process and apply concepts discussed in the chapter.

- Annotated lists of **Online Resources** at the end of each chapter provide quick access to supplemental material.

- An **Instructor's Manual** is available online to adopters by contacting your local Allyn & Bacon representative.

From watching actual classroom video footage of teachers and students interacting to building standards-based lessons and web-based portfolios . . . from a robust resource library of the "What Every Teacher Should Know About" series to complete instruction on writing an effective research paper . . . **MyLabSchool** brings together an amazing collection of resources for future teachers. This website gives you a wealth of videos, print and simulated cases, career advice, and much more.

Use **MyLabSchool** with this Allyn and Bacon Education text, and you will have everything you need to succeed in your course. Assignment IDs have also been incorporated into many Allyn and Bacon Education texts to link to the online material in **MyLabSchool** . . . connecting the teachers of tomorrow to the information they need today.

VISIT www.mylabschool.com to learn more about this invaluable resource and Take a Tour!

Here's what you'll find in

VideoLab ▶

Access hundreds of video clips of actual classroom situations from a variety of grade levels and school settings. These 3- to 5-minute closed-captioned video clips illustrate real teacher–student interaction, and are organized both topically *and* by discipline. Students can test their knowledge of classroom concepts with integrated observation questions.

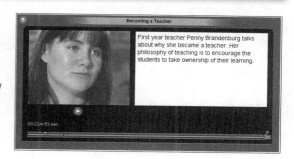

◀ Lesson & Portfolio Builder

This feature enables students to create, maintain, update, and share online portfolios and standards-based lesson plans. The Lesson Planner walks students, step-by-step, through the process of creating a complete lesson plan, including verifiable objectives, assessments, and related state standards. Upon completion, the lesson plan can be printed, saved, e-mailed, or uploaded to a website.

Here's what you'll find in (mylabschool™

Where the classroom comes to life!

Simulations ▶

This area of MyLabSchool contains interactive tools designed to better prepare future teachers to provide an appropriate education to students with special needs. To achieve this goal, the IRIS (IDEA and Research for Inclusive Settings) Center at Vanderbilt University has created course enhancement materials. These resources include online interactive modules, case study units, information briefs, student activities, an online dictionary, and a searchable directory of disability-related web sites.

◀ Resource Library

MyLabSchool includes a collection of PDF files on crucial and timely topics within education. Each topic is applicable to any education class, and these documents are ideal resources to prepare students for the challenges they will face in the classroom. This resource can be used to reinforce a central topic of the course, or to enhance coverage of a topic you need to explore in more depth.

Research Navigator ▶

This comprehensive research tool gives users access to four exclusive databases of authoritative and reliable source material. It offers a comprehensive, step-by-step walk-through of the research process. In addition, students can view sample research papers and consult guidelines on how to prepare endnotes and bibliographies. The latest release also features a new bibliography-maker program—AutoCite.

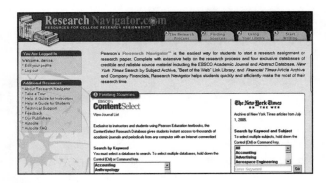

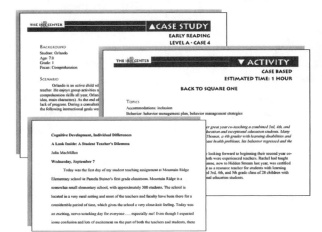

◀ Case Archive

This collection of print and simulated cases can be easily accessed by topic and subject area, and can be integrated into your course. The cases are drawn from Allyn & Bacon's best-selling books, and represent the complete range of disciplines and student ages. It's an ideal way to consider and react to real classroom scenarios. The possibilities for using these high-quality cases within the course are endless.

FIFTH EDITION

Human Resource Leadership for Effective Schools

John Seyfarth

Virginia Commonwealth University

PEARSON
and

Boston ■ New York ■ San Francisco
Mexico City ■ Montreal ■ Toronto ■ London ■ Madrid ■ Munich ■ Paris
Hong Kong ■ Singapore ■ Tokyo ■ Cape Town ■ Sydney

Senior Editor: Arnis E. Burvikovs
Editorial Assistant: Erin Reilly
Marketing Manager: Erica DeLuca
Production Editor: Gregory Erb
Editorial Production Service: Omegatype Typography, Inc.
Composition Buyer: Linda Cox
Manufacturing Buyer: Linda Morris
Electronic Composition: Omegatype Typography, Inc.
Cover Administrator: Kristina Mose-Libon

For related titles and support materials, visit our online catalog at www.ablongman.com.

Between the time website information is gathered and then published, it is not unusual for some sites to have closed. Also, the transcription of URLs can result in typographical errors. The publisher would appreciate notification where these errors occur so that they may be corrected in subsequent editions.

ISBN-10: 0-205-49929-5
ISBN-13: 978-0-205-49929-8

Library of Congress Cataloging-in-Publication Data

Seyfarth, John T.
    Human resource leadership for effective schools / John T. Seyfarth.—5th ed.
        p.   cm.
    Includes bibliographical references and index.
    ISBN 0-205-49929-5
    1. School personnel management—United States. 2. School management and organization—United States. I. Seyfarth, John T. Human resources management for effective schools. II. Title.

    LB2831.5.S46 2008
    371.2'2010973—dc22

                                                        2006052778

Printed in the United States of America

10 9 8 7 6 5 4 3 2 1   RRD-VA   11 10 09 08 07

To Susie and Chuck

CONTENTS

9   Compensation and Rewards   165

PREFACE

The first edition of this book appeared 16 years ago, written with the premise that personnel decisions in schools should be evaluated in terms of their potential impact on student learning. Though hardly revolutionary, that way of thinking did not receive a lot of attention at the time. However, it seems safe to say that has changed. There is general agreement today that decisions about personnel cannot be viewed apart from their effect on what goes on in classrooms. The repercussions of every personnel decision reach beyond the people and events immediately involved, touching other programs, other teachers, other students, and even other schools. We have become aware that every decision administrators make should be viewed for its implications, however small, for instruction.

There have been many changes in the landscape of public schooling since the first edition of this book appeared. Many of those changes have had a part to play in our changing views about student learning. The passage of No Child Left Behind (NCLB) and its implementation in the schools has been one of the most significant events in education in recent years. Some of the effects of that legislation have been positive, others not so positive. Among the positive outcomes:

Parents and the general public now have access to much more information about school performance.

Administrators and teachers have access to data on student performance that they are able to use for spotting and correcting weaknesses in programs.

Increased attention is being given to upgrading the quality of the teaching force and to ensuring that teachers are not assigned to teach out of their subject field.

Among the not-so-positive outcomes:

Test scores have become the single measure by which school quality is judged, eclipsing all other metrics.

School districts are spending much more time than in the past gathering and reporting data to the federal government.

The federal government has become the dominant player in setting educational policy.

With so much attention given to the quality of teachers, little has been done to upgrade the quality of administrators and administrative practices in schools.

Only time will tell whether NCLB will achieve the goal for which it was intended. So far it has had a modest positive effect on student test scores, but recently those gains appear to have leveled off and even, in some cases, have fallen. Some experts believe that further advances in student achievement must await improvements in teachers' working conditions.

The fifth edition of this text has undergone major revisions. It has much new material and even has a new title that reflects current terminology. In response to reviewers' comments, **more case studies have been added**. Every chapter except the first now has case studies related to the content of the chapter. To make room for the additional case studies, two chapters were merged, resulting in one less chapter than the fourth edition. Popular features such as Plan of the Chapter, Summary, Suggested Activities, and Online Resources have been updated. This edition makes **more use of the Internet**, which has matured into a source of current and useful information about human resources practices in schools, including some information that is not available from traditional sources. This edition also correlates to the Educational Leadership Constituent Council (ELCC) Standards when discussing pertinent issues such as personnel selection and evaluation.

Supplements to This Text

An **Instructor's Manual** and **Test Items** are available to adopters by contacting your local Allyn & Bacon representative. The Educational Leadership website, **www.ablongman.com/edleadership,** offers a wide range of resources that are useful for students and faculty.

mylabschool is a collection of online tools for your success in this course, on your licensure exams, and in your teaching career. Visit www.mylabschool.com to access the following:

- Video footage of real-life classrooms, with opportunities for you to reflect on the videos and offer your own thoughts and suggestions for applying theory to practice
- An extensive archive of text and multimedia cases that provide valuable perspectives on real classrooms and real teaching challenges
- Allyn & Bacon's Lesson and Portfolio Builder application, which includes an integrated state standards correlation tool
- Research paper assistance using Research Navigator™, which provides access to three exclusive databases of credible and reliable source material: EBSCO's ContentSelect Academic Journal Database, The New York Times Search-by-Subject Archive, and "Best of the Web" Link Library
- Career Center with resources for Praxis exams and licensure preparation, professional portfolio development, and job search and interview techniques

Acknowledgments

I am indebted to the students, colleagues, and practitioners whose experiences and insights I have drawn on for this book. I wish also to thank my reviewers for their thoughtful suggestions. The reviewers for this edition were: Michael Cunningham, Marshall University; Ann Hassenpflug, University of Akron; Ernest Noack, Western New Mexico State University; and Charles Ryan, Wright State University.

John Seyfarth
Richmond, Virginia

Human Resource Leadership for Effective Schools

CHAPTER

1

HUMAN RESOURCES LEADERSHIP AND EFFECTIVE SCHOOLS

Most personnel decisions have either a direct or indirect impact on student learning. When a decision is made to employ a teacher, counselor, or aide, when a new personnel evaluation plan is implemented, when a teacher is dismissed, or when a compensation plan is adopted, there are implications for the quality of instruction. These and other personnel decisions should be made with attention to their potential effect on instruction and student learning.

Unfortunately, many personnel decisions in schools are made for other reasons. Schools can do a better job of recruiting, hiring, inducting, and evaluating teachers. Professional development programs can be improved. More thought can be given to rewarding teachers who improve their knowledge and skills, and additional effort can be made to hire teachers who are fully qualified for the positions they hold. Richard F. Elmore, professor of education at Harvard, wrote, "Human resources is by far the weakest dimension of general management in school systems, but it is potentially the highest value-added management practice" (Gewertz, 2005).

It is the goal of this book to help improve the practice of human resources leadership in schools. Identifying applicants who will turn out to be effective teachers requires considerable knowledge and skill. Those who say "I know a good teacher when I see one" imply that teacher selection is intuitive, when, in fact, predicting which applicants will be successful in the classroom requires a good deal of knowledge and skill, and perhaps even some luck. This book is intended to help current and future administrators become more effective human resources leaders.

PLAN OF THE BOOK

This book covers all aspects of human resources leadership in schools, starting with planning for staffing needs and selecting personnel and progressing to professional development programs, evaluating employee performance, and terminating employees whose performance is not satisfactory.

The book is intended to help practicing and prospective school administrators gain a better understanding of human resources functions, including interviewing, collective bargaining, grievance adjudication, employee evaluation, and reduction-in-force. The following chapters include discussions of the chapter topics, along with activities and case studies designed to increase readers' knowledge and understanding of issues and practices related to that topic. Lists of online resources and references are available at the end of each chapter.

HUMAN RESOURCES LEADERS

All school administrators are, in a sense, human resources leaders because they work with and make decisions about people. School principals daily make important choices about people. They interview and select teachers, provide leadership for the growth and development of those teachers, evaluate their performance, and develop strategies to correct any performance deficiencies they observe.

All of the functions involved in human resources leadership should make a contribution, either directly or indirectly, to student learning. If any function is not currently helping to enhance student knowledge, it should be redesigned in such a way that it will do so.

The key to student academic achievement is the teacher. Good teachers help students learn while they are in their classrooms, but the beneficial effects of good teaching continue after the students have moved on. Researchers have found that children who were taught by a good third-grade teacher continued to show above-average achievement gains in the fourth and fifth grades. The beneficial effects from repeated exposure to effective teachers are compounded. Students who have three strong teachers in a row attain achievement test scores that are 50 percentile points greater on average than the scores of students who are taught by three ineffective teachers in a row (Loeb, 2001). Thus, it is important that school systems set a goal of placing an effective teacher in every classroom, but to ensure that students learn they must do more than simply hire competent personnel. School districts must also ensure that the culture and working conditions in schools support and facilitate teachers' work.

MODEL OF STUDENT LEARNING

Figure 1.1 depicts a model of student learning showing how the human resources leadership functions contribute to student achievement. The heart of the model

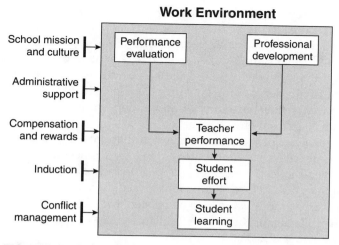

FIGURE 1.1   **Relationship of Human Resources Functions to Student Learning**

is the link between teacher behavior, student effort, and student learning. Two human resources leadership functions (performance evaluation and professional development) act directly to influence teachers' behavior in the classroom. Through professional development teachers learn new methods of teaching and become familiar with new material and technologies. Evaluation provides feedback that helps teachers improve their performance.

Ideally, these activities occur within a work environment that reflects a mission and culture that are characterized by administrative support and by the availability of adequate compensation and rewards, high-quality induction programs, and the use of appropriate conflict-management strategies. When these elements are in place and operating effectively, an environment is created that facilitates teachers' work and enhances student learning.

The search for ways to improve student performance began in earnest in the early 1980s, after the National Commission on Excellence in Education (1983) warned that poor-quality schools were a threat to the nation's security. That warning prompted actions by the federal government and the various states to improve the quality of instruction in American schools. A number of states established standards for student achievement and began requiring standardized tests in core subject areas to track students' progress toward achievement of the new standards. The states also instituted tougher regulations over teacher certification, adopted revised procedures for teacher evaluation, and reduced class sizes in the early grades and in critical subjects such as English. Recent research indicates that these efforts have begun to pay off.

According to data from the National Assessment of Educational Progress (NAEP), student scores in mathematics rose between 2000 and 2003, with 31 percent of fourth-grade students and 27 percent of eighth graders reaching the "proficient" level of performance in 2003, up from the 22 percent of fourth graders and 25 percent of eighth graders who scored at that level three years earlier. In reading, 24 percent of fourth graders attained the proficient level in 2003, the same percentage as in 2002. Twenty-nine percent of eighth graders were proficient in reading in 2003, down from 30 percent one year earlier.

The initial analysis of these data suggested that providing additional instructional resources to teachers had contributed to the improvement in test scores and that implementing even modest increases in support for schools serving children from low-income families also helped. Reductions in class size, especially in prekindergarten and the early grades, were also associated with improved student performance (Grissmer, Flanagan, Kawata, & Williamson, 2000; Manzo & Galley, 2003; Smith, Molnar, & Zahorik, 2003).

Smaller classes and more funding for instructional materials both contribute to teachers' feelings of efficacy, which may account, at least in part, for the observed improvements. The researchers found that providing additional instructional materials to teachers or hiring more teachers in order to reduce class size had a more beneficial effect on achievement than increasing teachers' salaries (Grissmer et al., 2000).

According to some researchers, teachers' salaries have no relationship to student achievement. Hanushek (2001, p. 175) stated "there is virtually no relationship between teacher salaries and student achievement." However, there is agreement that the quality of teachers in low-income and inner-city schools is below that in some suburban localities (Lankford, Loeb, & Wyckoff, 2002). These discrepancies in quality can be addressed by adjusting salaries to compensate for the competitive disadvantages in teacher recruitment experienced by schools with low student achievement.

Resource Allocation

We know very little about how to allocate resources optimally for the improvement of student learning. We do not know, for example, whether using funds to purchase instructional materials results in greater achievement gains than if the same amount were spent on professional development. Nor do we know whether hiring fewer teachers and using the salary savings for instructional aides is a smarter strategy than hiring more teachers to reduce class size.

We also need to learn more about ways of combining resources to achieve synergy. We know that high-quality induction programs help new teachers get off to a good start and lead to improvements in student learning. But can the effect of high-quality induction be enhanced by combining it with intensive, stimulating professional development programs? We don't know the answer to that and many other questions having to do with allocation of resources.

As experiments with new approaches to school improvement have continued, a picture has emerged of ideal practices that should be part of school reform. Thompson (2003) depicted what he called a high-performance school system with eight features that have been shown to contribute to increasing student achievement. The eight are described in the paragraphs that follow.

Standards-based. Challenging standards define what students should know and be able to do at each level.

Clear mission. The high-performance system adopts as its mission enabling all students to meet challenging standards and develops policies and procedures for managing budgets and human resources that contribute to that goal.

School climate. Schools and district offices maintain nurturing, supportive, respectful relationships with students, parents, and others.

Assessment. High-performance districts assess school performance and use the results to provide prompt and targeted assistance to schools that need help.

Professional development. Ongoing, high-quality professional development opportunities designed to help achieve the district mission are provided for all employees in these districts.

Resources. Resources, including personnel, funds, time, and material, are distributed in such a way as to support powerful instructional practices in all schools.

Data collection. Schools are seeking assistance in analyzing, organizing, and interpreting data for the purpose of making program improvements (Lafee, 2002). This process is referred to as data-driven decision making and is defined as the process of selecting, gathering, and analyzing data to identify instructional or student achievement problems and acting on those findings (Streifer, 2002).

Communications. High-performance districts communicate frequently with patrons and other internal and external stakeholders to keep them abreast of the schools' performance and to invite their participation in decisions about school programs.

ORGANIZATIONAL EFFECTIVENESS

Organizations monitor a variety of outcomes to show how effectively their programs are performing. Police departments measure success by the number of citations issued and the percentage of crimes solved; a popular magazine relies on the number of new subscriptions and revenue from advertising to judge its impact; an architectural firm considers the value of the commissions it receives and the number of awards won as indicators of its influence.

Profits are a preferred measure of effectiveness for retail establishments, whereas manufacturers plot productivity trends. Trucking companies track the number and cost of accidents involving their trucks, and colleges, universities, and hospitals rely for approval on accreditation by professional groups.

Outcomes and Governing Philosophies

Public schools in the United States were founded for the purpose of teaching literacy. That mission is still important, but over time schools have acquired a variety of other functions. Today, in addition to teaching literacy and numeracy, the schools are expected to help students learn habits of healthy living, acquire skills to earn a living, and develop understanding and respect for people from other cultural and religious backgrounds. There is always a divergence of opinion about which of these outcomes is most important, and their rankings shift periodically in response to events. After the Russians became the first nation to launch a satellite, Americans heard about the need to improve instruction in science and mathematics, and Congress promptly passed legislation for that purpose.

As public expectations for schools shift, school administration philosophies also change. When schools are charged by parents and policymakers with raising student achievement, administrators focus on efficiency. When inequality in society gains prominence in public debates, administrators look for ways to improve equality. When a mechanistic approach to running schools threatens to overwhelm humanitarian values, administrators espouse a human relations orientation. When schools are charged with mediocrity, administrators focus on improving school quality. These philosophies of school governance are described in the sections that follow.

Efficiency.   Schools review student performance on tests measuring learning gains for prescribed content as indicators of their effectiveness. Test scores are an efficiency measure, and the current emphasis on efficiency is not new to schools. Public schools went through a long period in the early twentieth century during which efficiency was a prominent goal. At that time the new profession of educational administration was charged with the task of preparing schools to accommodate a flood of children from immigrant families. Pressed by rapidly rising school enrollments and limited resources, administrators turned to the corporate world looking for ways to manage crowded and sometimes chaotic schools. From industry they borrowed the ideas and methods of scientific management, which placed high value on efficiency.

Leaders who value efficiency look for straightforward measures of organizational output and seek ways to achieve the best results at the lowest cost. Efficiency continued as an emphasis in schools until the emergence of the human relations movement during the 1930s.

Human Relations. The human relations movement was in part a backlash against the impersonality of a managerial philosophy based solely on efficiency. Researchers found that when workers were invited to offer ideas on increasing productivity, output rose. No matter what suggestions they offered the result was the same—productivity seemed to benefit when their ideas were adopted. Ultimately, the researchers decided that it was not the changes in the way the work was performed that made the difference in productivity but the fact that workers were asked for their opinions.

The movement that grew out of these findings emphasized open lines of communication between managers and workers and advocated worker participation in work-related decisions. Most teachers expect to have a voice in decisions about their work, so worker participation was not a radical new concept in schools. Teachers held strong views about teaching, and most were willing to share them. So the human relations movement had less of an impact in schools than in other settings.

Equality. Equality came into prominence with the U.S. Supreme Court's decision that segregated schools violated the constitutional rights of minorities (*Brown* v. *Board of Education of Topeka*, 1954, 1955). Interest in equality of educational opportunity broadened during the 1970s to include not only racial minorities but also females and students with mental and physical disabilities. The Education for All Handicapped Children Act mandated far-reaching changes in programs serving students with disabilities. It also required expansion of services and added safeguards to protect procedural rights of these students.

Quality. The quality of school programs is an issue that surfaces periodically, often in connection with national crises. The National Commission on Excellence in Education (1983) aroused the nation's concern when it declared that the United States was threatened by a rising tide of mediocrity as a result of the deteriorating quality of education. The commission's report was the best known of many such studies at that time that sounded similar themes.

These concerns led to an energetic effort to identify through research teaching techniques that would lead to reliable increases in student achievement. The idea was to identify instructional methods used by successful teachers that other teachers could then adopt and that would lead to steady gains in learning. This research went by the name of process-product research, and it was aimed at identifying teaching strategies that seemed to work equally well in all subjects and with children of all ages.

Although process-product research enhanced our understanding of some of the factors that contribute to student achievement and disproved the claim that schools made no difference and that student achievement was solely attributable to students' IQ and family factors, it nevertheless left many questions unanswered. Most of the research was carried out in urban elementary schools, and it was not clear if similar results would have been obtained had the studies had been conducted in rural areas or in middle or high schools.

Concerns also arose about uncritical acceptance of the findings of the process-product studies. Most of the studies relied on correlational statistics, which show whether two variables are related in some systematic way. For example, a correlation might show whether reducing class size is associated with increased student achievement (a negative correlation) or if lengthening the school day is accompanied by higher achievement (a positive correlation). The problem with this approach is that correlations cannot be used to establish cause and effect. Does reducing class size actually produce increased achievement, or does some unnamed intervening factor lead to the learning gain? Correlational studies cannot answer such questions.

Some critics charged that the definition of *effectiveness* used in the process-product research was too narrow. Typically, process-product studies compared the behavior of teachers whose students attained above-average learning gains with those of teachers whose students had lower or no gains. Learning gains were measured by test scores, while other important outcomes such as good citizenship and demonstrated leadership were ignored.

The hope that process-product research would lead to a prescription for school improvement was not realized. Although the studies identified certain teaching behaviors that had an effect on student learning, the research did not make clear the conditions under which those behaviors were most likely to produce positive results, nor did they show administrators how to help teachers acquire those behaviors. The research was incomplete in that respect.

School-Based Management

Important structural reforms were undertaken in schools in response to the National Commission's (1983) report. School-based management (SBM) was advocated as a way to move instructional decisions closer to the classroom and make school teachers and administrators more accountable. Proponents of SBM argued that personnel at the school level—that is, teachers and principals—were in the best position to know which instructional methods worked with their students. A National Education Association (1991) survey showed that about one-third of all schools had adopted some form of school-based management by the early 1990s. However, that did not prove to be a panacea, and interest in it waned as policymakers continued to seek ways to make school personnel more accountable.

NO CHILD LEFT BEHIND

Accountability meant that the schools tracked student performance and published the results, taking action when necessary to correct problems of low achievement (Raywid, 2002). Schools that achieved exemplary results received no rewards, and those that lagged suffered no penalties. That changed with the passage of the No Child Left Behind (NCLB) legislation, which was signed into law in 2002.

NCLB introduced a new level of accountability in education by requiring schools to administer state-approved tests and analyze the results by student subgroup. It provides penalties for schools that fail to make adequate yearly progress (AYP) in raising achievement scores among all student subgroups.

NCLB provides that Title I schools that do not make AYP for two consecutive years must allow students who choose to do so to transfer to another public school or public charter school in the same district that is not classified as needing improvement. After three years of failing to make AYP, a Title I school must offer supplemental educational services to low-income students after school, during the summer, or on weekends (Renter & Hamilton, 2003).

NCLB also requires that every classroom have a "highly qualified" teacher; the definition of *highly qualified* in the legislation refers to holding a college degree and full teacher certification, along with evidence that the teacher knows the subject he or she teaches. Knowing one's subject does not require a degree in the subject because passing a state-approved test is also acceptable. The states are free to add additional requirements to the definition of *highly qualified*, although it is unlikely many will choose to do so because increasing the requirements will make it more difficult to attract teachers, especially in shortage areas (Walsh, 2003).

NCLB has been the subject of much criticism because of its reliance on standardized tests as the sole indicators of student performance and, hence, of school success. One of the most frequent complaints about the use of standardized tests for accountability purposes is that this use leads to an overemphasis on raising test scores and results in a narrowed curriculum. Koretz (2002) had that charge, among others, in mind when he wrote that

> overly simplistic reliance on achievement tests in accountability systems can produce perverse incentives and seriously inflated estimates of gains in student performance (p. 753).

The "perverse incentives" Koretz (2002) refers to include the temptation for teachers to "teach to the test," which can have the effect of producing impressive-appearing gains in test scores even though students' actual understanding of the domain of knowledge on which they were tested has improved little. When teachers teach to the test, they spend a disproportionate amount of time on tested content and neglect other subject matter. Indeed, Koretz cited research from Kentucky showing that fourth-grade teachers in that state, whose students were tested on science, spent more time teaching that subject and less time teaching mathematics, whereas in the fifth grade, where students were tested on mathematics and not science, the opposite effect occurred.

Critics of the use of standardized test results for accountability charge that, in addition to narrowing the curriculum, the practice diverts time from instruction to allow time to prepare students to take the tests and creates dilemmas for teachers arising from feelings of incompetence, anger, and, in some cases, guilt (Leithwood, 2001).

The use of test scores as the sole indicator of school performance is also criticized for neglecting a wide range of other types of student knowledge, skills, and dispositions that are equal in value to the skills measured by standardized tests. Some educators have expressed concern that the attention to accountability and reliance on student achievement data in assessing schools' performance is forcing schools to neglect other equally important student outcomes, including the socioemotional aspects of children's development (Allen, 2003).

Sirotnik (2002) noted that parents "demand . . . that future citizens develop intellectually well beyond 'the basics'" and identified some of the performances that are neglected by the accountability system mandated by NCLB.

> A responsible accountability system will include many forms of assessment that tap directly into the actual performances that students are expected to demonstrate, [including] reading, writing, speaking, problem solving, experimenting, inquiring, creating, persisting, deliberating, [and] collaborating . . . (p. 666).

One effect of NCLB has been to substantially increase the amount of information about school performance available to parents and the general public. Most states now maintain websites with extensive information about student achievement in the schools. Three examples of such sites are described here.

Texas. Texas reports results of students' performance on the Academic Excellence Indicator System by state and district average; school mean; and ethnic group mean for reading, math, writing, and science for grades 3 through 11. Every school also receives an overall grade (www.tea.state.tx.us/cgi/sas/broker).

Michigan. The Michigan School Report Card publishes average yearly progress (AYP) scores in language arts and math on the Michigan Educational Assessment Program for all schools in the state. Each school also receives a composite grade (https://oeaa.state.mi.us/ayp).

Florida. Florida's School Accountability Report carries the percentage of students meeting high standards in reading, math, and writing and the percentage of students who made gains in reading and math. That site also shows the percentage of students in the lowest quintile who made gains and shows the performance of students on free or reduced lunch and the percentage of minority students in each school (http://schoolgrades.fldoe.org).

SUMMARY

Sound human resources leadership has a direct impact on schools' instructional effectiveness. Correct decisions about teacher selection, induction, evaluation, and growth and development can contribute to improved student achievement. A respected scholar described human resources leadership as the weakest dimension of school administration but one with the potential for a substantial value-added return. Issues that have held the attention of administrators have varied over time in response to public concerns and the prevailing political and economic climate in the country. Efficiency was a focus of school administration early in the twentieth century, followed a few years later by a human relations emphasis, and, beginning in midcentury, by attention to equality and quality. Currently the emphasis is back on efficiency, with particular attention paid to accountability, following mandates in the No Child Left Behind legislation.

ONLINE RESOURCES

American Association of School Administrators (www.aasa.org)

> AASA is an organization for school superintendents. Click on the Educational Issues button to locate information about the organization's views of No Child Left Behind.

Center on Education Policy (www.ctredpol.org)

> Click on the Index of Topics button and then on Teachers to access a policy brief entitled "What School Districts Are Doing to Improve Teacher Quality in High Need Schools."

Education Trust (www2.edtrust.org/edtrust)

> This site has access to a report entitled "How Poor and Minority Students Are Shortchanged on Teacher Quality."

Achievement Alliance (www.achievementalliance.org)

> This organization has a more positive view of No Child Left Behind than most professional education organizations. The site proclaims, "We believe No Child Left Behind is the nation's best hope for raising academic performance of all students."

Center for the Study of Teaching at the University of Washington (www.ctpweb.org)

> This center has published several reports on school reform, including one entitled "Support for Teachers' Work in the Context of State Reform" and another entitled "Teacher Retention and Mobility."

REFERENCES

Allen, R. (2003, November). Building school culture in an age of accountability. *ASCD Education Update, 45*, 1, 3, 7–8.

Brown v. Board of Education of Topeka, 347 U.S. 483 (1954).

Brown v. Board of Education of Topeka, 349 U.S. 294 (1955).

Gewertz, C. (2005, August 10). Staff investment pays dividends in Maryland district. *Education Week,* pp. 1, 16.

Grissmer, D., Flanagan, A., Kawata, J., & Williamson, S. (2000). *Improving student achievement.* Santa Monica, CA: Rand.

Hanushek, E. A. (2001). The truth about teacher salaries and student achievement. In W. M. Evers, L. T. Izumi, and P. A. Riley (Eds.), *School reform: The critical issues* (pp. 174–176). Stanford, CA: Hoover Institution Press.

Koretz, D. M. (2002, Fall). Limitations in the use of achievement tests as measures of educators' productivity. *Journal of Human Resources, 37,* 752–777.

Lafee, S. (2002, December). Data-driven districts. *School Administrator, 59*(11), 6–7, 9–10, 12, 14–15.

Lankford, H., Loeb, S., & Wyckoff, J. (2002, Spring). Teacher sorting and the plight of urban schools: A descriptive analysis. *Educational Evaluation and Policy Analysis, 24*(1), 37–62.

Leithwood, K. (2001). School leadership and educational accountability: Toward a distributed perspective. In T. J. Kowalski and G. Perreault (Eds.), *21st century challenges for school administrators* (pp. 11–25). Lanham, MD: Scarecrow Press.

Loeb, S. (2001). Teacher quality: Its enhancement and potential for improving pupil achievement. In David H. Monk and Herbert J. Walberg (Eds.), *Improving educational productivity* (pp. 99–114). Greenwich, CT: Information Age.

Manzo, K. K., & Galley, M. (2003, November 19). Math climbs, reading flat on '03 NAEP. *Education Week,* pp. 1, 18.

National Commission on Excellence in Education. (1983). *A nation at risk: The imperative for educational reform.* Washington, DC: U.S. Government Printing Office.

National Education Association. (1991). Site-based decision making: The 1990 NEA census of local associations. Washington, DC: Author.

Raywid, M. A. (2002, February). Accountability: What's worth measuring? *Phi Delta Kappan, 83,* 433–436.

Renter, D. S., & Hamilton, M. (2003, May). First signs of the new accountability. *Principal Leadership, 3,* 10–12.

Sirotnik, K. A. (2002, May). Promoting responsible accountability in schools and education. *Phi Delta Kappan, 83,* 662–673.

Smith, P., Molnar, A., & Zahorik, J. (2003, September). Class-size reduction: A fresh look at the data. *Educational Leadership, 61,* 72–74.

Streifer, Philip A. (2002). *Using data to make better educational decisions.* Lanham, MD: Scarecrow Press.

Thompson, S. (2003). A high-performance school system. In F. M. Duffy, *Courage, passion, and vision* (pp. 101–112). Lanham, MD: Scarecrow Press.

Walsh, K. (2003, June 4). A blessing in disguise. *Education Week,* pp. 28, 30.

CHAPTER

2

PLANNING FOR STAFFING NEEDS

Schools must compete with other organizations to recruit and retain competent, motivated employees. To ensure that they are able to attract the number and quality of personnel they need in order to be effective, schools must anticipate their future staffing needs and recruit qualified applicants.

PLAN OF THE CHAPTER

The following topics are discussed in this chapter: (1) recruiting teachers, (2) projecting school enrollments, (3) determining staff allocations, (4) a model of the selection process, (5) essential functions, and (6) identifying selection criteria.

RECRUITING TEACHERS

Teacher shortages are a recurring reality that most human resources administrators must face. A recruitment program that operates year after year, during periods of both shortages and abundance, is the best way of avoiding extreme shortages because it is difficult to gear up to recruit teachers during periods of short supply if the effort has languished during the years of plenty.

Maintaining an ample supply of qualified applicants is a primary mission of human resources managers, but, in addition to attracting applicants, school districts must also be prepared to move quickly to obtain commitments from the most highly qualified prospects. Some teacher shortages are created as a result of inefficient hiring practices. The National Commission on Teaching and America's Future concluded, after studying the problem of teacher supply and demand, that some school districts used inefficient and outdated hiring practices and as a result lost the most promising candidates to other districts that acted quickly to make an offer and secure a commitment when an especially strong applicant was interviewed (Darling-Hammond, 2000).

Teacher aides and paraprofessionals are a source of potential teachers. Many individuals in these positions would like to become teachers, and they understand better than most people what teaching entails. By offering paraprofessionals tuition assistance to help offset the cost of obtaining a teaching credential, school districts can create a continuing supply of committed teachers. Some districts encourage paraprofessionals to think of their jobs as stepping stones to teaching positions (Black, 2002).

Because of the difficulty in finding qualified applicants, states and districts have devised innovative ways of recruiting qualified applicants. Massachusetts offers $20,000 signing bonuses paid over four years to teachers who meet certain criteria (National Governors Association, 1999). The South Carolina Teaching Fellows Program was created by the General Assembly of that state in 1999. It provides fellowships for up to 200 high-achieving high school seniors who receive $6,000 per year for up to four years in return for agreeing to teach in the state for a comparable length of time (South Carolina Center for Teacher Recruitment, 2000). The Department of Defense works with school districts in a collaborative "Troops to Teachers" program that provides financial assistance to former military workers and school districts to help prepare defense workers for careers in education (Taylor, 1994).

Determining Need

To determine how many teachers must be hired before the opening of school, planners need to know about how many students will enroll in the schools in the fall and how many of the previous year's teachers will return to the classroom. Because precise enrollment figures are not available until after school starts, planners must rely on estimates for planning purposes. A method for calculating enrollment projections is discussed in the next section. School districts conduct surveys of teachers in the spring, asking whether they plan to leave their jobs before the next school year. Their responses are used to develop preliminary estimates of the number and types of vacancies expected, even though the numbers are subject to change.

The large majority of teachers remain in their jobs from year to year. The National Center for Education Statistics reported that between the 1999–2000 and 2000–2001 school years about 85 percent of public school teachers returned to the school in which they had taught the previous year, whereas about 8 percent changed jobs, either moving to a different school in the same district or to a job in a different district. Slightly more than 7 percent left teaching altogether. Thus, an average district could expect to have to replace between 12 and 15 percent of its teachers each year.

Depending on the makeup of the teaching force, attrition in a given district may be higher or lower than the national average. A district with a large number of teachers nearing retirement age will have high attrition. And a district with a large number of teachers in their twenties and early thirties can also expect above-average turnover because young people are the most mobile segment of the population. Districts in which a majority of teachers are in their forties and fifties usually have low attrition rates.

PROJECTING SCHOOL ENROLLMENTS

Enrollment projections enable administrators to anticipate future enrollments and recruit and hire teachers and other personnel needed to staff the schools, but enrollment projections are only as useful as they are accurate. Underestimating enrollments may mean that class sizes will have to be increased or more teachers hired; overestimating results in more teachers being hired than are needed. Accurately estimating future enrollments requires a good bit of skill as well as luck. The longer the range of a prediction, the greater the possibility for error.

Long-term predictions on school enrollments in the United States made in the early 1960s proved to be far from accurate because those who made them used assumptions that turned out to be faulty. Planners assumed that the birthrate would continue unchanged for the foreseeable future. They failed to anticipate the advancements in birth control that made family planning easier and more practical. As a result, the birthrate dropped and so did school enrollments. Enrollment projections are only as accurate as the assumptions on which they are based.

The National Center for Education Statistics (2005) expects total public school enrollments (PK–12) to rise slightly from the 2002 total of 48.2 million to 48.7 million in 2009 and 49.9 million in 2014. However, enrollments in grades PK–8 in 2009 are projected to drop slightly (34.1 million in 2002, 33.9 million projected in 2009) before rising to 35.7 million in 2014. Secondary (9–12) enrollments are projected to increase to 14.9 million in 2009 from the 2002 total of 14.1 million, dropping to 14.3 million in 2014.

However, national estimates of enrollment are of limited value for planning at the local level. A district's enrollment rises or falls as a result of many factors, some of which are independent of national trends. Thus, it is important for administrators at the district level to be aware of local developments that may affect school enrollments.

Colleges and universities graduate more teachers than are actually needed in some subject areas and too few in others. Because not all graduates who prepare to teach actually enter the profession, data on the number of people who graduate from teacher preparation programs are not an accurate guide to teacher supplies. Recent research has shown that only about 6 out of 10 graduates of teacher preparation programs actually take jobs in the field, and, of those who do enter teaching, between one-third and one-half leave the profession within the first five years (National Governors Association, 1999), although there is debate about how many of those who resign actually transfer to teaching positions in other districts or eventually return to the classroom after a break (Wayne, 2000).

Cohort Survival Method

The method that is used most often to predict future enrollments is called the *cohort survival method*. The word *cohort* originally referred to a division of soldiers in the Roman army. It has since come to mean any group of people who begin a venture together. People who were born in the same year or who were initiated into a college fraternity at the same time are examples of cohorts. For purposes of predicting school enrollments, we consider a cohort to be any group of students who start school together. A cohort may lose members when individuals move away or drop out of school, or gain members when students transfer into a school.

The cohort survival method is based on the assumption that the future will be like the past. For the short term, that is usually a safe assumption. Drastic changes in population do not normally occur within the space of a year or two, nor do people's habits change quickly. However, in school districts near military bases or in communities with industries that are sensitive to economic fluctuations, relatively large variations in enrollment can occur with no advance warning.

The cohort survival method is most accurate in districts in which school enrollments are relatively stable or in which enrollment trends are consistent. The method is less accurate in predicting enrollments for districts with fluctuating enrollments. The accuracy of any prediction diminishes as the distance from the predicted event increases. Predicting enrollments one year in advance is more accurate than predicting enrollments 5 or 10 years ahead. There are two reasons for loss of accuracy over time. Unforeseen events can affect school enrollments, and errors in predicting near-term enrollments compound over time, creating ever-larger distortions.

Persons who calculate enrollment projections for school districts try to limit error to less than 1 percent of actual enrollments. A 1 percent error rate means that for a projection of 1,000 students, the actual enrollment will fall between 990 and 1,010, and that for a projection of 10,000 students, the actual enrollment will fall between 9,900 and 10,100. For small errors, districts are usually able to accommodate the difference by increasing (or decreasing) class sizes slightly or hiring an additional teacher or two. However, larger errors have more significant repercussions.

If enrollments exceed the projection by only 100 students, a district may have to employ several additional teachers and locate space for that many more classes. If projections call for more students than actually enroll, the district may be responsible for paying salaries for some teachers who are not needed.

Most districts that use cohort survival analysis prepare separate projections for each school and then combine them to obtain a district total. Because most districts now maintain automated enrollment data, it is fairly simple to carry out the necessary calculations at the district office. The results are usually reviewed by principals, who are sometimes aware of impending events, such as a plant closing or construction of a new subdivision, that will affect their schools' enrollments. With this information, adjustments are made and the final predictions prepared. Projecting an accurate district total is somewhat easier than predicting correct enrollments for individual schools because district enrollments are generally more stable.

Projecting First-Grade Enrollment

In preparing enrollment projections for kindergarten, data on the number of births five years earlier are used. In the example shown in Table 2.1, projections over a five-year period in a district with increasing enrollments are averaged to obtain the mean enrollment ratio. In actual practice, enrollment figures for 10 years or even

TABLE 2.1 Kindergarten Enrollment Projections for a District with Growing Enrollments

YEAR OF BIRTH	LIVE BIRTHS	STARTED KINDERGARTEN	ENROLLED	ENROLLMENT RATIO
1996	2,073	2001	2,019	.9740
1997	2,097	2002	2,044	.9747
1998	2,105	2003	2,069	.9829
1999	2,118	2004	2,093	.9882
2000	2,121	2005	2,136	1.0071
2001	2,206	2006		

Step 1. Divide the enrollment (Column 4) by the number of live births five years earlier (Column 2) to obtain the enrollment ratio (Column 5). A ratio greater than 1.00 means that the number of kindergarten students exceeded the number of children born five years earlier.

Step 2. Add the enrollment ratios and divide by 5 to obtain the mean enrollment ratio.

Step 3. Multiply the number of live births in 2001 by the mean enrollment ratio to obtain the projected 2006 enrollment.

more are used in the calculations. Using more years produces more reliable estimates (Schellenberg & Stephens, 1987).

Retention Ratios

To project enrollments for grades 2 through 12, a retention ratio is calculated by dividing each year's enrollment at a given grade level by the previous year's enrollment at the next lower grade level. This procedure is repeated for each of five years prior to the current year. A mean retention ratio is obtained, and the mean is multiplied by the current year's enrollment in the next lower grade level to obtain the enrollment projection for the upcoming year. This procedure is illustrated in Table 2.2, using hypothetical data to project enrollments in grade 7 for a district with decreasing enrollments. When projected enrollments are obtained for all grades, they are added to the kindergarten projections to obtain the projected districtwide total enrollment.

When enrollment trends are evident, allowance should be made by adjusting the projection either up or down. If the enrollment ratio has increased each year for the previous five years, there is a good chance that it will continue to increase (although perhaps at a declining rate), and using the average for the previous five years will underestimate the enrollment. However, if the trend shows a decline over a five-year period, the enrollment ratio is likely to overestimate enrollments. Depending on the direction and magnitude of the trend, an adjustment of the final enrollment figure may be needed.

Most administrators prefer to underestimate rather than to overestimate enrollments because the potential cost to the district is smaller in the case of underestimates. Enrollments that exceed projections slightly can often be accommodated by increasing class sizes, but once a teacher has been hired there is no way

TABLE 2.2   Seventh-Grade Enrollment Projection for a District with Falling Enrollments

YEAR	SIXTH-GRADE ENROLLMENT	YEAR	SEVENTH-GRADE ENROLLMENT	RETENTION RATIO
2000	2,964	2001	2,847	.9605
2001	2,496	2002	2,391	.9579
2002	2,473	2003	2,378	.9616
2003	2,280	2004	2,132	.9351
2004	2,144	2005	2,117	.9874
2005	2,057	2006		

Step 1. For a given year divide the seventh-grade enrollment by the previous year's sixth-grade enrollment to obtain that year's retention ratio (Column 5).

Step 2. Find the sum of the five retention ratios and divide by 5 to obtain the mean retention ratio.

Step 3. Multiply the number of students enrolled in grade 6 in 2005 by the mean retention ratio to obtain the projected number of seventh-grade students for 2006.

that the money for his or her salary and benefits can be recaptured (unless a contingency clause has been included in the contract).

A sizable one-time increase or decrease in the retention ratio affects the mean ratio and may bias enrollment estimates. For example, in Table 2.2 the ratio for 2004 (.9351) is lower than the other ratios and is probably an aberration. When it is used to calculate the mean retention ratio, the obtained figure is likely to underestimate actual enrollments. When this happens, an adjustment is made to correct the estimate.

DETERMINING STAFF ALLOCATIONS

School systems rely on enrollment projections to determine how staff resources will be allocated. Teachers, aides, counselors, librarians, and assistant principals are assigned on the basis of the number of students expected to enroll in each school. If the enrollment projections indicate that a school will have an increase in enrollment, a decision must be made whether additional staff are needed and, if so, in which positions or grade levels. Schools that lose students may have to give up positions.

Information about resignations and retirements are taken into account, and a determination is made on the number of employees who must be employed, transferred, or laid off. If additional staff members are needed, action is taken to initiate interviews with qualified applicants.

In recent years school districts have begun to consider other factors, in addition to enrollments, in deciding how to allocate staff resources. Schools with large numbers of children with learning disabilities or children from poor families may receive additional human resources, and some districts have given each school latitude to decide what combination of teachers, administrators, counselors, aides, and technicians it needs.

A MODEL OF THE SELECTION PROCESS

Selecting school personnel involves matching applicants' qualifications to the selection criteria for a given position. To the extent that a good match is achieved, employees will be successful and effective. However, when a district hires an applicant whose qualifications don't match the selection criteria, that person is likely to experience frustration and do low-quality work. Figure 2.1 shows a model of the selection process.

Preparing a Job Description

The first step in the hiring process is to develop a job description for the position to be filled. A standard description consists of these components:

1. Job title
2. Summary description
3. Duties and responsibilities
4. Qualifications
5. Terms of employment

The summary describes the general type of work (e.g., instruction, selling, supervising, negotiating, operating, monitoring, reporting, etc.), identifies the

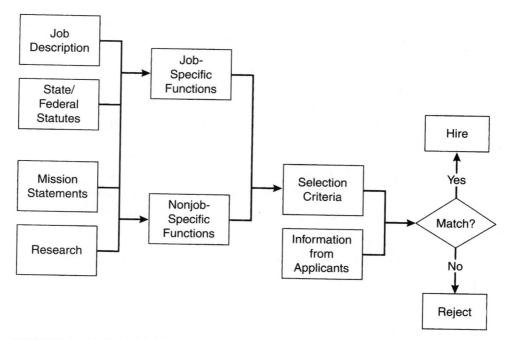

FIGURE 2.1   Model of the Selection Process

employing organization, and indicates the title of the individual to whom the job holder reports. It may also tell whether the job holder works under close or not-so-close supervision, and whether he or she has frequent or infrequent contact with other employees, customers, and outside contacts.

The section headed duties and responsibilities specifies the tasks the job holder performs; tells with whom and for whom the tasks are performed; indicates how frequently the tasks are performed; and identifies the materials, tools, or equipment used on the job.

The qualifications section lists the type and level of education required for the job. It also identifies degrees, licenses, or certifications required; the amount and type of previous work experience expected; personality characteristics desired; and special skills needed.

Terms of employment identifies the job location, unique or unusual working conditions, and the availability of resources or aids. This section may also contain information about salary and fringe benefits, working hours, and the start date for the job. Exhibit 2.1 shows an example of a job description for an elementary school teacher.

EXHIBIT 2.1

JOB DESCRIPTION FOR ELEMENTARY SCHOOL TEACHER

SUMMARY
Full-time position teaching third grade in Fairview Elementary School (enrollment: 540 students in grades K–4). Teacher reports to the principal.

DUTIES AND RESPONSIBILITIES
Establish clear objectives for lessons

Follow district curriculum guide; cover all required content

Instruct students individually and in groups using teaching methods appropriate for the students and the subject

Evaluate students' work and report to parents on student progress

Establish and enforce rules of behavior in the classroom

Collaborate with other third-grade teachers to plan instruction

Serve on committees and perform other duties as directed by the principal

QUALIFICATIONS
BA or MA degree in an appropriate subject with a valid teaching certificate

Three letters of reference

Teaching experience preferred

TERMS OF EMPLOYMENT
School year of 180 days, beginning August 15.

ESSENTIAL FUNCTIONS

The Americans with Disabilities Act (ADA) has brought about changes in the process of selecting employees. The legislation introduced the concept of essential functions, duties associated with a particular job that are critical for success in that job. For a chemistry teacher, an essential function of the job involves planning and presenting instruction considering the students' level of understanding of the material. Equally important, the teacher must establish rules and procedures for handling chemicals safely. That requires the teacher to know which chemicals react when they are mixed together and which ones are toxic or caustic.

For some jobs, the essential functions include physical demands such as bending, climbing, balancing, standing, sitting, lifting, carrying, hearing, seeing, and so on. The ability to use tools or special equipment may also be an essential function. For teachers, the ability to use a computer is essential. To determine whether a task is an essential function, consider the amount of time a worker spends on that task. A school custodian spends a great deal of time sweeping and mopping floors, and both activities are essential functions of the position.

However, even though the time devoted to a task may be small, if serious consequences are likely to ensue when the task is not performed, the task is classified as essential. An example is removing snow from sidewalks around a school. The time spent shoveling snow is not long, except perhaps in states in the snowbelt, but the consequences of not removing snow could be serious if someone slips and falls on a slick sidewalk. Therefore, removing snow is considered an essential task.

Collective bargaining agreements must be consulted in determining essential tasks. If the union contract specifies that custodians will not replace broken windows, that task would not be listed as an essential function of the position.

Consider the position of school counselor. Counselors are expected to provide information and advice to help students choose colleges or make vocational plans. In a particular situation a counselor also might be expected to visit middle schools to counsel students there on the transition to high school. Suppose an applicant for a counseling position were confined to a wheelchair and was not able to travel to middle schools without assistance. Would the district be justified in rejecting that applicant in favor of someone who could travel?

The answer probably depends on whether visiting middle schools is considered an essential function of the job. Because relatively little of the counselor's time is devoted to that task and other people may be available to do it, it is unlikely that the visits would be considered essential.

Changing Expectations

Teachers are hired to help students learn. They are expected to perform other duties as well, including maintaining records of students' attendance and academic accomplishments, serving on curriculum committees, and carrying out various managerial responsibilities. All of these are job-specific criteria, but none is more important than helping students to acquire knowledge, skills, and attitudes of respect for self and others.

Expectations held for teachers have changed in recent years, and the selection criteria for hiring should reflect those changes. Teachers are now expected to cover prescribed content and to help children, including those with learning difficulties, to master that content. They are also expected to help children construct meaning, rather than simply memorize facts. Increasingly, teachers are expected to be familiar with and use instructional technologies (Burnaford & Hobson, 2001).

The Interstate New Teacher Assessment and Support Consortium (INTASC), a collaborative effort involving the Council of Chief State School Officers and other groups, has developed a set of principles that explicitly or implicitly incorporate all of the expectations described in the previous paragraph. These principles constitute useful job-specific criteria for selection of both beginning and experienced teachers. The principles are based on research on teacher effectiveness and relate to the core task of teaching—presenting instruction that leads to student learning— while ignoring less central aspects of the teacher's role. Exhibit 2.2 shows the 10 INTASC principles.

IDENTIFYING SELECTION CRITERIA

Selection criteria identify the attitudes, knowledge, and skills that a school district values in the teachers it hires. Selection criteria are derived from research on effective teaching and from knowledge of the instructional program and of the nature of the school and community in which the vacancy is located. Some criteria, such as an earned college degree in an appropriate field or possession of a valid teaching certificate, are required. Others are preferred but not required. For example, some districts express a preference for a person with previous teaching experience or demonstrated knowledge of a particular curriculum.

The standards developed by INTASC describe the knowledge and skills desirable in beginning teachers, although few beginning teachers possess all of the qualities named in the 10 principles. The principles can also be used to construct generic selection criteria. The following discussion shows how selection criteria can be formulated from several INTASC principles.

Principle 1. A knowledge criterion based on INTASC Principle 1 might read:

Criterion 1. The applicant must have majored in the subject area or earned credit hours equal to a major, with a GPA of B or better in all courses in the field.

A skill criterion based on Principle 1 is:

Criterion 2. The applicant demonstrates the ability to create learning experiences that are meaningful for students.

EXHIBIT 2.2

INTASC PRINCIPLES FOR BEGINNING TEACHERS

Principle 1: Teacher understands the central concepts, tools of inquiry, and structures of the disciplines and creates learning experiences that make subject matter meaningful for students.

Principle 2: Teacher understands how children learn and develop and provides learning opportunities to support their intellectual, social, and personal development.

Principle 3: Teacher understands how students differ in their approaches to learning and creates instructional opportunities that are adapted to diverse learners.

Principle 4: Teacher understands and uses a variety of instructional strategies to encourage students' development of critical thinking, problem solving, and performance skills.

Principle 5: Teacher uses individual and group motivation and behavior to create a learning environment that encourages positive social interaction, active engagement in learning, and self-motivation.

Principle 6: Teacher uses knowledge of effective verbal, nonverbal, and media communication techniques to foster active inquiry, collaboration, and supportive interaction in the classroom.

Principle 7: Teacher plans instruction based on knowledge of subject, students, the community, and curriculum goals.

Principle 8: Teacher understands and uses formal and informal assessment strategies to evaluate and ensure the continuous intellectual, social, and physical development of the learner.

Principle 9: Teacher is a reflective practitioner who continually evaluates the effects of his or her choices and actions on others (students, parents, and other professionals in the learning community) and who actively seeks out opportunities to grow professionally.

Principle 10: Teacher fosters relationships with school colleagues, parents, and agencies in the larger community to support students' learning and well-being.

Source: The Interstate New Teacher Assessment and Support Consortium (INTASC) standards were developed by the Council of Chief State School Officers and member states. Copies may be downloaded from the Council's website at http://www.ccsso.org.

In evaluating an applicant for a position in which Criterion 1 is used, one would need to review the college transcript, but in evaluating whether an applicant can create meaningful learning experiences (Criterion 2), it would be necessary to observe the individual teaching a lesson or to hear from someone, such as a former principal, who had made such an observation. An interviewer might also get at this criterion by asking the applicant, "Can you give me an example of a lesson you taught that made the study of the Great Depression meaningful for your students?"

That question is an example of one that would be used in a behavior description interview (BDI). Such questions ask about past behavior and are better predictors of future performance than more hypothetical questions (Clement, Kistner, & Moran, 2005). A BDI question asks the applicant to explain how he or she performed certain tasks or achieved certain results on a previous job. Such a question is a more reliable indicator of how the person will most likely perform in the job for which he or she is being interviewed than a question such as "How would you teach your students about the Great Depression?" that calls for a hypothetical response.

Principle 2. INTASC Principle 2 also implies both knowledge and skill criteria. In this case the applicant's knowledge is best shown through a demonstration of the skills named in the principle (supporting intellectual, social, and personal development). The criteria might be worded like this:

Criterion 3. The applicant develops a lesson plan that shows he or she understands children's intellectual development.

Criterion 4. The applicant develops a lesson plan that shows he or she understands children's social development.

Criterion 5. The applicant develops a lesson plan that shows he or she understands children's personal development. Instead of developing a lesson plan, the criteria might say, "The applicant teaches a demonstration lesson that shows. . . ."

In many school districts today there is more concern about children's intellectual development than their social and personal development, and for that reason, those districts might decide to use Criterion 3 and ignore the other criteria.

Principle 3. INTASC Principle 3 also deals with both knowledge and skill, and asking an applicant to demonstrate the skill again yields evidence of knowledge, as shown in this example:

Criterion 6. The applicant develops a lesson plan (or teaches a demonstration lesson) that adapts learning opportunities to diverse learners. Criterion 6 might be evaluated by use of a critical incident. That technique is discussed in Chapter 3.

All of the INTASC principles describe knowledge and skills that are important for teachers to possess. However, it is probably not realistic to expect applicants to meet all the criteria that can be generated from the INTASC principles. Those responsible for preparing the criteria for a given position should focus on the qualities that are most important for success.

Exhibit 2.3 contains a sample of selection criteria for teachers based on the INTASC principles. Many educators believe these criteria are important in order for student learning to take place. Some of the criteria in Exhibit 2.3 refer to actions taken in previous jobs. For example, Item 10 (Teacher tells how he/she has worked with

EXHIBIT 2.3

HIGHLY VALUED TEACHER SELECTION CRITERIA (BASED ON INTASC PRINCIPLES)

1. Teacher accepts responsibility for helping all students to learn.
2. Teacher tells how he/she has communicated an affirming belief in all students' abilities to learn.
3. Teacher plans/presents lessons that capture students' interest and actively engage them.
4. Teacher plans/presents lessons that demonstrate extensive knowledge of the subject.
5. Teacher plans/presents lessons that include optional activities for learners with diverse abilities, interests, and backgrounds.
6. Teacher plans/presents lessons that encourage student inquiry and critical thinking.
7. Teacher tells how he/she has encouraged students to show mutual respect and to interact with one another in supportive ways.
8. Teacher reflects on lessons he/she has taught and explains how they might have been improved.
9. Teacher tells how he/she maintains close, supportive, working relationships with colleagues.
10. Teacher tells how he/she has worked with parents to support children's learning.
11. Teacher tells how he/she has used formal and informal assessment strategies to evaluate students.

parents to support children's learning) could be assessed by asking the applicant a BDI question (Give examples from a previous job that show how you involved parents in their children's learning). For a person with no previous teaching experience, the interviewer would reword the question to ask how that might be done.

Items 3–6 in the exhibit use the phrase "plans/presents." To assess those criteria, the applicant might be asked to develop a lesson plan that would meet the criterion or to teach a demonstration lesson that would fulfill it. If there is no opportunity for the applicant to actually plan or present a lesson, the interviewer would ask the applicant how he/she might do that.

Incorporating Mission Statements

Selection criteria should be written with the school's mission in mind. The mission statement identifies the distinctive elements of a school's program and suggests the knowledge, skills, and attitudes that are desirable of teachers in the school. In a school with a mission to prepare students to be good citizens, those who are involved in selection of teachers should look for applicants with an extensive knowledge of our government and of the Constitution.

School mission statements typically do three things: They name the distinctive features of the school's environment, describe the curricular emphasis or instructional processes unique to the school, and list outcomes that the staff hope to achieve. Here's a simple example of a mission statement for an elementary school:

> The mission of Andrews Elementary School is to create a safe, nurturing atmosphere [*environment*] in which students work with outstanding teachers and staff [*process*] to acquire a foundation for lifelong learning [*results*].

Exhibit 2.4 shows examples of these three elements of a mission statement that can be combined in a variety of ways to create new and unique statements. The following mission statements were formed by choosing one or more elements at random from each column of Exhibit 2.4:

> Example 1: The mission of Beaufort Middle School is to maintain a spirit of exploration that motivates students to use the tools of inquiry to make sense of the world around them.

> Example 2: The mission of Columbus High School is to offer a challenging learning climate in which students acquire problem-solving skills that enable them to become active, involved, and productive citizens.

> Example 3: The mission of Delray High School is to offer hands-on learning opportunities to help students acquire the knowledge and skill they need to prepare for successful and fulfilling careers in the food service industry.

The development of a mission statement engages members of the school community in discussions that lead eventually to a statement of common purpose. This process may also bring out strongly held views that highlight differences among members of the community regarding processes and goals. When that happens, there is value in clarifying terms. Many of the words we use carry multiple meanings, yet we often assume without verification that others share our definitions of key terms. In order for a mission statement to serve as a guide to action, members of the community must agree on what it means. One way to do that is through a mission review.

Mission Review. In performing a mission review, the members discuss the wording of the mission statement and examine various interpretations of the phrasing. This can lead to revealing differences in members' interpretations of terms such as *safe environment, lifelong learning, diversity*, and *academic excellence*. Through these discussions, participants explore the various meanings implied by these terms and work toward adoption of definitions that everyone accepts (Lydon, 1999).

When a group reaches consensus on the meanings they wish to assign to terms in the mission statement, the hard work of bringing the mission to fruition begins.

EXHIBIT 2.4

MATRIX OF ELEMENTS FOR CREATING SCHOOL MISSION STATEMENTS

ENVIRONMENT	PROCESS	RESULTS
Safe	Address unique needs of students	Become lifelong learners
Clean	Work with experts	Think critically
Nurturing	Work with students and families	Develop social competence
Enriched	Challenge students	Learn independence
Motivating	Inspire students	Gain academic competence
Friendly	Work together	Learn self-acceptance
Warm	Teach students	Achieve personal success
Welcoming	Help students	Learn important values
Professional	Teach problem-solving skills	Gain knowledge
Open	Educate students	Make wise decisions
Learning	Prepare for a career	Become productive individuals
Supportive		Reach potential
Challenging		Be successful learners
Diverse		Be self-fulfilled individuals
		Become lifelong learners
		Be active, involved citizens
		Succeed in life
		Think critically
		Make responsible choices
		Make wise decisions

A technique that is used to initiate this process is called visioning (Institution for Educational Leadership, n.d.). Visioning involves constructing mental images of a future in which the goals identified in the mission statement have been achieved. An example of a visioning activity that can help school staffs to operationalize selection criteria for new teachers is to think about the attributes of teachers who would help the staff to achieve the results identified in the mission statement.

Visioning also serves another purpose. It enables individuals to imagine a different situation from the one in which they find themselves and encourages them to consider actions that will help to make the vision a reality. By imagining a future that is different from the present, members of the community are prepared to begin the change process.

SUMMARY

Schools must compete with other organizations to recruit and retain competent, motivated employees. Recruiting is an ongoing activity. The process of planning for staffing schools begins with development of enrollment projections and estimates of the number of teachers who will leave to retire or take other jobs. The cohort survival method is the most widely used method for calculating enrollment projections. It is reasonably accurate for short-term projections in school districts where enrollments do not fluctuate markedly from year to year. Teacher selection begins with the development of a job description and selection criteria.

Selection begins with the preparation of a job description, which includes the title, a list of duties and responsibilities, qualifications, and terms of employment. Job descriptions identify the essential functions of a position—that is, the functions for which the position exists. The next step is to identify the selection criteria. Lists of duties such as the standards for teachers prepared by the Interstate New Teacher Assessment and Support Consortium (INTASC) can be drawn upon in writing the selection criteria.

SUGGESTED ACTIVITIES

1. Work in teams to write a job description for a position held by one member of the group. Designate one individual as "resource" and interview that person to obtain information.

2. Write an advertisement for a publication such as *Education Week* using the job description you developed for Question 1.

3. Obtain a job description for a support position (counselor, school psychologist, visiting teacher, etc.). Use it to identify essential functions for the position.

4. For the job you currently hold or one that you have held in the past, list the selection criteria that could be used to choose a replacement for you.

ONLINE RESOURCES

National Commission on Mathematics and Science Teaching for the 21st Century (www.ed.gov/americacounts/glenn)

This site, which contains the report of a citizen's panel headed by former Senator John Glenn, recommends ways of increasing the nation's supply of teachers of mathematics and science. Among other ideas, the panel recommended summer institutes, more financial aid, and better pay for teachers.

National Teacher Recruitment Clearinghouse (www.recruitingteachers.org)

The clearinghouse brings individuals seeking teaching jobs and districts attempting to locate qualified applicants together. It provides links to departments of education and advice to districts on websites for recruiting and retaining teachers.

National Center for Education Statistics (www.nces.ed.gov)

NCES provides a variety of statistical information about public and private schools, including results of surveys on school safety and crime in schools, scores on National Assessment of Educational Progress tests, and a nationwide school locator.

National Institute for Excellence in Teaching (www.talentedteachers.org)

The institute replaces the Teacher Advancement Program, which was sponsored by the Milken Family Foundation. It seeks to help meet the need for talented teachers by accelerating development of comprehensive reforms in schools.

Journal of Research in Rural Education (www.umaine.edu/jrre/19-3.htm)

An article by R. S. Grip ("Projecting Enrollments in Rural Schools") tests the accuracy of the cohort survival method of projecting enrollments for schools with fewer than 600 students. The author concludes that the method is reasonably accurate in the short term.

Occupational Information Network (http://online.onetcenter.org)

This site features detailed job descriptions of most occupations. It was developed by the U.S. Department of Labor in collaboration with a group called the O*Net Consortium.

CASE STUDIES

Case No. 1

Annette Bradley, director of instruction, is talking with Monica Phillips, principal of West Lake High School. They are discussing teaching vacancies at Phillips's school.

MS. PHILLIPS: I've got vacancies in English, history, and PE.

MS. BRADLEY: Have you interviewed anyone yet?

MS. PHILLIPS: Just one person for the English position.

MS. BRADLEY: What about history and PE? We have a couple of strong applicants in history.

MS. PHILLIPS: Actually, I want to get your thoughts about holding off on the history. I really need another counseling position.

MS. BRADLEY: You want to hire a counselor instead of a history teacher?

MS. PHILLIPS: That's right.

MS. BRADLEY: Why?

MS. PHILLIPS: We ought to be sending more of our graduates to college. Last year only 42 percent enrolled and some of those only lasted one semester. Parents of our students—most of them—didn't go to college. They want their kids to go, but some kids are not taking the courses they need in order to get in. I need a counselor to advise students what courses to take, help them find financial aid, things like that.

MS. BRADLEY: What about Betty Wilcox?

MS. PHILLIPS: She does a good job, but she needs help.

MS. BRADLEY: How will you cover history?

MS. PHILLIPS: We can get by if you'll approve a half-time position.

MS. BRADLEY: How did your students do on the history section of the state tests?

MS. PHILLIPS: They could have done better.

MS. BRADLEY: Taking away a teaching position isn't going to help.

MS. PHILLIPS: Actually, I'm only taking half a position.

MS. BRADLEY: I'd like to see your class schedule, with classes and anticipated enrollments. I'll talk with Frank Houser, our pupil personnel person, to see what he thinks. Have you mentioned this to him?

MS. PHILLIPS: Yes. He's all for it.

Questions

1. Ms. Bradley seems to think Ms. Phillips's proposal may be shortsighted. Do you agree? Explain your thinking.
2. If you were the director of instruction, what questions would you have asked that Ms. Bradley did not ask?
3. What is your opinion of shifting a teaching position from one department to another or from an academic subject to a service activity such as counseling? In general, do you believe that allowing schools to make their own decisions about staffing is a good idea?
4. How might Ms. Phillips achieve her goal of increasing college attendance among graduates of West Lake High School without giving up a teaching position?

Case No. 2

Look at the following job description and edit it, taking out any parts that violate the law or that you think are not needed.

Summary. Position—Teacher of first- and second-year English at Mesa High School. The Mesa High School building was recently repainted. The school has 1,500 students, 60 percent white, 30 percent Hispanic, and 5 percent other.

Students on free lunch account for 20 percent. Brian Vermillion is the principal of Mesa High School.

Duties and Responsibilities. Teach five sections of English, serve on school committees, attend department meetings, and sponsor school yearbook or debate team. Coach of debate team must travel with the team to four debates a year. Teacher must maintain a neat, orderly classroom and participate in district professional development programs. Need to follow the district curriculum and prepare students to take State Mastery Tests in April. Assign, collect, and read at least one written assignment each month and return them to students with comments.

Qualifications. Successful applicant must hold a BA in English or English Education and have a valid teaching certificate. Two years of teaching experience, not including student teaching, required. Prefer a young person who is able to establish rapport with ninth- and tenth-grade students. Submit two letters of reference, including one from a former work supervisor. Must be bilingual (English and Spanish).

Terms of Employment. Teachers report August 20. Classes start August 28. Winter holiday: December 20–January 2. Spring break: April 4–14. Free parking, reduced price lunch, health insurance, retirement, other benefits.

REFERENCES

Black, S. (2002, May). Not just helping hands. *American School Board Journal, 189,* 42–44.

Burnaford, G., & Hobson, D. (2001). Responding to reform: Images for teaching in the new millennium. In P. B. Joseph & G. E. Burnaford (Eds.), *Images of schoolteachers in America* (pp. 229–243). Mahwah, NJ: Erlbaum.

Clement, M. C., Kistner, W., & Moran, W. (2005, May). A question of experience. *Principal Leadership, 5,* 58–61.

Darling-Hammond, L. (2000). *Solving the dilemmas of teacher supply, demand, and standards.* New York: National Commission on Teaching & America's Future. (ERIC Document Reproduction Service No. ED463337).

Institute for Educational Leadership. (n.d.). *Visioning.* Retrieved from www.e-lead.org/resources.asp?ResourceID=19.

Lyddon, J. W. (1999). *Strategic planning in smaller nonprofit organizations.* Retrieved from www.wmich.edu/nonprofit/Guide/guide7.htm.

National Center for Education Statistics. (2005). *Projections of education statistics to 2014.* Retrieved from www.nces.ed.gov/programs/projections/app_a1.asp.

National Governors Association. (1999). Teacher supply and demand: Is there a shortage? Retrieved from www.na.org/pubs/issueBriefs/2000/000125Teachers.asp.

Schellenberg, S., & Stephens, C. (1987). *Enrollment projection: Variations on a theme.* Paper presented at the annual meeting of the American Educational Research Association, Washington, DC.

South Carolina Center for Teacher Recruitment. (2000). [Online.] Available: www.scctr.org.

Taylor, T. (1994). *Troops to teachers: Guidelines for teacher educators.* (ERIC Document Reproduction Service No. ED 366591).

Wayne, A. J. (2000, September). Teacher supply and demand: Surprises from primary research. *Education Policy Analysis Archives, 18*(47). Retrieved from epaa.asu.edu/epaa/v8n47.html.

3 EVALUATING AND SELECTING APPLICANTS

The process of selecting school personnel involves assembling information about applicants and evaluating individuals against the selection criteria for a position. The quality of those who are offered jobs is determined by the selection criteria used and the accuracy and comprehensiveness of the information gathered. A well-designed selection process will lead to job offers for high-quality candidates, but whether those offers are accepted depends on other factors. Those factors must be considered if a district is to attract the kinds of teachers and support personnel needed in order to develop a first-class educational program.

PLAN OF THE CHAPTER

This chapter covers the following topics: (1) sources of information about applicants, (2) interviewing for selection, and (3) transfer policies and student learning.

SOURCES OF INFORMATION ABOUT APPLICANTS

There are seven sources of information about applicants. They are the application form, licensure and certification, transcripts, references, test scores, background checks, and interviews. All seven yield information about aspects of an applicant's qualifications. Transcripts and test scores are indicators of academic ability and performance, and references provide insight into an individual's work in other settings. Interview responses add context and help evaluate information obtained from other sources. The value of these information sources varies. References and interview responses are generally regarded as more useful than the other sources, and transcripts and test scores are considered least useful. In making hiring decisions, administrators seek to determine whether an applicant can perform the essential functions of the position for which he or she is being considered.

Application Form

The application form is the basic tool for collecting information about applicants. It is important that the form ask for essential information and that applicants not be asked for information that serves no useful purpose or that might be used for discriminatory purposes. The form should be designed so that human resources personnel can easily determine what position the applicant is applying for and whether he or she is minimally qualified for the job. An example of an application form for the hypothetical Montrose school district is shown in Exhibit 3.1.

Questions that are not related to qualifications for performing a job should not appear on the application form because such information may be used for discriminatory purposes. Districts may ask about conviction of a crime if it pertains to a bona fide occupational qualification or business necessity, but inquiries about an applicant's arrest record should be avoided. Questions dealing with race or ethnic background, religion, sex, or age should not be asked, although that information may be collected anonymously on preemployment inquiry forms. The legal ramifications of requesting this type of information are discussed in more detail in Chapter 11.

Other questions that are likely to be suspect are inquiries related to marital status or name of spouse, maiden name of female applicants, questions about the number and age of children or plans to have children, child care arrangements, organizational memberships, whether an applicant's spouse objects to the applicant's traveling, and whether an applicant is the principal wage earner in the family. Employers are safe in asking if an applicant has commitments that would interfere with regular attendance on the job and, if language fluency is a requirement on the job, whether the applicant is able to read, write, or speak other languages.

Employers may ask if an applicant is over 21 years of age and whether he or she is a citizen of the United States. Noncitizens may be asked if they hold a valid work permit issued by the U.S. Citizenship and Immigration Services. Rather than asking applicants questions about medical conditions, employers are advised to describe the nature of the essential functions required on a job and ask applicants whether they will be able to perform those tasks and what accommodations, if any, they will need in order to perform them.

Licensure and Certification

All states have standards for licensure and certification of teachers. A license is issued when an individual meets requirements imposed by the state, such as completing a preparation program or achieving a minimum score on a test of content knowledge or professional practice. Some states issue new graduates a temporary certificate that is valid for two or three years during which time the individual must perform satisfactorily in order to qualify for a standard certificate.

Certification signifies that an individual qualifies to teach a particular subject or age group. National certification is available through the National Board for Professional Teaching Standards (NBPTS). NBPTS certification is granted to teachers who

EXHIBIT 3.1

APPLICATION FOR EMPLOYMENT

Montrose Public Schools

Position for which you are applying (subject and grade)

First choice _____

Second choice _____

Third choice _____

Name _____ Soc. Sec. No. _____

Address _____ City _____ State _____

Type of license _____ Issuing state _____

Subjects you are licensed to teach

1. _____ 3. _____

2. _____ 4. _____

Educational Background

Degrees	Institution granting	Date	Major

1. _____

2. _____

3. _____

Student Teaching Experience

Date completed _____ School and district _____

Grade and subject _____

College supervisor name and address _____

Cooperating teacher name and address _____

(continued)

EXHIBIT 3.1   CONTINUED

Teaching Experience (list positions, most recent first)

Employer _____

Title _____

Dates (started) _____   (ended) _____

Reason for leaving _____

Supervisor's name and title _____

Employer _____

Title _____

Dates (started) _____   (ended) _____

Reason for leaving _____

Supervisor's name and title _____

Employer _____

Title _____

Dates (started) _____   (ended) _____

Reason for leaving _____

Supervisor's name and title _____

Non-Teaching Work Experience

Employer _____   Address _____

Position _____   Dates employed _____

Supervisor's name and address _____

List student activities you would be willing to sponsor.

_____   _____

_____   _____

EXHIBIT 3.1 CONTINUED

Additional Information

Are you a citizen of the United States? _____

Can you perform all essential functions of the position with or without reasonable accommodation? _____ (If accommodation is needed, explain below.)

Have you ever been suspended, dismissed, nonrenewed, or asked to resign from a position? _____ (If yes, explain below.)

Has your teaching license ever been suspended or revoked? _____ (If yes, explain below.)

Have you ever been convicted of or pled guilty to a misdemeanor or felony (except for a traffic offense)? _____ (If yes, explain below.)

have voluntarily completed a rigorous evaluation of their content knowledge and teaching skill. Board certification is available in about two dozen fields (Berry, 2005a).

Alternative Certification. Forty-four of the 50 states accept some alternative certification plans for teachers. Passport to Teaching, sponsored by the American Board for Certification of Teacher Excellence, is one of the better known of these programs. It is designed to attract career changers and is recognized by five states (Florida, Idaho, New Hampshire, Pennsylvania, and Utah) (www.abcte .org/passport).

The website of the National Center for Alternative Certification lists and describes alternative certification programs by state. (See Online Resources at the end of this chapter.) However, some of what are being called alternative certification programs are actually emergency certificates under a new name. Alternative certification is especially appealing to older people and to members of minority groups, many of whom have limited access to traditional programs.

Troops to Teachers is an alternative certification program for former members of the military. It was established by the Department of Defense in 1994 to help service personnel obtain teaching certificates. Financial aid and job hunting assistance are offered for individuals who agree to teach in high need schools. (See Online Resources.)

An alternative certification program that has received a lot of attention is Teach for America (TFA), which helps place recent college graduates in schools. Once placed, the trainees take courses leading to teaching certificates. In a recent year, about 17,000 new graduates applied for the program, including graduates of Ivy League colleges. The program is selective; only about one out of eight applicants is accepted. Program supporters believe that its value is shown by its ability to attract to teaching people who otherwise might not consider careers in the classroom. Critics argue that the program has limited value because of the high attrition rate (most TFA teachers leave the classroom within two years). Critics also cite research showing that TFA teachers are no more effective in producing student learning gains than those who earn certification in traditional programs (Berry, 2005b).

There is little evidence that teachers who enter the classroom via an alternative route are more or less effective than those who follow a more traditional path. In fact, as critics of teacher certification are fond of pointing out, there is little evidence that certification requirements of any kind are related to teacher effectiveness (Finn & Madigan, 2001). There is some research, however, that shows that teachers with alternative certification have higher attrition rates than teachers from more traditional backgrounds. Because alternative certification programs vary greatly in quality, it seems likely that any statement about these programs would be true of some but not of others. Research is needed to determine what characteristics are found in alternative certification programs that produce teachers who are effective in the classroom and who are likely to remain in the field.

Transcripts

Some districts have attempted to simplify the application process by dropping the requirement that transcripts be submitted with the application. It is important that a transcript be obtained at some point in the selection process, however, in order to verify that the individual has indeed completed an approved course of study and received a college degree. Imposters have succeeded in posing as teachers, ministers, and physicians without holding degrees and, in a few cases, without ever having attended college. An official transcript bearing an embossed seal from the issuing institution is acceptable as valid evidence of an applicant's having attended that institution.

The transcript provides useful information about an applicant's academic achievements and course of study. Although a high grade point average is no guarantee that an applicant will be successful in the classroom, other things being equal, individuals who do well academically in college generally achieve better results with children than those who are average achievers or below.

References

Administrators often discount letters of reference, which tend to be one sided, praising the applicant's positive qualities while avoiding mention of weaknesses.

Some principals are reluctant to put critical comments into writing for fear of legal repercussions, although about one-half of the states have immunity laws that protect administrators against defamation suits. References can be a valuable source of information if handled in the right way. The following pointers will help improve the quality of information obtained from references:

1. Ask applicants to include among their references the names of supervisors on previous jobs. Supervisors can evaluate former employees' knowledge, attitudes, work habits, leadership, initiative, and cooperation.
2. Ask applicants to sign a release form giving permission to contact previous supervisors. Fax a copy of the release form to the reference.
3. Contact references by phone to verify the former employee's dates of employment, job title, and level of responsibility. Ask about the employee's reliability, teaching ability, and relationships with co-workers, administrators, and parents.

Test Scores

All but a handful of states require prospective teachers to take and pass one or more tests of content knowledge and/or professional skills. Some of these tests were developed by the states, but increasingly states are relying on tests prepared by testing companies. The Praxis tests developed by the Educational Testing Service are in use in 42 states (Sack, 2005). Praxis I assesses an individual's basic knowledge, and Praxis II covers knowledge of content fields. Praxis III is designed to be used by trained assessors to observe and rate teachers in four domains: organizing content knowledge, creating an environment for learning, teaching, and teacher professionalism. In some states, new teachers must receive a satisfactory rating on Praxis III in order to receive a two-year provisional certificate; in other states, passing Praxis III is required in order for provisionally certified teachers to receive a standard certificate.

Arizona will soon begin requiring new teachers to demonstrate their teaching skills on videotape. Beginning teachers there are granted a temporary three-year certificate and must prove their proficiency in order to receive extended certification. Connecticut and Indiana have similar programs. The assessment used by Arizona was developed by the National Board for Professional Teaching Standards as part of its program of voluntary teacher certification (Keller, 2005).

Opposition to required testing of prospective teachers has declined in recent years because the quality of the tests has improved and states have broadened testing programs to include more subjects and higher cutoff scores. Teacher unions generally acquiesce in testing prospective teachers but oppose testing of employed teachers. The National Education Association (2000) said that "competency tests must not be used as a condition of employment, license retention, evaluation, placement, ranking, or promotion of licensed teachers."

Background Checks

Before an applicant is hired, an effort should be made to determine whether he or she has a criminal record. Failure to check can be a potentially serious error. Some states now require all applicants for teaching positions to be fingerprinted and to submit to a criminal background check (Abercrombie, 1998). Criminal databanks with information about persons convicted of child abuse, kidnapping, and other violent crimes are now available in most states, and the U.S. Department of Justice, through its National Sex Offender Registry Assistance Program, leads an effort to make information on all sex offenders available to local law-enforcement officials. Also, private firms can be hired to conduct preemployment background checks on applicants, including their criminal history, employment and credit history, drug screenings, and education verification. A list of companies that perform these services can be located on the Internet by entering "employee background" or "employee screening" in a search engine.

However, even the most careful screening program may occasionally fail and allow a criminal to slip through. Administrators need to be alert to information that could signal a possible problem. Omissions and inconsistencies on the application form should be checked out. These are usually oversights, but one should never assume that. Gaps on the employment record should also be investigated. It is better to investigate and find nothing than to hire a person who later turns out to have a criminal record.

Some districts now require applicants to sign an affidavit swearing that they have not engaged in behavior that would preclude them from being hired to work in a school. An example of one such affidavit is shown in Exhibit 3.2.

Highly Qualified

No Child Left Behind requires all teachers of core subjects to be highly qualified. They must hold a bachelor's degree, be fully licensed and certified, and be able to demonstrate knowledge of their subject field. The knowledge requirement can be met by a major in the field or an equivalent number of credits. Current teachers can meet the requirement for knowledge of content without having to return to school or take a test by complying with HOUSSE (High Objective Uniform State Standard of Evaluation) standards. Teachers who teach more than one core subject must meet the "highly qualified" standard in every subject they teach. State plans for meeting the "highly qualified" requirement of NCLB can be reviewed online through the U.S. Department of Education website (www.ed.gov/programs/teacherqual/hqtplans/index.htm).

INTERVIEWING FOR SELECTION

Applicants for a teaching position usually participate in two rounds of interviews—a screening interview and one or more selection interviews. The screening interview eliminates from consideration individuals who do not meet the district's

EXHIBIT 3.2

SAMPLE AFFIDAVIT

I have not at any time pled guilty to or been convicted of any of the acts listed below, and I have never been terminated from a position or threatened with termination for committing any of these acts:

- rape or sexual assault
- drug or alcohol abuse
- sexual harassment
- molesting or sexually exploiting a child
- indecent exposure

Have you ever been accused of any of these actions? _____. If yes, explain below the circumstances and disposition of the charges.

_____

_____

Date _____ Signature _____

Date _____ Witness _____

_____

_____

current needs or who for various reasons are not qualified to teach. This interview is usually conducted by a member of the human resources department. Selection interviews are used to determine which applicant is the best qualified for a specific vacancy. In some schools selection interviews are conducted by a team that includes the principal, one or more teachers, and possibly a parent.

Screening Interview

In the screening interview, the staff member assesses applicants' educational preparation (institutions attended, degrees, major, and grade point average), teaching experience (amount and relevance), beliefs about teaching, and ability to contribute to the instructional program. Some of this information is available on application forms, and the interview allows the questioner to verify or expand on that information and to fill in any missing pieces. If the interviewer concludes that the applicant does not meet the district's standards, the applicant is so informed and the application is set aside. Those who meet the standards and who qualify for one of the open positions are scheduled for a selection interview.

Selection Interview

Members of the interview team assess the applicant's suitability for a specific vacancy. If the position is for a teacher of middle school math, the interviewers will ask about the applicant's experience with children of middle school age and about his or her knowledge of the math curriculum. These interviewers may also return to topics that were touched on in the screening interview, including questions pertaining to the applicant's beliefs about teaching and previous teaching experience.

Questioners at the selection interview try to determine whether an applicant is likely to be a good fit for the school where he or she will be working. They want to know if this person has taught children with similar backgrounds and whether his or her teaching style and philosophy of teaching are compatible with those of other teachers in the department or grade level.

Interviewers also look at applicants' potential contributions to the school and district. An applicant with National Board certification or one who has published professional articles or a book brings recognition and promise to the job that other applicants may lack. Similarly, an applicant who has developed and marketed a series of videotaped mathematics lessons for middle school students has experience that can be of considerable potential value to the district. Questions in the selection interview are generally unstructured or semistructured. This format allows interviewers to evaluate the individual's communication skills and ability to "think on one's feet."

Interview Team.   The composition of the team conducting second-round interviews is important. The most common practice, according to one study, is for principals to conduct second-round interviews alone. In less than half of the districts surveyed did teams include teachers, and parents took part in fewer than 10 percent of the schools (Liu, 2003).

Teams with a broad base of membership have the advantage of bringing additional points of view to the selection process. However, keeping a team interview on track can be a challenge for the leader. It occasionally happens that two team members with divergent opinions on an issue will get into an argument. Thankfully, such disagreements are rare, but other problems unfortunately are fairly common. One problem frequently encountered in group interviews involves irrelevant questions. A team member who asks a question that has already been answered wastes everyone's time. Questions such as "I went to Ohio State too; what years were you there?" are appropriate for helping an applicant to make a connection and feel more at ease, but if they are asked at the wrong time, they can sidetrack the interview. Selection interviews are often tight on time, and questions that don't help the team to make an accurate assessment of an applicant's qualifications can lead to a poor decision.

In order to avoid missing important information, interviewers should be briefed in advance about the areas of inquiry for which they will be responsible, and the interview leader should be prepared to corral any members who digress too much. Every question asked in a selection interview, other than the rapport-building queries in the first few minutes of the session, should be designed to shed light on one of the selection criteria. A question that doesn't have the potential to yield useful information about an applicant may be a waste of time.

An experienced team leader begins the interview process by introducing the applicant and the members of the team. The next few minutes are devoted to comments designed to frame the interview and put the applicant at ease. The bulk of the interview time is saved for questions designed to elicit information that will help the members of the team evaluate the applicant. Those questions may be intermixed with questions for elaboration or clarification of previous answers. A few minutes near the end of the interview should be saved for questions from the applicant.

It is important that the team leader maintain a reasonable pace of questioning and give all the members of the team a chance to speak. Otherwise, as the time grows short, interviewers may be forced to rush their questions or skip some they would like to have asked. It is advisable to let interviewers know in advance about how much time they will have and to call time when they exceed the limit.

Technical Issues

Taking notes during or immediately after an interview can help to avoid confusion. An interviewer who meets a half dozen applicants during a day may find that the details of those conversations become murky as the day wears on. Consider an interviewer who believes that the young woman from Indiana who was applying to teach music had said she hated math when she was a student, but on checking his notes he discovers that that comment actually came from the woman who taught high school English in Tennessee. Most people who have conducted several back-to-back interviews within a few hours have had similar experiences. In the example, attributing the comment to the wrong person would probably have caused no harm, but in other cases misplaced memories can lead to confusion.

Reliability and Validity

Two important qualities of any measuring instrument are reliability and validity. Although these concepts are sometimes confused with one another, they are not the same.

Reliability. Reliability refers to a measure's consistency. If you step on your bathroom scale one morning, you expect the register to show that your weight hasn't changed much from the previous day. If the scale shows a big swing, the scale is probably unreliable. If two interviewers use a standardized interview format to assess an applicant, we expect them to reach similar conclusions. If they disagree—one says "hire her" and the other disagrees—the interview lacks reliability.

Validity.   Validity refers to whether an instrument actually measures what it purports to measure. One would not use a ruler to measure temperature because it's not designed for that purpose and the results would be meaningless. In the same way, using a poorly designed question in an interview can yield meaningless results. Interview questions are meant to elicit information that indicates how an applicant is likely to perform on some specific aspect of a job. If the questions lack validity, they will result in misleading conclusions.

Validity is also affected by the interviewer's mindset. When two people interact, both individuals form impressions that are influenced by their values, beliefs, and biases. To avoid drawing incorrect inferences, interviewers need to be aware of possible biases inherent in the process. Researchers have identified five reactions of interviewers that sometimes color their judgments. They are the contrast effect, the halo effect, negative information bias, confirmation bias, and social merit bias.

> *Contrast effect.* When an interviewer mentally compares an applicant with an individual who was interviewed earlier, the contrast effect takes place. All applicants should be judged solely on the basis of their qualifications. Comparing applicants is likely to result in a poor choice.
>
> *Halo effect.* When an interviewer's overall opinion of an applicant is colored—either negatively or positively—by the answer to one question the halo effect is responsible.
>
> *Negative information bias.* Interviewers tend to attach disproportionate weight to negative information obtained during an interview, with the result that promising applicants may be eliminated from consideration on the basis of fairly inconsequential information. Interviewers can avoid this problem by carefully weighing negative information to determine whether it is important enough to disqualify the applicant. If not, it should be given appropriate consideration.
>
> *Confirmation bias.* Research has shown that information obtained early in the interview has a greater influence on the interviewer's evaluation of the applicant than information that is revealed later. Put another way, interviewers tend to make their up their minds quickly and spend the remainder of the interview seeking to confirm their earlier judgments (Razik & Swanson, 2001). This bias works to the disadvantage of prospects who, because of shyness or social anxiety, are less likely to make positive first impressions.
>
> *Social merit bias.* Human beings are attracted to individuals with certain physical or social qualities. For example, we tend to have a positive impression of people who are tall, good-looking, and well-groomed and react less favorably to those who have physical disabilities or disfiguring conditions or who dress more simply. Because physical appearance has only a slight relationship to the ability to be an effective teacher, it should not be allowed to influence hiring decisions.

Interviews are subject to the same legal scrutiny as written tests but are less likely to be the subject of a legal challenge. Nevertheless, interviewers should be aware that when courts do examine interviewing practices, questioning techniques are often a subject of scrutiny. Questions should be job relevant, and the same questions should be asked of all applicants.

An interview is more likely to yield valid information if the interviewer has had appropriate training. Trained interviewers acquire the ability to put applicants at ease by extending a warm greeting and starting the interview with a joke or small talk. They avoid using words that are likely to arouse defensiveness. They let applicants do most of the talking, and they use body language to show they are interested in what the applicant has to say.

Experienced interviewers are careful to phrase questions in ways that reduce the chance of a socially desirable response. They do that by using open-ended questions or offering alternatives. An interviewer who asks "When you introduce new spelling words, do you ask students to use them in a sentence?" she will probably get a "Yes" answer because the applicant will think that that is the preferred response. A better strategy is to ask an open-ended question such as "How do you introduce new spelling words to your class?" Another possibility is to offer optional answers: "Do you ask students to write sentences or definitions, or something else?"

Observing Body Language

An applicant's answers are the most important source of information in an interview, but there are also other ways to obtain information that can be useful. Body language, including facial expressions, eye contact, posture, animation, eye blinks, throat clearing, and pauses, can yield clues to the individual's state of mind. However, relying too heavily on such impressions can be risky. Consider an interviewer who reacts favorably to an applicant who reminds him of a beloved aunt. If he is not aware of the origin of his feelings, the interviewer may award the applicant a higher rating than her qualifications justify.

Probes.   Probes are questions that ask an applicant to give more information or to clarify a previous answer. Such questions often bring out facts or opinions that were not revealed in the initial response and thus increase the validity of the interview. If an applicant says she thinks homework is a waste of time, an interviewer might probe for more information by rephrasing the comment as a question: "You don't think students learn much from doing homework?" Probes may also be worded as embedded questions, as shown in these examples:

"I'd like to hear more about your thoughts on that subject."
"I'm not sure what you have in mind."
"I hadn't thought about that. Why do you say that?"

Interviewers must be somewhat skeptical in order to be effective because applicants who are eager to make a good impression are likely to be tempted to embellish the truth or omit negative information altogether. Conventional wisdom suggests that a person who is lying will give himself or herself away because of nervousness, but in fact, many people are able to lie without appearing at all nervous to a casual observer. Interviewers must rely on other means of detecting omissions and exaggerations. One such method that trained interviewers use when they suspect lack of truthfulness is to continue asking questions. The more questions an applicant must answer, the more difficult it becomes to continue to conceal the truth (Vrij, 1999).

Designer Interviews

Several researchers have developed interviews for specific purposes. One of these is the Haberman interview. Martin Haberman has developed a screening interview that can be used to identify teachers who are likely to be successful in urban schools. Following are some of the qualities measured by the Haberman interview that are particularly important for teachers in urban schools:

Persistence (refuses to give up on children with behavioral problems)

Survives in bureaucracy (ignores or works around bureaucratic hurdles that discourage some teachers)

Values student learning (makes student learning his or her highest priority)

Comfortable with diversity (able to connect with and teach students from varied backgrounds)

Organization and planning (ability to manage a complex classroom)

The Haberman interview is available online.

Critical Incident Interview

Critical incident interviews have been used for selection of police officers, emergency services personnel, forest rangers, software engineers, social workers, and auditors, among others. The technique involves asking a candidate to read a description of a true-to-life event that could happen on a job and to explain how he or she would respond in that situation. A critical incident is an event that could mean the difference between success and failure on the job. An example of a critical incident for a police officer is a situation in which the officer is preparing to handcuff a suspect who suddenly pulls a gun. The police officer must decide instantly what action to take. Failing to take immediate and decisive action could result in the officer's injury or death.

In this type of interview, after an applicant reads the description of an incident, he or she is given a few minutes to think about a response. The applicant is rated on the quality of the answer. In all a person might be asked to respond to three or four such stimulus events in the course of an interview.

When the individual explains what action he or she would take, the interviewer may ask questions for purposes of clarification. In scoring an applicant's response, the interviewer considers whether the applicant uses sound judgment, whether the proposed action solves the problem, and whether the applicant uses all of the relevant information available in the written account. The best critical incidents are those without clear-cut "right" and "wrong" answers, and in which a variety of responses are possible, ranging from some with great merit to others that are not well thought out.

Not all critical incidents involve emergencies, although many do. A good many classroom situations require an immediate decision by a teacher but are not considered emergencies. An example is a child who disagrees with the teacher on a factual issue. The teacher must decide how to respond without being defensive while showing respect for the child's opinion.

Exhibit 3.3 is an example of a critical incident that could be used with an applicant for a job as high school physical education teacher. Read the critical incident and tell what you would look for in a response from someone you were considering for the job before you read further.

A good answer to the question raised by the incident described in Exhibit 3.3 should do two things—clarify the purpose of the team competition and offer support for the girl. The teacher should have discussed the instructional objectives of the lesson before starting the exercise. If she or he did not, then the instructor should do so as soon as Mark voices his complaint. The activity is not meant to see which team can perform best on these tests. It is designed to give everyone an opportunity to engage in fairly strenuous physical activity. If the teacher fails to make that clear at the start, then students' competitive instincts will take over and they will assume that the point is to see which team is best.

EXHIBIT 3.3

CRITICAL INCIDENT: HIGH SCHOOL PE TEACHER

You are teaching high school physical education. Your classes have both boys and girls and range in size from 24 to 36 students. Today, you have organized your first-period class into six teams of six students, each with an equal number of boys and girls. The plan is to have the teams engage in a series of activities that include running, climbing, and sit-ups. One boy, Mark Miller, complains that his team is at a disadvantage because a girl on the team has a deformed foot and cannot run fast. "Put her on somebody's else's team," Mark says. "We don't want her. She'll just make us lose." Several students on the other teams voice similar sentiments. One says, "You keep her. We don't want her."

How will you handle this situation?

The second issue in this situation is to offer support for the girl whom Mark wants off his team. The teacher should reassure the girl that, in spite of what Mark said, she is on the team to stay and that her value to the team is not diminished by her disability. At some point, perhaps immediately, the teacher should lead a discussion on issues of respect and tolerance for those who are different. Mark's comment is hurtful, and the teacher should explain, as gently as possible, that criticizing classmates because of physical limitations is not acceptable. Because Mark was not the only student to criticize the girl, everyone in the class should hear the teacher's remarks.

This incident illustrates a point that teachers sometimes forget: In any class, whether physical education or physics, students are learning about the subject, but they are also learning how to get along with others and how to be helpful rather than critical toward those who are less gifted or less privileged. This critical incident could help a selection committee tell how well an applicant understands that point and acts on that understanding.

An applicant who proposes to move the girl to another team or who suggests that she sit out some of the activities is ignoring the girl's feelings and reinforcing the notion that winning is all-important. An applicant who gave such a response would probably be eliminated from further consideration.

Perceiver Interview

The perceiver interview is a type of structured interview in which standard questions are asked of all applicants. The questions are meant to derive information about applicants' values and philosophy, style of interacting with other people, and ability to analyze problematic situations common in teaching.

Teacher applicants who are interviewed using the perceiver protocol are rated on 12 themes. Among the themes are empathy (acceptance of others' feelings), rapport drive (ability to maintain an approving relationship with each student), and activation (ability to stimulate students to think, to feel, and to learn). Interviewees are also rated on individualized perception (perceiving students as individuals), input drive (searching for ideas and materials to help students learn), and innovation (trying new ideas and techniques in the classroom). Developers of the perceiver interview believe that applicants who are rated high on the 12 themes are more effective in the classroom. However, a recent study testing that proposition found only a modest relationship between the ratings and teachers' subsequent behavior on the job (Young & Delli, 2002).

Rating the Applicant

Research has shown that note-taking improves an interviewer's ability to recall information about the applicant at a later time. Detailed note-taking can be a distraction, but writing key words and phrases rather than complete statements minimizes the disruptive effect and allows the interviewer to accurately reconstruct

EXHIBIT 3.4
APPLICANT RATING FORM

Name of applicant _____

Rater _____ Date _____

Rate the applicant from 1 (low) to 5 (high) on each item.

	(Circle one)				
1. Educational preparation	1	2	3	4	5
2. Teaching experience—amount	1	2	3	4	5
3. Teaching experience—type and quality	1	2	3	4	5
4. Knowledge of diverse students	1	2	3	4	5
5. Ability to adapt instruction	1	2	3	4	5
6. Using a variety of instructional strategies	1	2	3	4	5
7. Using sound assessment practices	1	2	3	4	5
8. Oral communication	1	2	3	4	5
9. Written communication	1	2	3	4	5
10. Responsiveness to parents	1	2	3	4	5
11. Cooperation with colleagues	1	2	3	4	5
12. Receptiveness to others' ideas	1	2	3	4	5

the interview later. It is common practice to use a checklist or rating scale to evaluate applicants immediately following an interview. An example of a rating scale that can be used for this purpose is shown in Exhibit 3.4.

TRANSFER POLICIES AND STUDENT LEARNING

Employees seek to transfer from one school to another for a number of reasons. Some want to transfer for convenience, whereas others seek to move to schools with better programs, facilities, or equipment. Still others hope to work with particular teachers or administrators or want to be assigned to a school with school-based management.

In many districts an effort is made to act on transfer requests before decisions are made to hire new teachers. This allows teachers who are already employed by the district to have the first choice of vacancies. Such a policy is helpful in sustaining teacher morale, but it can create problems when selection decisions are delayed while employed teachers are given the option to interview for vacancies.

Many teaching vacancies are filled by teachers who transfer from one school to another in the same district. Some teachers transfer voluntarily, whereas others are reassigned as a result of declining enrollments or termination of programs. In districts with union contracts that grant more senior teachers the right to choose a school, the principal of the receiving school has limited control over the selection and may be required to accept a teacher whom he or she would have passed over if given the option. A recent study found that 40 percent of all transferring teachers in the districts examined went to schools in which the principal had, at best, a limited voice in the selection decision. To avoid being forced to take a teacher with a poor performance record, some principals said they delayed reporting teaching vacancies to the district, and some admitted that they would excess a poor performer in order to retain a more effective teacher (Matthews, 2005). The research report is available online at www.tntp.org.

Districts often postpone hiring new teachers until all current staff members have been placed. That practice prevents having to pay salaries to teachers who may not be needed. However, the delay sometimes means that the most desirable applicants are lost to districts that move more quickly. Researchers in one study found that districts that waited until May to offer contracts to new applicants often lost the best prospects (Levin, Mulhern, & Schunck, 2005).

Equity in Transfer Practices

Transfer decisions may cause inequities in the distribution of teacher talent. School districts strive to place effective teachers in all schools, but personnel policies may operate to redistribute talent so that more effective teachers wind up in the same schools. Relying solely on seniority in granting teacher transfers means that experienced teachers are likely to gravitate toward more desirable schools, and the less desirable schools end up with younger, less experienced teachers. Because teachers are likely to be attracted to schools where achievement is high, this maldistribution of talent reinforces existing disparities in student learning.

No Child Left Behind contains a provision that requires state education agencies to take steps to ensure that teacher talent is distributed equitably among schools. This feature of the legislation has received much less attention than the "highly qualified" requirement, but in the long run it could have equally great significance for the quality of instruction. The provision states that children from poor and minority families may not be taught at higher rates than other children by inexperienced, unqualified, or out-of-field teachers (Keller, 2006).

Of course, experience is not necessarily synonymous with ability, and many inexperienced teachers are very capable, but the problem with open transfer policies is that the most able teachers do not remain long in schools that have little to offer in the way of rewards and prestige. In a profession in which there are limited opportunities for vertical mobility, teachers gravitate toward schools with better teaching conditions, reputations for quality programs, or better facilities. This can create a problem for administrators who may be left with no alternative other than staffing less popular schools with beginning teachers.

SUMMARY

There are seven principal sources of information about applicants—the application form, licensure and certification, transcripts, references, test scores, background checks, and interviews. The application form should be designed to show quickly what position is being applied for and whether the applicant meets the minimum qualifications for that job. All states require that teachers be licensed and certified. Most states now accept alternative forms of certification. Praxis III, a test developed by the Educational Testing Service, is used by some states for certification purposes. No Child Left Behind contains a provision that charges state officials with monitoring teacher assignments to ensure that students from poor and minority families receive an equitable share of instruction from experienced teachers. Two types of interviews used in selecting teachers are the screening interview and selection interview.

Screening interviews are conducted by district office staff members in order to eliminate applicants who for various reasons do not fit the district's current personnel needs. Selection interviews are led by a principal, perhaps with assistance from teachers, and are designed to determine whether an applicant is suited for a particular vacancy. An applicant may go through several selection interviews before receiving an offer of employment. Human resources personnel should be aware of potential biases in interviews, including the contrast effect, halo effect, social merit influence, and confirmation bias. Critical incident interviews use written scenarios as the basis for employment interviews. An applicant is shown a description of a problematic situation from the job and asked what action he or she would take. Transfer policies that have the effect of concentrating teacher talent in a few of the most desirable schools are receiving increased scrutiny from parents and policymakers.

SUGGESTED ACTIVITIES

1. Read the following responses to an interviewer's question of two applicants for a seventh-grade teaching position. What do you learn about the applicants from these responses? What follow-up questions might you ask each? Based on this one response, which applicant do you believe would be the better choice?

   Interviewer: What classroom rules do you establish for your students?

   Applicant 1: I assume by the time they reach seventh grade students know the basic rules of behavior, such as not disrupting class, paying attention, not using bad language, turning in homework on time, and so on. When a student breaks one of those rules, I remind him or her about it. The only other rules I have deal with moving throughout the building and taking care of equipment and materials. I go over those the first day of school. When a student breaks a rule, I deduct points from his or her grade. I don't put students on detention because that simply makes more work for me.

Applicant 2: I've found that having a few critical rules that everyone knows makes my job a lot easier. So I set aside some time every day during the first week or two of school to talk about rules. I post the rules and tell students what each rule means and explain why we need it, and I try to answer any questions they may have. I find that this helps because later in the year, if someone gets in trouble for breaking a rule, she or he understands why the rule is important.

2. Which of the following questions would you be likely to ask, and which ones would you avoid when interviewing applicants for a teaching or administrative position? Explain your answers.

   a. Does the applicant have previous teaching experience?
   b. Is the applicant a native-born or naturalized citizen?
   c. Is an applicant willing to work on religious holidays?
   d. Has the applicant ever been arrested?
   e. What is the applicant's sexual orientation?
   f. Does the applicant have a master's degree?
   g. Does the applicant speak a foreign language?

3. Suppose you are the principal of a school and one of your teachers, whose spouse is being transferred to a position in another city, asks you to write a letter of reference. You have misgivings because the teacher is not effective. Discuss your ethical responsibilities in this situation and tell what you would do.

4. Following are some responses given by teacher applicants in response to interview questions. State a probe you might use if you were interviewing this person and wanted more information.

   a. "I try not to sugarcoat the truth when I'm talking with parents. I believe 'honesty is the best policy.' "
   b. "If my students haven't learned the material, I don't see the point of last-minute cramming to try to get them ready for state tests."
   c. "My students were the rowdiest in the school when I arrived. One month after I got there, they were so well-behaved people couldn't believe it."

5. Read the following comments made by an interviewer to a staff member about an applicant and tell which effect is illustrated (halo effect, contrast effect, confirmation bias, negative information bias, or social merit bias).

   a. "When he said that he never flunks students, that did it for me. I immediately rejected him in my mind."
   b. "She was well-dressed and was obviously from a well-to-do family. She would make a great addition to our faculty."
   c. "Susan was a strong applicant, but Lorraine, the teacher from Des Moines that I interviewed yesterday, had a lot more going for her."

ONLINE RESOURCES

National Center for Alternative Certification (www.teach-now.org)

This is a searchable database with information about alternative routes to teacher certification.

Teach for America (www.teachforamerica.org)

This organization places recent college graduates in teaching jobs for two years in underresourced schools in urban areas and some rural locations. Participants receive five weeks of training before starting their assignments.

Troops to Teachers (www.dantes.doded.mil/dantes_web/troopstoteachers/index-test.htm?Flag=True)

The Troops to Teachers program was established in 1994 by the Department of Defense to help ex-military personnel obtain teacher certification.

JobWeb (www.jobweb.com/Resources/Library/Intereviews/Interviewers_92_01.htm)

This site lists favorite interview questions and answers of recruiters for business firms. Examples: What do you see yourself doing in five years? Tell about a time you had to work with someone who was difficult to get along with. Tell how you handled an ethical dilemma.

Teacher Quality Newsletter (www.ccsso.org/content/PDFs/TQI080706.pdf)

This online newsletter is published by the Council of Chief State School Officers and reports actions by schools aimed at recruiting and retaining quality teachers and improving teacher quality.

CASE STUDIES

Case No. 1

Mariah Gladstone, principal of Bailey Road Middle School, needs a mathematics teacher for the new school year starting in two weeks. The human resources department has no applications from qualified persons. Ms. Gladstone is considering the following possibilities:

Joseph Martin, a recently retired mathematics teacher, is willing to teach a half day.

Abby Winston, the wife of a graduate student at a local university, is qualified to teach math, but she can't promise she will be available during the second semester.

By increasing class sizes in the department to 35 students and putting off advanced classes for one year, it will be possible to get by without hiring a teacher.

Craig Norman, biology teacher at Davis High School in the district, is qualified to teach math and would be willing to transfer if someone is available to teach his biology classes. Human resources has a qualified applicant to teach biology, but the principal at Davis does not want to lose Norman.

Renee Crisp, a student at a local university, is preparing to teach math and is willing to take the job at Bailey Road if offered. However, she will not be certified until she takes student teaching in the spring.

Question
1. Rank these options in order, from most to least desirable, as you would recommend them to the superintendent. Be prepared to give reasons for your ranking.

Case No. 2

Alberta Martin has applied for an elementary school teaching position with your school district. She has eight years of experience teaching in another state but has not taught in the past four years. She holds a temporary teaching certificate in your state, and her references, although old, are all favorable. According to the application form, she left her last teaching position in the middle of the school year. Her most recent job was as a cashier at a Target store in another state, a position she held for a year and a half. She moved to your state three months ago.

Questions
1. If you were interviewing Ms. Martin for a position in your district, would you have concerns about hiring her? Explain.
2. Tell what questions you would ask during the interview and how you would assess her answers in order to decide whether to consider her for employment.
3. Who else would you like to contact in evaluating Ms. Martin's application?

Case No. 3

Marilyn House has applied to teach middle school English in your district. A human resources department staff member contacted the principal of the middle school where she taught for five years before moving to your city and reported the following conversation with the former principal:

PRINCIPAL: Is this a confidential conversation?

INTERVIEWER: Yes, it is.

PRINCIPAL: Well, I have to tell you I was personally happy when Ms. House said she was moving. She was a very creative teacher, but she caused me a lot of problems.

INTERVIEWER: Can you tell me about the problems you had with her?

PRINCIPAL: She couldn't get along with other teachers. She claimed the other teachers were jealous of her because she was a better teacher.

INTERVIEWER: Was that true?

PRINCIPAL: It may have been true, but it didn't help that she pointed it out.

INTERVIEWER: Exactly what kinds of problems did she have with other teachers?

PRINCIPAL: All the parents wanted their kids in her room, and that caused hard feelings. She let other teachers know how popular she was, and naturally they resented that. She's not a very diplomatic person.

INTERVIEWER: I take it you would not hire her again?

PRINCIPAL: If she applied to teach here again, I would have a long talk with her and lay out what I expect of her. If she agreed to those terms, I'd probably take her back.

INTERVIEWER: Thank you. You've been very helpful.

PRINCIPAL: Now don't tell Ms. House what I've said. She'd be hopping mad if she found out what I've said.

Questions

1. How would you rate the value of the information provided by the former principal?
2. What action would you take next with regard to Ms. House's application?

Case No. 4

Betty Moreland is applying to teach fifth grade at Madrid Elementary School. Betty completed alternative certification in May. The Madrid principal, Jackie Holland, interviewed Ms. Moreland and rates her "average" but thinks she will probably need more supervision in the first year than most beginning teachers. Ms. Holland must decide whether to offer Ms. Moreland the job or consider two other applicants. Both of those applicants have taught in other districts. One taught fourth grade for three years, and the other taught second grade for one year. Fifth graders must take state achievement tests in March, and Ms. Holland wants a teacher who will have students ready for the tests. Ms. Holland is an experienced principal, and the superintendent says she is noted for helping new teachers get a good start. The superintendent has told her that if she does not hire Ms. Moreland, she will probably be hired to teach at another school in the district where she may not receive as much support.

Questions

1. Suppose you were principal of Madrid Elementary. Would you hire this applicant? Explain your reasons.
2. In deciding which applicant to hire, how much weight would you give to previous experience? If an applicant had taught a different grade, would you give the same or less credit as for experience in the grade for which you are hiring?
3. Would you be influenced in your decision by the superintendent's comment? Explain.

Case No. 5

You are director of human resources for a district with 15 elementary schools. You have become aware that one of the schools (Elm Park) has an unusually large number of teachers who have indicated they will not return to the school next year. The school has had a very low teacher turnover rate in the past. The principal, Charlotte Sterling, is finishing her second year at the school, her first principalship. The superintendent asked you to find out what led to the increased attrition at Elm Park. You met with the principal, who explained that some of the teachers are retiring and that others are leaving for other reasons. She said some of the teachers don't agree with her approach to instruction but that she doubts that has had much effect on teacher turnover. She said that she expects all teachers to use a method she introduced to the school, which had been successful in other similar schools. She told you the method works best when all teachers employ it.

Questions
1. Do you regard high attrition at a school as evidence that a problem exists? What are possible causes of the high teacher turnover at Elm Park? Of those causes, which ones call for corrective action?
2. Tell what actions the superintendent might consider taking to correct the problem at Elm Park School.
3. In gathering information for your report to the superintendent, you will need to talk to people in the district office and in the school. List the people you will talk to and tell what you hope to learn from each.

REFERENCES

Abercrombie, K. (1998, April 29). Right to teach in California denied without prints. *Education Week,* p. 5.

Berry, B. (2005a, December). Recruiting and retaining board-certified teachers for hard-to-staff schools. *Phi Delta Kappan, 87,* 290–297.

Berry. B. (2005b, October 19.) Teacher quality and the question of preparation. *Education Week,* pp. 32, 34.

Finn, C. E., Jr., & Madigan, K. (2001, May). Removing the barriers for teacher candidates. *Educational Leadership, 58,* 29–31, 36.

Keller, B. (2005, October 26). New teachers in Arizona must prove skills via videotape. *Education Week,* p. 27.

Keller, B. (2006, August 30). In every core class, a qualified teacher. *Education Week,* pp. 42–45.

Levin, J., Mulhern, J., & Schunck, J. (2005). Unintended consequences: The case for reforming the staffing rules in urban teachers union contracts. Retrieved from www.tntp.org/newreport.

Liu, E. (2003, April). *New teachers' experiences of hiring: Preliminary findings from a four-state study.* Paper presented at the annual meeting of the American Educational Research Association, Chicago.

Mathews, J. (2005, November 17). Teacher transfer rules hurt schools, study says. *Washington Post,* p. A10.

National Education Association. (2000). NEA 2000–2001 resolutions. Retrieved from www.nea .org/cgi-bin/AT-resolutionssearch.cgi.

Razik, T. A., & Swanson, A. D. (2001). *Fundamental concepts of educational leadership* (2nd ed.). Upper Saddle River, NJ: Prentice-Hall.

Sack, J. (2005, November 9). NCATE approves single cutoff score on teacher tests. *Education Week,* pp. 3, 18.

Vrij, A. (1999). Interviewing to detect deception. In A. Memon & R. Bull (Eds.), *Handbook of the psychology of interviewing* (pp. 317–326). New York: Wiley.

Young, I. P., & Delli, D. A. (2002, December). The validity of the Teacher Perceiver Interview for predicting performance of classroom teachers. *Educational Administration Quarterly, 38,* 586–612.

4 SELECTING ADMINISTRATIVE AND SUPPORT PERSONNEL

Finding qualified candidates to fill vacancies in schools is an ongoing challenge in most districts. This chapter examines the procedures used to fill vacancies in administrative and support positions in schools and describes the duties performed by the individuals who hold those jobs. Finding the right people for these positions is critical in order for schools to run smoothly and offer effective instructional programs.

PLAN OF THE CHAPTER

This chapter covers the following topics: (1) selection procedures, (2) use of tests for selection of administrators, (3) selection of principals and assistant principals, (4) skills of effective leaders, (5) women in administration, and (6) selecting other support personnel.

SELECTION PROCEDURES

Selection procedures for administrative and support personnel are similar to those used in the search for teachers. The steps are as follows:

1. Prepare a job description
2. Announce the vacancy
3. Review applications and eliminate those who do meet the selection criteria
4. Conduct first-round interviews
5. Select finalists and conduct in-depth interviews
6. Make selection
7. Notify applicants

Preparing a Job Description

In preparing a job description, the first step is to carry out an analysis of the position to identify the essential functions performed by the job holder. This information can be obtained from interviews with individuals holding the position, or questionnaires they fill out, observations, or descriptions of vacancies advertised by other districts. Following is a list of duties of elementary school principals derived from advertisements appearing in *Education Week* during May of 2006. The items are grouped according into areas of responsibility.

BUILD PARENT AND COMMUNITY RELATIONS
Create partnerships with parents and community
Maintain an open door policy for parents and staff
Maintain visibility in the school and community

SUPERVISE STAFF
Facilitate meetings and professional development opportunities
Conduct employee performance evaluations
Provide leadership for building relationships

FACILITATE THE INSTRUCTIONAL PROGRAM
Establish a climate conducive to learning
Provide strong educational leadership and a collaborative management style
Manage and analyze student assessments and related data
Develop a shared vision to guide staff and parents in meeting the learning needs of all students

MAINTAIN A SAFE, ORDERLY ENVIRONMENT
Provide consistent, child-friendly discipline skills

Announcing the Vacancy

Most districts announce all administrative, supervisory, or counseling openings to current employees in order to give those who may be interested the opportunity to apply. Some negotiated agreements contain a clause requiring that teachers be notified of administrative and counseling vacancies. An issue of concern to individuals who are interested in moving up is whether vacancies are filled from within the district or from outside. Some school districts have ironclad policies of filling all vacancies from within, whereas others hire the most qualified candidate, regardless of location. Consistently hiring from within the district has the advantage of helping maintain high teacher morale, but it runs the risk of developing inbred thinking. Hiring outsiders often brings fresh thinking into the system.

School districts are recruiting more actively to fill administrative vacancies because the pool of prospective administrators is shrinking. As older principals retire, fewer teachers are applying to fill the vacancies. In one recent survey, 60 percent of superintendents reported that their districts faced a shortage of qualified principal candidates. It is not uncommon for a district to receive fewer than a dozen applications for a principal vacancy; as a result districts that have traditionally filled administrative vacancies from within are being forced to look outside the immediate locality for replacements (Cusick, 2003).

Some districts advertise nationally in publications such as *Education Week* and the *New York Times* to attract applicants for administrative positions, and in states that allow it school districts may recruit principals from the managerial ranks of business. The requirement that principals have teaching experience eliminates that option in other states. Some experts have argued that more people could be attracted to careers in administration if starting salaries were increased and working conditions improved (Archer, 2003).

Currently, principals earn between $10,000 and $25,000 more than classroom teachers, but they also work more days each year, and their workdays tend to be longer than those of teachers. Secondary principals also spend a considerable amount of time working evenings, attending school sports events, board meetings, and committee sessions. Many teachers believe the additional compensation is not adequate for the extra work required (Cusick, 2003).

Screening the Applicants

With the growing emphasis on accountability in schools, the process of screening and selecting administrators is changing. The criteria used for selection of administrators now emphasize the ability to develop strong school cultures and to facilitate the work of teachers in order to produce gains in student achievement. Evidence of the ability to work effectively with parents and community leaders also receives more attention than in the past.

School superintendents in Georgia and Tennessee, when asked what they believed were the most important qualifications for principals to possess, rated knowledge of learning theory and curriculum development among the most important. The leadership skills they rated highest included team building and the ability to communicate effectively (Lease, 2002). Other skills that the superintendents felt principals should possess included proficiency in human relations and public relations, planning, and technology. They also valued principals with knowledge of diversity, multicultural and gender issues, and school law. Budgeting, finance, and facilities management were rated lower in importance by the superintendents (Lease, 2002).

In another study, superintendents were asked what skills were most likely to lead to a principal's failure to succeed on the job. The five deficiencies cited most often by the respondents were principals' inability to work cooperatively with faculty and staff, failure to develop positive community relations, making poor decisions, and ineffectiveness in solving problems. Lack of leadership in curriculum and instruction was also cited frequently as leading to failure by a principal (Matthews, 2002).

Under No Child Left Behind, administrators are responsible for providing leadership to achieve yearly progress for all students, leading ultimately to proficiency in critical subject matter. The law does not define the process by which this goal is to be achieved, instead leaving that decision to policy makers and managers of the educational enterprise. Much of the responsibility for achieving this ambitious objective will rest directly on the shoulders of principals, and they can expect to be held accountable for progress toward the goal. Accordingly, no task the principal performs will exceed instructional improvement in importance.

The Interstate School Leaders Licensure Consortium (ISLLC) identified six standards for programs preparing school leaders. All statements begin with the phrase "A school administrator is an educational leader who promotes the success of all students by. . . ." They then identify actions by which administrators achieve the goal of success for all students. These actions include developing a vision of learning; nurturing a school culture conducive to learning; managing the organization in an efficient and effective manner; collaborating with families and community members; understanding and responding to the political, economic, and legal context of schools; and acting ethically and with integrity. The complete text of the six standards is available on the website of the Council of Chief State School Officers (www.ccsso.org/content/prdfs/isllcstd.pdf).

Interviewing and Checking References

A number of suggestions for conducting selection interviews with teachers were presented in the previous chapter. Most of the advice presented there applies also to interviewing for administrative and support positions. First-round interviews are intended to narrow the field to the most promising prospects.

At this point, applicants' references are reviewed. It is common practice to contact applicants' previous and current employers to verify information on the application form. Even though an employer may have furnished a written recommendation, it is still wise to follow up by telephone. However, no reference should be contacted unless the applicant agrees. Some applicants wait to inform their current employer that they are seeking to change jobs until they are informed that they are among the finalists for a new position.

Announcing Decisions

Completion of second-round interviews is normally followed in short time by an announcement of the selection decision. The decision may be delayed if two equally strong prospects are vying for the position or if none of the finalists appears qualified. In the latter case, the decision may be made to reopen the search and interview additional applicants.

When a decision is made to hire an individual, that person normally receives word promptly, but the mail moves more slowly for those who were not chosen. Courtesy dictates that all active applicants (that is, those who participated in second-round interviews and have not withdrawn) are informed when the decision is made, but this practice is by no means universally observed.

Applicants from within the district who made the list of finalists should receive a personal communication, either in the form of a letter or a telephone call, informing them of the reasons they were not chosen and suggesting ways they might improve their chances of selection in the future. Those who are unlikely to receive serious consideration for future openings should be notified tactfully of that fact and encouraged to pursue other opportunities. Candidates from outside the district should be informed when a decision has been made and encouraged to apply again in the future if their qualifications warrant that.

USE OF TESTS FOR SELECTION OF ADMINISTRATORS

Human resources directors and their staffs have begun using written and oral tests to help screen applicants for administrative positions. Individuals who respond to hypothetical situations requiring judgment and decision making reveal a good deal about their leadership ability. The information gained from such sources is reliable and useful, even though it is not an infallible predictor of leadership success. Two types of instruments currently used for selection purposes are written tests and assessment centers. Descriptions of these techniques follow.

Written Tests

Educational Testing Service (ETS) markets two tests that are designed to assess the skills of prospective school administrators: the School Superintendent Assessment and the School Leaders Licensure Assessment (SLLA). According to the ETS website, 18 states use one or both of these tests, either as a requirement for or as an alternative route to certification. The SLLA, which is used primarily to certify future principals, is a six-hour test in four parts. All four parts involve descriptions of situations that the principal of a school might face. Candidates are asked what action they would take in each situation or what factors would influence their decision. They may also be asked about possible consequences of a decision or what issues are raised by the situation described.

Assessment Centers

An assessment center is a collection of exercises that seeks to simulate on-the-job experiences in order to measure job-related skills. When used with school administrators, assessment centers focus on leadership abilities, oral and written communication, planning and organizing, decision making, taking initiative, and sensitivity. The types of activities that are typical of an assessment center include leaderless groups, role-play activities, in-basket exercises, and problem analysis.

Originally, assessment centers used live raters observing individuals engaged in assessment exercises and rated them. However, that approach was quite costly; the newer versions rely on objective test items and videotaped interactions among participants. A number of universities and school districts operate joint assessment centers to assist in selecting leaders for schools. Assessment center ratings are positively correlated with performance in a variety of jobs.

SELECTION OF PRINCIPALS AND ASSISTANT PRINCIPALS

Principals are responsible for all aspects of school operations. Their primary responsibility is to provide leadership for the instructional program. Principals perform seven essential functions:

1. Plan, develop, supervise, and evaluate the instructional program
2. Select, assign, and evaluate staff and provide opportunities for their professional growth and development
3. Maintain two-way communication with parents and the community
4. Enforce appropriate standards of student conduct
5. Use due process procedures in dealing with students and staff members
6. Maintain safe, clean, and attractive buildings and grounds
7. Keep accurate records of enrollment, attendance, disciplinary actions, and funds received and expended

No principal can single-handedly run a school, which means that he or she must delegate many of the duties associated with these responsibilities to members of the school staff and must rely on those individuals to achieve the hoped-for results. Thus, the principal depends on the performance of others. However, because the principal bears ultimate responsibility, he or she must be able to select employees who are knowledgeable and competent, and must provide guidance and supervision to ensure that they perform effectively.

Accountability

Leaders hold employees accountable for accomplishing the organization's mission. Too often, accountability is overlooked or ignored. Before No Child Left Behind established the goal of raising all children, regardless of their social, ethnic, or economic backgrounds, to grade level in critical subjects such as reading and mathematics, there was no generally accepted standard by which the performance of teachers, counselors, aides, and administrators could be judged. Now it is possible to determine whether a school is moving at a reasonable pace toward that goal. Regardless of whether one agrees with the goals of NCLB, there is no doubt that having measurable goals is a necessary first step toward creating accountable schools.

Hess (2006) described accountability as a lever for improving schools, yet he found in surveying course offerings in principal preparation programs that very little class time was devoted to the topic. Does that finding suggest that the professors in those programs believed that other topics were more important? Perhaps. However, most professors would agree that future principals need to be able to provide leadership for improving school performance. Accountability is a tool for doing that. As part of the process of creating accountability in schools, principals must be able to collect, understand, and apply data.

Minneapolis Public Schools has developed a process for achieving accountability in its schools. The process consists of five steps: (1) monitoring results, (2) evaluating, (3) planning for improvement, (4) implementing improvement, and (5) reporting to the community (Minneapolis Public Schools, n.d.). These steps can be applied to individuals, departments, and schools. Every teacher can follow these steps to improve his or her instruction, and departments and schools can do the same. By stressing to employees the importance of performing these actions on an ongoing basis, administrators can help to establish accountability as a habit.

Selection of Assistant Principals

Assistant principals work closely with the principal on tasks assigned by the principal. The workload may be divided among administrators in several ways. In schools with only one assistant, it is not uncommon for both the principal and assistant to perform any and all administrative duties, whereas in schools with several assistants, each one may have responsibility for a specific function. In some schools each assistant principal supervises one or more subject areas or grade levels, whereas in other schools the principal serves as instructional leader and designates one assistant to be in charge of student conduct, another to be responsible for finances and building maintenance, and so on.

Assistant principals often say that their university coursework failed to prepare them adequately for the job. In a recent survey, assistant principals cited several critical skills that they did not learn about in their preparation programs. These skills included motivating teachers, resolving conflicts, developing a curriculum for the "real world," working effectively with teams, improving instruction, and dealing with the politics of the job (Weller & Weller, 2002).

At one time an assistant principal's lack of experience was not considered a matter of great concern because the principal was ultimately responsible for the school and it was believed that an assistant principal's shortcomings could be compensated for by the principal's greater knowledge and expertise. It was not unusual for a new assistant principal to take several years to learn the job. However, most districts now expect the assistant principal to start contributing immediately. It is unusual for an individual with no administrative experience to be selected as an assistant principal. Most have had experience as interns, summer school principals, or heads of special projects. The workload in most schools is such that everyone on the team must do his or her part.

Districts now give much more care and thought to the process of selecting assistant principals and offer workshops and internships to help novice assistant principals learn the job more quickly and with less stress. In Kentucky, assistant principals serve as interns during their first year on the job, and their performance is evaluated by a committee composed of a mentor principal, the district superintendent, and a university professor of educational leadership (Kirkpatrick, 2000).

Given the scope and importance of the evolving role of the assistant principal, the selection criteria for the position should be the same as those used in selecting principals. The differences in the selection criteria used for the two positions usually have to do with depth and length of experience, with the principal expected to have more varied experience, and with counterbalancing qualifications. That is, an effort is usually made to select an assistant principal whose subject field and administrative experiences complement rather than duplicate those of the principal.

SKILLS OF EFFECTIVE LEADERS

Leadership is a matter of mastering certain skills, and these skills can be learned. When filling a vacancy for a principal or assistant principal, it is advisable to look for individuals with leadership ability. Some of the skills that good leaders demonstrate are as follows:

Assertiveness. People with this skill are able to gain a hearing for their views without being disrespectful or argumentative. Assertiveness and aggressiveness are quite different. Aggressive people promote their views even at the cost of offending others.

Interpersonal communication skill. People with this skill regularly use communication techniques that increase trust and help others to be receptive. These techniques include listening, tone of voice, eye contact, and body language.

Persuasiveness. People with this skill are able to present their views in a convincing manner.

Optimism. People with this skill are hopeful and positive. They are not easily deflected from the pursuit of a goal by the obstacles they encounter, and their enthusiasm is not dampened by setbacks.

Stability. People with this skill are predictable and emotionally available.

Calmness under pressure. People with this skill remain serene during a crisis, helping others to avoid panic or extreme anger.

Well-organized. People with this skill are able to conceptualize ways of accomplishing a complex task by combining the efforts of a number of people leading to the achievement of a desired outcome.

Problem-solving ability. People with this skill enjoy encountering novel difficulties and designing unique and elegant approaches to dealing with them.

Planning skills. People with this skill monitor trends in order to be prepared for future developments. They prepare in advance for both expected and unexpected contingencies.

There are also some skills that may lead to problems for a person in a position of leadership. Striving for perfection is one of those. Writers, designers, artists, and architects are noted for being perfectionists, a skill that helps them succeed in their work but that can lead to problems in other settings. People who seek perfection are inclined to be impatient with others and may refuse to delegate tasks because they believe they can do the job better themselves. People with strong perfectionistic tendencies often do not perform well as members of a team. However, advocating high standards is not the same as being a perfectionist. Perfectionists tend to be critical without being helpful. An effective leader sets high expectations for the performance of others but helps them find ways to meet those expectations.

There are also other skills that can lead to problems for those in leadership positions. Extroverts usually make effective leaders, but some extroverts have a strong need to be well liked, which sometimes makes it difficult for them to take unpopular positions. People who are inclined to be direct are often effective leaders. Those who work with them say they always know where they stand with this type of leader. However, directness also has a downside. Other people sometimes perceive directness as abrasive and may be hurt or offended by comments that are too direct.

WOMEN IN ADMINISTRATION

Some progress has been made in recent years in achieving gender and racial equity in school administration, although the number of women and minorities serving as school administrators continues to be small. The proportion of K–12 principalships (public and private) held by women increased from 35 percent of the total in 1993–1994 to nearly 44 percent in 1999–2000 (National Center for Education Statistics, 2002). During the same period, the number of African American principals in schools grew from 10 to 11 percent of the total (National Center for Education Statistics, 2002). The number of women superintendents is also slowly increasing. Title IX and the Women's Educational Equity Act have helped to open doors, and because women now make up a majority of students in principal preparation programs, it is inevitable that school administration will in time become a largely feminine occupation.

In spite of these gains, vestiges of discrimination remain. Women administrators report that they are sometimes criticized for characteristics, such as being ambitious or task oriented, that are acceptable from men. A female superintendent of a large urban district in the northeastern United States tells about her experience as a middle school principal wanting to hire a woman assistant principal and being told by the district superintendent that it wasn't wise to have two women administrators in one school.

Mentors Helping Women

Historically, women who have held leadership positions have been helped by mentors or sponsors to attain and succeed in those positions. Researchers who studied the careers of graduates of Stanford University law school wrote that "the mentoring relationship has a significant influence on the career decision-making and perhaps even on the success of women in business" (Tucker & Niedzielko, 1994). That statement is also true of women in fields other than business or law.

Women, more often than men, acknowledge having had help from a mentor. Men appear to rely more on a group of acquaintances, a kind of "personal old boys' network" in the words of one researcher, and are less likely to acknowledge a single individual as a mentor or sponsor.

When they are available, women provide career assistance to other women, but many women have male mentors. Perhaps because until recently there were few women in executive positions in school systems, women have had no choice but to rely on men. However, women have begun to develop Internet-based professional networks with other women in leadership roles. One such network is www.advancingwomen.com.

Women leaders are described as fostering participation and involvement of colleagues and subordinates. They tend to validate others, delegate authority, and allow for a free flow of information. Women leaders are also inclined to share decision making with others. However, it wouldn't be accurate to say that those characteristics are true only of women. Most effective leaders, whether male or female, exhibit some or most of those qualities.

Sexist Stereotypes.   In the past women were held back by sexist stereotypes. They were depicted as weaker than men and as indecisive and frivolous. Those notions have been largely discredited, but there is a temptation to replace old stereotypes with new ones. Men are sometimes depicted as authoritarian, closed to input from others, aggressive, and insensitive. Those are also stereotypes, and although there are men who fit those descriptions, most do not.

Gender and Leadership Style

The idea that men's and women's leadership styles are distinctive is a recognition of differences that are rooted in both biology and socialization. From there an assumption is sometimes made that women are better suited for certain leadership positions than men, and vice versa. That is not a new idea. Women have been disproportionately assigned to leadership roles in elementary schools, whereas slots in middle and high schools have been reserved for men, based on the belief that women are more nurturant than men and that young children need a nurturing presence. Yet that pigeonholes people and ignores their adaptability. It doesn't follow that men are not suited for positions in elementary schools or that women are less effective as leaders of middle schools and high schools.

Some recent research suggests that people's gender identities may contribute to or hinder their success in a profession, although not in ways that one would necessarily expect. An intriguing study examined careers of graduates of Stanford University. People who received MBAs from Stanford in 1987 were followed to see how well they fared in their careers. The graduates were divided into four groups, based on their gender and expressed preference for work environment. Men who preferred to work in an "aggressive" organization were labeled "masculine-identified males," whereas men who wanted to work for a company that valued "supportiveness and solidarity" were labeled "feminine-identified males." Women were classified into two groups in the same way (feminine-identified women and masculine-identified women).

Eight years after graduation, these four groups were compared. The masculine-identified men had the highest salaries, but the feminine-identified women did almost as well. They had started off earning less, but at the time of the study they had reached salary equity with the masculine-identified men, even though they worked, on average, 13 percent fewer hours. Feminine-identified men also did well. They earned salaries that were comparable to the masculine-identified men while working 10 percent fewer hours. The group with the lowest salaries were the masculine-identified women. The researchers concluded that the aggressive style of these women annoyed colleagues and supervisors and limited their success on the job. This study lends support to the impression that aggressive women are at a disadvantage professionally in our society. The study is available online at www.gsb.stanford.edu/news/research/ob_womencareers.shtml.

SELECTING OTHER SUPPORT PERSONNEL

Schools employ a variety of support personnel to help teachers in their work and to provide various types of services to children and their families. Exhibit 4.1 lists some of the titles held by people in support positions in schools. The amount of education required in these positions varies from high school to Ph.D. level. Among the people who have an important impact on instructional programs are psychologists, guidance counselors, library/media specialists, instructional aides, and substitute teachers.

School Social Workers

School social workers, also known as visiting teachers, were introduced in schools in the early 1900s. They were added to school staffs to improve communication

---

EXHIBIT 4.1

EXAMPLES OF SUPPORT PERSONNEL EMPLOYED IN SCHOOLS

Adult education and literacy specialist	Equipment repair assistant
Athletic trainer	Maintenance worker
Behavior technician	Media specialist
Bus driver	Paraprofessional
Bus route coordinator	Secretary
Child nutrition worker	Social worker
Custodian	Teacher aide
Educational psychologist	Teacher assistant

---

between families and the schools and to provide assistance to teachers and administrators in working with children who had academic, social, or emotional problems or whose home conditions posed a potential threat to their security and well-being.

Social workers perform liaison functions with community agencies, including social welfare organizations, law enforcement agencies, and medical service providers. If a child is in trouble with the police, a social worker will contact the police to find out what the child's offense was and will work with the family to obtain legal representation and help prevent a future recurrence. A social worker may also be called on to appear as a witness in court proceedings against families that refuse to send children to school or are suspected of neglect or abuse.

Typically, social workers work with individual students who have been referred by teachers for such problems as poor attendance, behavior problems, suspected abuse or malnutrition, social maladjustment, or health problems. They may be asked to investigate the home life of a child who falls asleep in school or who comes to school without lunch money. Often, social workers quietly collect food or clothing for children whose families are not able to buy them, or they may put the family in touch with a church or individual who can offer assistance.

Specialized training prepares social workers to use a variety of psychological techniques and casework methods to alleviate problems of children and families. They need to have strong communication skills and must be able to work effectively with a variety of people in situations that may be dispiriting or even dangerous (Allen-Meares, Washington, & Welsh, 1996).

Social workers are expected to be proactive child advocates and must be able to work effectively with families that may be suspicious or even hostile. They must maintain good working relationships with personnel in community services agencies, churches, and the courts. Among the criteria to look for when hiring a school social worker are the desire to help children, the ability to confront recalcitrant parents and officials, and the courage to take action to remove children from deplorable home conditions when necessary.

School Psychologists

Psychologists first appeared in schools near the beginning of the twentieth century. One of the first duties they were assigned—and one on which they continue to spend a good deal of time—is performing diagnostic services for special education placement. Psychologists report that, on average, they devote about 70 percent of their time to assessment activities; 20 percent is spent consulting with parents, teachers, administrators, and other professionals; and 10 percent is allocated to direct intervention with students (Fagan & Wise, 1994).

They also assist in administering, scoring, tabulating, and interpreting the results of standardized tests; help teachers to develop diagnostic tests; and offer advice on preparing instructional materials for students with particular learning needs. Psychologists are frequently asked to conduct professional development sessions for teachers on instructional strategies for children with learning disabilities, attention deficit disorder, and/or mental retardation.

A candidate for a position as school psychologist needs to have extensive professional preparation, including a master's degree or Ph.D. Among the important personal qualities necessary for success as a psychologist in schools are warmth, empathy, and ability to relate easily to a wide variety of people. Psychologists must be familiar with a wide range of psychological and diagnostic instruments and be able to administer and interpret the results of these tests. They need to be well organized and behave at all times in an ethical manner. Communication skill and adaptability are other necessary qualities.

At one time, teaching experience was considered a requirement for school psychologists. In recent years, however, many states have eliminated that requirement and place greater emphasis on preparation and skill as a psychologist.

Guidance Counselors

The number of counselors in public elementary and secondary schools increased from about 14,600 in 1958 (*Digest of Education Statistics*, 1989) to 97,369 in 2002 (National Center for Education Statistics, 2002). However, even though counselors are more common in schools now than in the past, there is not total agreement about their role. Teachers, students, parents, and principals all have opinions about an appropriate role for counselors, but they sometimes disagree.

Guidance Counselor Functions. School guidance counselors perform eight vital functions in schools. These functions demonstrate the variety of activities that counselors are involved in and the number of groups with which they work:

1. Counselors collect and record information for student records.
2. Counselors communicate with teachers and specialists about students with learning or emotional problems.

3. Counselors confer with families who request assistance with children's academic, health, and social problems.
4. Counselors meet with individuals and groups of students to discuss class schedules, educational and career planning, and academic and interpersonal problems.
5. Counselors collect follow-up data from graduates on their educational and career experiences since graduation.
6. Counselors coordinate special student services provided by specialists such as psychologists and social workers.
7. Counselors write letters of reference for students seeking admission to institutions of higher education or applying for jobs.
8. Counselors coordinate state or district testing programs and assist in administering tests and interpreting results to students and families.

Individual counseling provides students with opportunities to have professional assistance in a caring, nonevaluative environment to solve problems and make decisions. Group guidance is developmental and preventive in nature. In group counseling, the counselor facilitates interaction among members of a group of students who are attempting to solve common developmental problems. Counselors may also train teachers to provide group guidance services.

Secondary school counselors assist students in making career plans and selecting courses appropriate for those plans, and provide guidance on how to meet high school graduation requirements. Career guidance and counseling is an organized group program that helps students prepare to select a career and enter the world of work.

Counselors often help to coordinate services provided by school and community agencies for a child. They serve as liaison from the school to community agencies and handle requests for information from community individuals and groups. Counselors also perform a public relations service by informing parents and members of the community about guidance and counseling programs and services.

Factors that are considered in selecting counselors are the recency and quality of training and, in particular, exposure to a well-planned and comprehensive internship. Positive personal qualities are especially important for counselors because of the closeness of the relationship between the counselor and the students with whom he or she works.

Traits that have been identified as essential to success in counseling include accurate empathic understanding, communication of respect, warmth, sincerity, and specific expression. Depending on the nature of the assignment, other criteria will be added to those essentials. Additional qualifications include knowledge of occupational opportunity structures, knowledge of requirements for entry into various occupations, and the ability to relate effectively to parents and teachers.

Library/Media Specialists

The work of a librarian or media specialist has evolved to include all forms of media, ranging from books and serials to films, CDs, DVDs, and the Internet. These specialists obtain and organize information so that it is easily accessible. They help teachers and students locate information and also instruct them on the use of the media center and on other topics, including technology.

Media specialists have three areas of responsibility—helping students and teachers locate information, instructing users in the use of various forms of technology, and administering the media center. Administering the center involves planning, purchasing, maintaining records, and supervising students and assistants. Purchasing instructional materials requires that the specialist have extensive knowledge of the availability of materials in all subject areas. Because most teachers don't have time to locate reviews of instructional materials, that job often falls to the media specialist.

A master's degree in library science is ideal preparation for a position as a media specialist, but schools are not always able to locate—or afford—people with these degrees. So they may rely on individuals who have had some courses on the basics of library operation. A good many school districts have a central office supervisor who assists media specialists with the technical details of the job.

Two attributes should be given primacy in the selection of media specialists. The first is an attitude that encourages students and teachers to use the media center and its materials extensively and often. Usage creates extra work for the staff because books, magazines, records, CDs, filmstrips, fiche, recorders, and projectors that are taken from shelves and drawers must be returned to them. However, care should be taken to hire media specialists who will welcome usage of the media center as an indicator that the center is contributing to the vitality of the instructional program.

The second attribute to look for in a prospective media specialist is recent training. Technology is moving at such a rapid pace that anyone who has not had a refresher course or workshop within the past year is probably out of date. This is one field in which training must be almost constant if a person is to keep up with the pace of change.

Instructional Aides

Instructional aides represent the largest group of support personnel in schools, numbering more than 1.3 million individuals (U.S. Department of Labor, 2002). Between 1990 and 1997 the number of aides in schools increased 40 percent, whereas the number of teachers rose only 15 percent (Ganser, 2002). Aides perform a variety of duties, ranging from helping young children don raincoats and boots on rainy days to passing out snacks and booting up computers. By relieving classroom teachers of menial tasks, aides allow them to devote more time to lesson planning and teaching. Aides are found in most special education classrooms and in nonspecial education settings where they work with children with disabilities to carry out provisions of individualized educational plans.

Some instructional aides tutor children or provide follow-up instruction using the teacher's lesson plan, thus providing students with individualized attention and reinforcement. Instructional aides also supervise students in hallways and the cafeteria. They record grades, set up equipment, and help prepare materials for instruction. Other duties performed by aides include grading tests and papers, checking homework, keeping health and attendance records, typing, and copying. They also stock supplies, operate audiovisual equipment, and keep the classroom in order (U.S. Department of Labor, 2002).

No Child Left Behind requires that instructional aides complete at least two years in an institution of higher education; hold an associate's degree or higher; or pass an assessment on their knowledge of reading, writing, and mathematics. A paper-and-pencil test may be used to meet the third requirement but other options are also acceptable. These requirements do not apply to aides who are employed in non-Title I schools or who do not teach students.

Two commercial tests are available for aides who do not currently meet one of the NCLB requirements. The ParaPro Test is published by the Educational Testing Service, and WorkKeys is a publication of ACT Inc. In addition to setting qualifications for instructional aides, NCLB establishes certain working conditions for aides. They must work in "close and frequent proximity" to a highly qualified teacher.

The demand for instructional aides is expected to grow in coming years as enrollments in special education and English as a second language programs expand. The continuing emphasis on accountability is also expected to spur the growth in demand for instructional aides who can help with instruction and provide remedial assistance to students. This change is already under way in many districts (Gerber, Finn, Achilles, & Boyd-Zaharias, 2001).

By raising the educational requirements for classroom aides, NCLB may have the effect of creating temporary shortages of qualified applicants, which in turn may force school districts to increase the salaries paid to these semiprofessional workers. The Bureau of Labor Statistics reported in 2000 that salaries paid to instructional aides ranged from $12,000 to $28,000, with the middle half earning between $14,000 and $22,000 (U.S. Department of Labor, 2002).

Substitute Teachers

Human resources administrators report that it is becoming more difficult to find good substitutes for teachers who are absent from their jobs. Because of the short supply of teachers in certain subject fields, some former substitutes have been pressed into full-time service, whereas others are limiting their substitute work because of difficult teaching conditions, heavy paperwork demands, and uncooperative students. Schools that provide support are the most likely to be able to find substitute teachers when they need them.

The National Substitute Teacher Alliance (NSTA) has developed a bill of rights designed to improve working conditions for substitute teachers and secure recognition for them. Most of the items on the bill of rights are supported by educators.

The first item calls for substitute teachers to receive respect as professionals. The second claims that they have a right to receive the information they need in order to plan successful learning experiences for students, and the third suggests they should be able to work in safety and to have a copy of procedures and policies for the school. It is in the interest of schools to abide by these declarations, yet the fact that substitute teachers have to plead for consideration is evidence that schools fall short. In many schools substitutes receive little or no information because teachers are too busy with other duties to consider the needs of substitutes.

Other items on the NSTA's bill of rights may be somewhat more controversial. One, for example, says that substitute teachers should have access to employer-provided health services, and another proposes that they be able to participate in the professional development programs available to full-time teachers. Health insurance is expensive, and most school districts are not ready to take on the added cost of funding health insurance for substitute teachers. Few districts provide training for substitutes, although many administrators see merit in the idea. Inviting substitutes to participate in professional development programs is a good idea that could have benefits for both full-time and part-time teachers. However, substitutes also need training designed especially to address their concerns. The bill of rights document can be viewed online at www.nsta.subs.org/substitute_teacher_bill_of_rights.htm.

The Substitute Teachers Caucus of the National Education Association advocates appropriate training in "guest teaching." Substituting is difficult work because the teachers do not know the students and are often unfamiliar with school policies and routines. It is common for teachers to be asked to have lesson plans on hand in case a substitute is required, but those plans are sketchy and not very useful. Substitutes often have little advance notice of where or what they will be teaching, so they have little opportunity to prepare.

Respondents in a recent study reported that substituting is most apt to be a positive experience in schools in which teachers are helpful, materials are easily located, and the teacher leaves lesson plans and suggestions for activities for students who finish their work early. All teachers, including substitutes, appreciate having well-behaved students; substitutes also like to have the names of two or three dependable students who are familiar with homework assignments and the classroom schedule. Survey respondents also reported that being informed about classroom rules, routines, and emergency procedures and having seating charts made their work easier (Tannenbaum, 2000).

Some schools use a report form to be completed by both the substitute and regular teacher. On the form, the substitute teacher can report how much material was covered, whether any problems arose, and note questions raised by students. The regular classroom teacher uses the form to thank the substitute or to make special requests (e.g., that furniture and supplies be put back in place next time). Both teachers see the other's report, and the principal also reviews them. In this way, two-way communication is maintained and the principal is alerted to any problems that may have arisen (Tannenbaum, 2000).

Secretaries and Administrative Assistants

A school secretary has important responsibilities. Much of the communication that goes on in a school originates with or passes through the school secretary. Given the importance of the position and the extent of the secretary's contacts with parents, teachers, and students, care should be taken in filling the position. Secretaries are often known by more students than any other single individual, with the exception of the classroom teacher and possibly the principal. Given the nature of this position and the extent of the secretary's contacts with the public, teachers, and students, careful selection for this position is critical.

The title "secretary" is being upgraded to "administrative assistant" as the duties of the position become more complex. Individuals in these positions have the following areas of responsibility:

1. Communicator (keep administrators, faculty, students, and parents informed, greet and help visitors)
2. Planner/scheduler (schedule meetings, reserve space, contact participants, make travel arrangements)
3. Information manager (maintain databases, locate information online, maintain files, prepare/print/distribute reports, take notes)
4. Financial manager (review and verify financial reports, track expenditures, authorize purchases, maintain inventory records)
5. Office manager (schedule work, supervise student and part-time employees, maintain an attractive and businesslike office, contact substitute teachers)
6. Student helper (contact parents when a child is ill, answer students' questions, supervise students referred to the office for discipline)

A necessary qualification for the position of secretary is the ability to tolerate frequent interruptions without undue frustration. Regardless of the importance of the task being worked on, the secretary is expected to put it aside to handle a request from a student or teacher. Rarely is the secretary able to finish a task without being interrupted at least once. To work in such an atmosphere requires patience, flexibility, and a sense of humor. Some of the tasks that secretaries perform, most notably financial record-keeping and check writing, require an atmosphere that permits concentration. In order to keep errors to a minimum, it is necessary to provide an opportunity for the secretary who performs those chores to retreat to a quiet, out-of-the-way room where there will be no interruptions. When selecting a secretary, it is important to recognize that not all individuals operate effectively in an atmosphere as busy as school offices often are. Care must be taken to select the person who can tolerate the noise and confusion without undue feelings of stress.

Because of their location in the center of the school's information flow, secretaries obtain considerable confidential information about teachers and students. Caplow (1976) noted that employees who have access to the manager of an organization and who possess information about other organization members acquire power that exceeds that allocated to them by the organization chart. He warned that such power can be a source of organizational problems and thus urged managers to keep the power of their assistants in check.

School Resource Officers

Random acts of violence against students and teachers have demonstrated that schools can no longer be regarded as safe havens from crime. The chance that a child will be injured at school is still quite small, but highly publicized incidents such as the shootings at Columbine High have heightened parents' fears and moved administrators to take action to improve school safety. As a result resource officers are now common in schools, and their presence has helped to improve the climate for learning.

Resource officers are police officers or sheriff's deputies who are assigned to serve in schools. Their primary duty is to protect lives and property by enforcing appropriate laws and board policies. They also perform a variety of other functions, including barring disruptive individuals from the building, investigating criminal activity, counseling students, serving as instructional resource persons, providing security at athletic and other school events, directing traffic, and arresting violators.

Because these officers are employees of a police department or sheriff's office, school officials have only limited say in their selection. Unfortunately, some law enforcement agencies view the job of resource officer as "baby-sitting" and give the job to the least experienced member of the staff. In fact, performing effectively in the resource role requires many of the same skills that are needed of a "street" cop—people skills, good judgment, and an alert mind (Bond, 2001).

To the extent that they are able to influence selection decisions, administrators need to emphasize the importance of choosing personnel who possess qualities that will help them to experience success in a difficult role. Officers should have previous law enforcement experience and be well informed about federal and state laws. They should have good communication skills, display an even temperament, and set a good example.

No school principal wants a "trigger happy" law enforcement person on the premises. A person who sees his or her role as an "enforcer" often arouses fear and even hostility among students. Successful resource officers rely on their abilities to earn students' respect by being friendly, firm, and fair. This respect goes further than a drawn weapon to reduce crime by students and the disruptive activities that are too common in some schools. One of the advantages of having a school resource officer in the building is that students who are headed for a confrontation with the law can be helped to see the danger they face and change their behavior. The mere presence of a law enforcement person in the school is a deterrent. When students understand that they can be arrested for actions that might otherwise merit nothing more severe than a detention, they tend to be more circumspect in their actions (Benigni, 2004).

The North Carolina Department of Juvenile Justice and Delinquency Prevention maintains an informative website that details the duties of school resource officers and gives an example of a memorandum of understanding between a sheriff's office and a school system establishing a school resource officer program. The site is located at www.ncdjjdp.org/cpsv/sro/sroagree.htm.

SUMMARY

Preparing a job description with required essential functions is the first step in filling an administrative or support position. The Educational Testing Service offers two tests that are used by states in certifying school leaders: the School Superintendent Assessment and the School Leaders Licensure Assessment. Among the essential functions performed by principals are planning and supervising the instructional program, selecting and evaluating staff, planning professional growth opportunities, and maintaining communication with parents and the community. Assistant principals are essential members of the administrative team in schools. Qualities of effective leaders include the ability to organize, projecting optimism and calmness in a crisis, and skill in oral and written communication. Men and women have different leadership styles but they include many common elements. Among support personnel necessary for efficient operation of a school are guidance counselors, library/media specialists, and secretaries.

SUGGESTED ACTIVITIES

1. Prepare a list of selection criteria you would use in hiring an instructional aide or a secretary. Then write a set of questions to help you evaluate how well a particular applicant meets those criteria.

2. Look at the following list of items that came to the attention of the principal of Hadley High School. As principal, you need to delegate some tasks. Decide to whom you would delegate each task (assistant principal, guidance counselor, social worker, department head, custodian, or bookkeeper), tell why you chose that person, and explain how you would evaluate that person's performance.

   a. An angry parent calls to complain about a teacher who assigns too much homework.

   b. The director of maintenance wants to talk to someone about setting up a schedule for repairing the driveway used by buses.

   c. The state university wants to send a recruiter to speak to juniors and seniors.

   d. A state agency asks for recommendations of four students to serve as summer interns.

   e. The bank left a message that there is a discrepancy in the previous day's bank deposit.

   f. Teacher evaluations are due in one week, and six teachers have not been observed.

g. A student who dropped out of school has applied for a job in a warehouse, and the supervisor calls asking for a reference.

h. A student was arrested for carrying a gun and threatening other students after school.

3. Consider the following leadership qualities. Tell why each is important and give an example of a situation in which that quality would be especially useful for a school administrator.

a. Optimism

b. Problem solver

c. Calm under pressure

d. Assertive

e. Persuasive

4. One of the tasks expected of school principals is to establish a climate conducive to learning in the school. Name three actions that a principal might take that would help make the climate in the school more supportive of learning.

ONLINE RESOURCES

Bureau of Labor Statistics, U.S. Department of Labor (www.bls.gov/oco/home.htm)

The *Occupational Outlook Handbook* is the authoritative source for information about occupations. Each of the thousands of entries includes a description of the type of work performed by members of the occupation, anticipated future demand for workers, qualifications, and salary ranges. It is a vital reference tool for counselors and human resource workers.

Harney County (Oregon) School District (http://www.burnsschools.k12.or.us/substitutes.htm)

This district has an online handbook for substitute teachers that contains a wealth of useful information, including a roster of teachers, school calendar, and district rules and policies. Districts planning to develop similar handbooks could use this publication at a model.

National Center for Education Statistics (nces.ed.gov//pubs2003/digest02/index.asp)

This site shows statistics on all levels of education in the United States, including enrollments, number of personnel, and their demographic characteristics.

CASE STUDIES

Case No. 1

Mary Ann Slaughter is secretary at Hoover Elementary School. She is the only clerical person in the office except for a part-time bookkeeper who works two days a week. A fifth-grade teacher, Bobbi Munson, is getting married in the summer and will resign her job in order to move with her husband to another city, where she plans to apply for a teaching job. Ms. Munson told the principal, Mary Rogers, about her plans, asking her to keep the information confidential. Ms. Rogers told her she would pass the information on to the director of human resources but would not tell anyone else. Two weeks later, Ms. Munson stepped into the principal's office and closed the door. She looked distressed.

"I didn't want you to say anything about my plans," she said.

Ms. Rogers frowned. "I didn't."

"You must have," Ms. Munson said. "Ms. Friar stopped me in the hall this morning and said, "Congratulations! I hear you're getting married.""

"Did she tell you how she knew?" Ms. Rogers asked.

"Yeah. She said Mary Ann Slaughter told her."

Rogers looked shocked. "Oh, no! I did mention it to Mary Ann. But I told her not to say anything."

"Well, obviously she ignored that suggestion."

"I'm so sorry, Bobbi. It was thoughtless of me. I know Mary Ann loves to talk, but I thought if I told her not to say anything. . . ." Her voice trailed off. "I really apologize. I have to talk to Mary Ann about this."

"I hope you'll do more than talk," Ms. Munson said. "I'm disappointed in you and Mary Ann both. I wouldn't have said anything if I thought it would get out."

Questions
1. What is the larger issue in this case?
2. Who is more at fault for Ms. Munson's loss of trust—Ms. Rogers or Ms. Slaughter or both?
3. What action should Ms. Rogers take now?

Case No. 2

James Hatori is principal of Ashbrook Middle School. He is interviewing Jennifer Garrett, an applicant for the position of guidance counselor at the school.

HATORI: I believe you've had some experience as a school counselor. Is that right?

MS. GARRETT: I was counselor at a girls' camp for two summers, and I did an internship at an elementary school while I was doing my graduate work.

HATORI: OK. So you've had some experience.

MS. GARRETT: Right.

HATORI: I want to ask you this question. Two weeks ago, I heard that a sixth-grade boy in this school had threatened to get a gun and "get even" with his enemies. I talked with the kid, and he denied saying it. I believed him, so I didn't take any action. But it worried me. He might have been lying to me. What would you do if you were counselor and you heard that a student had made a statement like that?

MS. GARRETT: I'd probably do what you did—talk to him.

HATORI: I hope you'd keep me informed.

MS. GARRETT: Probably.

HATORI: Why do you say "probably"? Is there a question in your mind?

MS. GARRETT: No, not really.

HATORI: How can you tell if a student's threat is serious?

MS. GARRETT: I think you treat all threats as serious.

HATORI: A counselor is supposed to be an expert. How do you know if a student is simply trying to sound important and isn't really likely to bring a gun to school and start shooting?

MS. GARRETT: You don't know. You have to use your best judgment. I wasn't trained to evaluate student threats. I'd take them all seriously.

HATORI: Every few weeks I read about a student somewhere who shoots someone at school. I don't want that to happen at Ashbrook.

MS. GARRETT: I wouldn't want it to happen here either. But there are some ways to get at how serious a student is.

HATORI: Like what?

MS. GARRETT: Does he have access to a weapon? Has he actually made plans? Does he name the people he wants to kill?

HATORI: Yeah, I'd say if the answer to those questions is "yes," he's pretty serious.

MS. GARRETT: The problem is the kid is not going to tell you those things.

HATORI: So how do you find out what's on his mind?

MS. GARRETT: I think you have to talk with students every chance you get, just to see how they're doing. Students who commit violent acts are alienated—usually they're harassed by other kids and want to get even. They think there's no one they can talk to.

HATORI: I try to be visible in the halls and on the bus deck and in my office. I'm available to talk to anyone anytime.

MS. GARRETT: That's good, but it's not enough. There needs to be a commitment to action.

HATORI: I'm committed to taking action.

MS. GARRETT: Teachers have to be committed too. If a kid mentions to a teacher that other people are harassing him, I'd like to know about it.

HATORI: I think I'd hear about it. Teachers tell me lots of things.

MS. GARRETT: Maybe, but in a couple of cases where kids erupted, they had talked to a teacher or an administrator beforehand and nothing was done to stop the harassment. We need to take those complaints seriously. These kids have low frustration tolerance.

HATORI: You can say that again.

Questions

1. In the interview, Hatori focused on preventing violence in the school and neglected other topics. What other questions should he have asked in order to evaluate Ms. Garrett as a prospective counselor?
2. How would you rate Ms. Garrett's answers to his questions?
3. Do you believe that spotting potential student troublemakers is an appropriate role for a counselor? If not, who should be responsible?
4. How would you rate Ms. Garrett as a candidate for the position of counselor at Ashbrook? Use a scale 1–5, where 1 = Reject and 5 = Make an offer. Explain why you gave the rating you did.
5. Do you agree with Ms. Garrett's advice to take all student threats seriously?

REFERENCES

Allen-Meares, P., Washington, R., & Welsh, B. (1996). *Social work services in schools* (2nd ed.). Boston: Allyn & Bacon.

Archer, J. (2003, June 4). Debate heating up on how to lure top-notch principals. *Education Week,* pp. 1, 12.

Benigni, M. D. (2004, January). When cops go to school. *Principal Leadership, 4,* 43–47.

Bond, B. (2001, April). Principals and SROs: Defining roles. *Principal Leadership, 1,* 52–55.

Caplow, T. (1976). *How to run any organization.* New York: Holt Rinehart.

Cusick, P. A. (2003, May 14). The principalship? No thanks. *Education Week,* pp. 44, 34.

Digest of education statistics. (1989). Washington, DC: U.S. Office of Education.

Fagan, T., & Wise, P. (1994). *School psychology: Past, present and future.* New York: Longman.

Ganser, T. (2002, December). The new teacher mentors. *American School Board Journal, 189,* 25–27.

Gerber, S. B., Finn, J. D., Achilles, C. M., & Boyd-Zaharias, J. (2001, Summer). Teacher aides and students' academic achievement. *Educational Evaluation and Policy Analysis, 23,* 123–143.

Hess, F. M. (2006, March). Looking beyond the schoolhouse door. *Phi Delta Kappan, 87,* 513–514.

Kirkpatrick, R. (2000, September). Recruiting and developing candidates for principal. *NASSP Bulletin, 84,* 38–43.

Lease, A. J. (2002, June). New administrators need more than good grades. *School Administrator, 59,* 40–41.

Matthews, D. (2002, September). Why principals fail and what we can learn from it. *Principal, 82,* 38–40.

Minneapolis Public Schools. (n.d.). *Accountability.* Retrieved from www.mpls.k12.us.Accountability.html.

National Center for Education Statistics. (2002). *Digest of education statistics, 2002.* Washington, DC: U.S. Department of Education.

Tannenbaum, M. (2000, May). No substitute for quality. *Educational Leadership, 57,* 70–72.

Tucker, M., & Niedzielko, G. A. (1994). *Options and obstacles: A survey of the studies of careers of women lawyers.* Washington, D.C.: American Bar Association.

U.S. Department of Labor Bureau of Labor Statistics. (2002). *Occupational outlook handbook, 2002–2003 edition.* Washington, DC: Author.

Weller, L. D., & Weller, S. J. (2002). *The assistant principal: Essentials for effective school leadership.* Thousand Oaks, CA: Corwin.

5 MOTIVATION OF PERSONNEL

All of the actions of a human being originate from inner motivation. However, in spite of extensive study, there are still many unanswered questions about human motivation. Human resources leaders must take human motivation into account in many phases of their work. This chapter examines our knowledge of job-related motivation and offers guidelines on applying that knowledge to the leadership of human resources in schools.

PLAN OF THE CHAPTER

The following topics are covered in this chapter: (1) nature of work motivation, (2) job satisfaction in teaching, and (3) job satisfaction and teacher turnover.

NATURE OF WORK MOTIVATION

Work motivation refers to conditions responsible for variations in the intensity, quality, direction, and duration of work-related behavior. Variations in the quality of work produced by employees may arise from either motivational or knowledge differences. If an employee is not achieving satisfactory results, it is necessary to ascertain whether the problem originates from lack of motivation, lack of knowledge, or both.

People are motivated to work for a variety of reasons, the most common being the need to earn money. Psychological drives, skills, and family situation are other factors that people consider in deciding what kind of work to do and where they want to work. The degree of fit between a person's work motivation and the job is usually an indicator of how well satisfied the individual will be with the job. Selection of employees involves an assessment of this fit for a given applicant. A person who enjoys being around people probably will not be satisfied in a job that involves little people contact, and one who values exercising authority is likely to be unhappy in a position that is devoid of power. Of course, human beings are very adaptable, and it is never safe to assume that an individual will not be happy in a given job, but by considering an applicant's work motivation, a human resources specialist can increase the probability that the person who is hired will be well suited for the position.

Theories of Motivation

Psychologists have advanced several theories to explain how people become motivated to perform a job and what factors within the individual or in the work setting influence the level of motivation experienced. Three theories are of particular interest to school administrators because of their potential for improving our understanding of work motivation among teachers. The three theories are:

1. *Expectancy theory:* Advocates believe that people are motivated by the opportunity to earn incentives.
2. *Equity theory:* Advocates believe that people expect a balance between effort expended and rewards received and lose motivation when that balance is missing.
3. *Goal-setting theory:* Advocates believe that people are motivated to achieve identified goals.

Each of these three theories has implications for administrative action. An administrator who believes that employees are motivated by expectancy will attempt to identify and distribute incentives to increase teacher motivation. One who believes in equity theory will try to provide more generous rewards to employees who work hard and withhold some rewards from those who put forth less effort. Administrators who subscribe to goal-setting theory will attempt to identify long- and short-range goals that are personally meaningful to employees and help the employees to achieve those goals. These theories are described in more detail in the following sections.

Expectancy Theory.   Psychologists who have studied human motivation have developed elaborate theories about the relationship between tangible rewards and employee performance. These theories help explain the conditions under which tangible rewards and recognition lead to an increase in employee productivity. One such theory is expectancy theory, which is based on the premise that workers perform tasks to gain incentives and that motivation is a function of the value of the incentive to the individual. Vroom incorporated three concepts into his model of expectancy motivation—valence, instrumentality, and expectancy—so the theory is sometimes referred to as VIE theory (cited in Pinder, 1984).

1. *Valence* refers to the positive or negative feelings attached to work outcomes. For example, money received for performing a job has positive valence for most workers, whereas working in a dirty environment has negative valence. For

teachers, student success has positive valence. Some work outcomes that have negative valence for teachers are unnecessary paperwork and being required to monitor hallways, restrooms, and bus-loading areas.

2. *Instrumentality* refers to the perceived connection between a work outcome and some object or event that has positive valence for an employee. An employee must believe that something he or she does on the job will lead to a desirable result in order for motivation to occur. According to the theory, a teacher who has been asked by the principal to serve on a textbook committee will be more motivated to serve if he or she believes that by doing so, something pleasant will be forthcoming. The teacher must believe that the task (serving on the committee) is instrumentally related to an incentive he or she values. That might be the principal's approval, or it might be the opportunity to improve the instructional program.

3. *Expectancy* refers to the employee's perception of the probability of successfully achieving a work outcome. In the preceding example, the teacher who has been asked to serve on the textbook committee may decide not to do it if she believes that she lacks the requisite knowledge and skills because she would not expect to be able to perform the task satisfactorily.

Expectancy theory suggests that instrumentality is a function of an individual's estimate of the probability that he or she can achieve certain results. When one's success is tied to the performance of others, as it is in programs that reward groups of teachers, then instrumentality is the sum of the individuals' estimates of success. In such a program, each teacher, in addition to considering his or her own ability to accomplish desired results, must attempt to determine whether other teachers will be successful. In that situation, instrumentality will be influenced by cohesiveness among teachers and the level of confidence they have in one another (Kelley, 1998).

Work outcomes include tasks performed on the job, but they may also include *opportunities.* For example, the chance to attend a workshop to improve one's skills is a work outcome, but most of us would not refer to it as a task. This distinction is important because with it we can use expectancy theory to help explain why teachers are sometimes not motivated to participate in staff development activities.

Expectancy theory is illustrated in Figure 5.1. The figure shows how a work situation leads to a condition of motivation or lack of motivation for an employee. The employee considers a work outcome, which might be an in-service program offering instruction on a new way to teach music. The teacher asks first, "Can I achieve the work outcome?" This might involve several other considerations, including "Do I have the time to take this in-service class?" "Is Tuesday afternoon a convenient time for me?" "Can I learn the material?" If the answer to any of these questions is *no,* the teacher will not be motivated for this particular work outcome. If the answer to all of the questions is *yes,* the teacher moves to the next decision block.

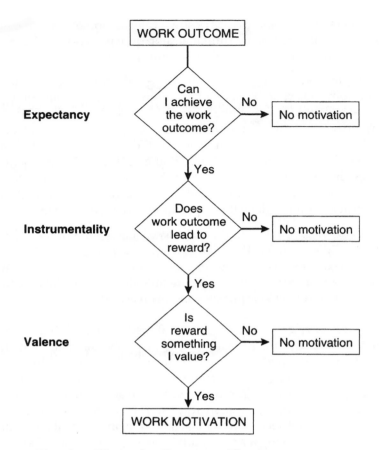

FIGURE 5.1   Flowchart Illustrating Expectancy Theory

At this point, the teacher considers whether there is an incentive to perform the outcome. The music teacher in the example might decide that the workshop could result in her acquiring new instructional techniques that would increase student interest in music or help her get a better job. If one of these outcomes has positive valence for the teacher, then she will be motivated to attend the workshop.

Consider another situation: A district offers a salary increment to teachers who agree to teach in schools with concentrations of low-achieving students. A teacher considers first whether he or she can perform the task. If the job involves working with children with learning problems, the teacher may decide that he or she lacks the necessary skills. However, if the teacher feels able and qualified to do the job and the salary increment is attractive, he or she will be motivated to accept the offer.

Applying Expectancy Theory. Using expectancy theory to motivate teachers is more likely to succeed if administrators follow these guidelines:

1. Select incentives that are valued by teachers. Direct financial incentives to teachers seem to have promise for attracting teachers to specific assignments, such as schools with large numbers of non–English-speaking students or schools located in neighborhoods with high rates of crime. They can also be used to achieve specific goals, such as raising achievement test scores. However, financial incentives do not work as well in raising the overall level of quality of teaching performance. These issues are discussed in more detail in Chapter 9.

2. Be sure that teachers understand the instrumental connection between work outcomes and incentives. If the connection between the work outcome and the incentive is not clear, no motivation will occur. Some merit pay programs fail because teachers do not understand what they must do to earn the merit increase.

3. Select work outcomes that are attainable. Teachers must believe that a work outcome is attainable in order for expectancy to affect their work behavior. Choosing work outcomes that are beyond the reach of most teachers defeats the purpose of using rewards and incentives.

4. Incentives are not effective when used to reward behavior that is expected or required of all employees. For example, teachers should not be offered incentives for arriving at school on time. Individuals may be given the choice of whether to seek a particular incentive.

Equity Theory. When rewards are distributed on the basis of performance, employees who do not receive a reward or who receive a smaller-than-average reward may feel they have been treated unfairly. It is, therefore, important to be aware of the issue of equity in distributing work-related rewards. Researchers who have studied equity find that employees compare themselves to people with whom they work who perform the same or similar jobs. An employee who feels that he or she worked harder but received a smaller reward than another employee will feel unfairly treated and will suffer a loss of motivation.

Reducing Tension. Equity theory suggests that if two employees—Allan and Barry—work equally hard but Allan receives a promotion and Barry does not, both will experience feelings of psychological tension. They may try by various means to allay this tension. One way they try to do that is by use of cognitive distortion. Barry may tell himself, "Maybe Allan works harder than I thought," or "Allan talks about how hard he works, and the boss believes him."

A second way to relieve psychological tension is to change one's inputs. Barry may decide not to work so hard, or he may elect to change his priorities on the job in order to devote more effort to activities that are rewarded. He may also act to change the comparison. One way to do that is to tell himself, "Allan may be a better salesman, but I'm a better manager." Or he may say, "A promotion is not worth it if I have to neglect my family to get it." Finally, Barry may leave the job altogether.

Allan may experience some of the same tension that Barry feels, and, if so, he will probably react in some of the same ways. For example, he might distort reality by telling himself, "I always thought Barry was kind of lazy." Or he may decide to change his inputs by working less hard in order to avoid further alienation from Barry.

Equity theory helps one to understand teachers' opposition to merit pay and other forms of performance-based compensation. Because most of these programs rely on principals' ratings to determine which teachers will receive salary increases, teachers fear that principals may reward their favorites and ignore all others. Teachers seem to be less concerned about inequities in the single salary schedule than they are about possible inequities in performance-based compensation plans.

Equity theory assumes that employees have accurate information about the amount of effort their colleagues expend, but in education that assumption is often faulty. Because teachers seldom observe one another's work directly, they lack complete information about the work habits of others. Nevertheless, they form judgments about which of their colleagues work hard and which do not, basing those conclusions on inconclusive evidence, such as how late a teacher stays at school and whether he or she takes work home.

Even though an employee may be misinformed about how hard colleagues work, it is the beliefs he or she holds that provoke the responses predicted by equity theory. Thus, the perception of inequity has the same effect on employee behavior as actual inequity.

Applying Equity Theory.   Using equity theory to motivate teachers is most likely to be successful when administrators follow these guidelines:

1. Differentiating rewards on the basis of performance will increase productivity but may also increase intragroup conflict. If harmonious relations and minimal conflict are important, distribute rewards equally among members.

2. Whenever possible, give all employees the chance to work toward rewards, but if rewards are offered to some groups and not others, make certain that the individuals understand and accept the reasons for the differentiation. Providing clerical assistance to employees who serve on a curriculum revision committee is acceptable, but providing such assistance to coaches who already receive a salary increment is likely to be perceived as inequitable.

3. Achieve a balance between the effort required and the value of the reward. Rewards that are of little value should be more easily attained than those that are of greater value. In education, the cost of incentive programs is always a concern.

Costs may be capped by limiting the number of incentive awards given, but a more equitable approach is to increase the amount of effort required to gain a reward, so that fewer people try for them.

4. In education, perceived inequities most often arise in connection with evaluating performance. If no objective and valid way of measuring performance exists, managers are vulnerable to charges of unfairly rewarding favorites. To avoid the charge, appoint a committee of teachers to set standards for deciding which individuals shall receive rewards.

Goal-Setting Theory. One reason that games are highly motivating is because they have clear and challenging goals. Whether playing bridge, video games, or touch football, participants understand the objective of the activity and enjoy the challenge of trying to attain it. A number of psychologists contend that clear-cut and challenging goals are as effective for motivating people in work settings as in recreational situations. Locke and Latham (1984) suggest that people gain a sense of accomplishment and efficacy from attaining goals, provided the goals are sufficiently challenging and success is not either impossible or meaningless.

Goal-setting theory has been shown to work in psychological laboratories as well as actual work environments when the goals are accepted by the people involved. Studies have shown that individuals who were assigned more challenging goals outperformed those who received moderately difficult or easy goals. Also, individuals who were given specific goals did better than those who were given vague admonitions such as "Do your best."

Goal setting is a form of self-leadership. Organizations use a variety of external control mechanisms for influencing employee behavior, including evaluation, rules and policies, and supervisory oversight. In recent years, however, organizations have begun to place more emphasis on internal controls. By working to achieve commitment by employees to the organizational mission and goals, these organizations hope that the need for external mechanisms of control will diminish.

Self-leadership refers to an inclination by an employee to engage in behaviors that contribute to the accomplishment of an organization's mission and that are performed in the absence of any external constraint. Employees engage in self-leadership because they are committed to the goals and purpose of the organization that employs them. In schools with school-based management, self-leadership assumes greater importance because these schools do not have access to the full range of external controls on employees that are available to districts with centralized administrative structures.

Locke and Latham (1984) stated that goals are motivating for employees even though they were not involved in setting them. Teachers may differ from other employees in that respect, however, because teachers believe that setting instructional goals is an important function of their jobs. Goals that are set by the administration are more likely to be accepted by teachers if the principal justifies the choice of goals and offers to provide support to members in attaining those outcomes.

Applying Goal-Setting Theory.   When goal setting is used as a motivational device for employees in schools, the following principles should be kept in mind:

1. Goal setting works better when employees are confident of their ability to achieve goals. Supervisors may need to provide interpersonal support for employees who lack confidence in their ability to achieve a goal. Individuals who are new to the job may be especially uneasy about identifying performance goals.

2. Performance goals should reflect the outcomes envisioned in the school's strategic plan and mission statement. Other documents that can be helpful in formulating goals are job models and incentive pay plans or career ladders.

3. Detailed feedback helps in several ways. It reduces uncertainty concerning which behaviors are most appropriate in the pursuit of goals, and it provides information about the relative importance of various goals. Feedback is more likely to be perceived accurately if it follows the performance without delay, is positive, and is given relatively frequently. The motivational value of feedback is influenced by the extent to which it conveys to the recipient a sense of competence.

4. Employees are more committed to performance goals that are chosen consensually by members of work teams.

Goal Setting and Teacher Evaluation.   Goal setting is commonly used in schools as part of the evaluation process. Teachers choose annual goals and are evaluated on their success in achieving them. In such programs, it is advisable for principals and teachers to discuss how goal attainment will be measured and to set a date for achieving the goals. The time limit is ordinarily one year, but interim reviews of teacher performance at periodic intervals during the year are recommended. Teacher evaluation schemes that involve teacher-selected outcomes are reviewed in more detail in Chapter 8. Goal setting as part of the evaluation process is most effective when these guidelines are followed:

1. Teachers are encouraged to select goals that conform to the school and district mission and to accountability requirements such as those found in NCLB.

2. When an organization asks employees to identify performance goals, it should commit itself to helping the employees achieve the goals they choose. To avoid the frustration and discouragement that arise from seeking unrealistic results, employees should be advised to select attainable goals, and supervisors should work to obtain the resources employees need in order to achieve them.

3. Employees should be assisted in writing goal statements that are clear and concise, describe measurable outcomes, and require a significant and continuing effort. Because most goal statements represent a year's work, a problem that is sometimes encountered is that the goals are too modest. A goal that can be accomplished within a month or two is not sufficiently challenging. Employees often think of goals as being an addition to their normal workload. In fact, the goal statement should incorporate the activities that are part of normal responsibilities.

4. Employees are understandably concerned about the possibility of being penalized if they select goals that are too difficult and they fail to achieve them. That fear can be reduced by giving individuals an opportunity to revise their goals if it turns out they are unable to accomplish as much as they had expected.

JOB SATISFACTION IN TEACHING

A persistent question in the minds of administrators and organizational psychologists has to do with the relationship between job satisfaction and performance. We sometimes assume that working conditions that increase employee satisfaction result in increased worker productivity. However, the evidence for such a proposition is weak. The correlation between employee satisfaction and worker productivity is low, and the direction of the relationship is not clear. Does satisfaction lead to improved performance, or does improved performance result in greater satisfaction? Or are both variables related to some other factor?

We know that workers' job satisfaction may be influenced by factors that are unrelated to productivity. Consider a vendor who sells beer in a sports venue. The vendor derives satisfaction from the opportunity to watch sporting events free of charge, and his satisfaction is not affected by the amount of beer he sells. Here are some other examples of workers whose job satisfaction is unrelated to productivity: a coin collector who takes tolls on an expressway and who enjoys searching for rare coins in the change deposited by drivers, a librarian who spends her free time reading, a salesperson in an exclusive dress shop who loves the generous discount she gets on the newest styles, and a church custodian who looks forward to practicing Bach fugues on the pipe organ during his lunch hour.

Career Anchors and Teacher Satisfaction

Schein (1990) introduced the concept of career anchor as a way of explaining the factors that motivate people in their work. A career anchor is the meaning a job holds for an individual or the purpose fulfilled by the job. For an engineer, a job might mean being able to solve difficult problems; for a politician, working for and receiving support from voters; and for an athlete, competing and winning on the playing field.

EXHIBIT 5.1
COMMON CAREER ANCHORS

Challenging goals	Clearly defined goals that require mental or physical stretching
Structure	Clearly stated rules and expectations; clear chain of command
Tangible rewards	Money in the form of wages and bonuses
Security	Protection against being laid off or terminated; provision of medical insurance, retirement benefits, and so forth
Helping people	Providing a valued service to individuals in need, sometimes referred to as "making a difference"
Affiliation	Opportunity to work and interact with compatible, like-minded people
Working conditions	Having a comfortable, attractive work setting and adequate resources for the job
Personal/professional growth	Opportunity to develop and use new knowledge and skills
Recognition	Receiving praise or awards for the quality of one's work
Variety	Performing routines and tasks that are new or unexpected
Interesting work	Deriving pleasure from the nature of the work itself, including the pace, the demands of the job, and acquiring specialized skills.
Influence or control	Supervising, directing, or exerting influence over other people
Autonomy	Working without close supervision; being free to make decisions about one's job independently

When a person is asked to name the features of a job that are most appealing, the responses are clues to the individual's career anchors. Exhibit 5.1 lists some of the reasons people give when asked what they look for in a perfect job (Freemantle, 2001; Ritchie & Martin, 1999). Understanding what employees like and dislike about their jobs can help them derive more satisfaction from their work. Most people have a sort of hierarchy of features they look for in jobs, including some qualities that are essential in a job and others that are nice but not required.

Rewards and Security.   Tangible rewards and recognition are commonly used motivators in all types of work settings. Money and praise are powerful motivators, and although most people say that money is not the most important motivator for them, salary increases or expansion of fringe benefits are nevertheless welcomed by almost everyone. Money is valued not only for what it will buy but also as a symbol of success and approval. Few people enter teaching expecting to make a lot of money, but for many the security that teachers enjoy helps to compensate for the relatively low salaries. Most teachers are assured of continued employment as long as they are reasonably effective in the classroom and do not break the law or violate community expectations. Fringe benefits such as medical insurance and a retirement plan add to the security of a teaching career.

Working with People.   People who like working with others often choose to teach because it is a job that involves constant interaction. Teachers spend most of every day with young people, and they also have opportunities to talk with colleagues. Contact with people is such an integral part of teaching that anyone thinking about a teaching career who doesn't enjoy interacting with others would be well advised to choose a different occupation.

Nature of the Work.   Some individuals are attracted to teaching by the nature of the job. Teaching is knowledge work, and helping students to understand new material is a fulfilling experience for many in the field. Teaching also involves a fairly high level of autonomy, although this autonomy is more limited now than in the past because of mandated curriculum prescriptions and accountability requirements. Nevertheless, teachers continue to enjoy a degree of autonomy that is absent from many other occupations. Another career anchor for some teachers is the opportunity for personal and professional growth. Teachers are expected periodically to take coursework or engage in other educational experiences in order to renew their professional credentials, a requirement that meets the need of many teachers for growth and learning.

Working Conditions.   Working conditions are a positive feature of most teaching positions. Teachers work in clean, comfortable surroundings, and many take pride in decorating their classrooms attractively. Teaching also involves variety, and people who are motivated by variety like teaching because no two days are the same. However, that is not to say teachers don't get bored. Those who crave very high levels of variety discover after a few years that the newness has worn off and boredom has set in. Some of these teachers seek a change of scenery, either by moving to a different school or grade level, or both, or they may obtain additional degrees to qualify for supervisory or counseling positions, or even leave the profession altogether to seek employment in other fields.

Exerting Influence.   Teaching requires one to influence students, and a person who genuinely dislikes influencing other people is not likely to be very happy in the classroom. Some teachers discover they are very good at persuading others, and these people often migrate to positions of greater influence within or outside of the profession. They may move into the position of department head, serve on a district curriculum committee, or accept an appointment as union representative in their school. Others choose an administrative career path and obtain a master's degree in order to become an assistant principal or principal and eventually move to a central office administrative position.

Structure.   All workers want to know what is expected of them and how they will be evaluated. They like information about what to do and what actions they should avoid. They like consistency and predictability in the people with whom they work, particularly those in higher-level positions. One way by which a supervisor creates structure for employees is by identifying clear goals for performance. Goals also give workers a standard by which they are able to judge their own performance. Employees vary in the extent to which they are able to tolerate ambiguous goals. Some are able to "go with the flow" better than others, and those who supervise employees soon discover that some of their workers have a much greater need for clear-cut rules and deadlines than others.

Sources of Dissatisfaction in Teaching

Teacher dissatisfaction is not a widespread problem. Most teachers like their work. However, mandated testing and the pressure that accompanies it have robbed teaching of some of its rewards. Individuals who entered the classroom expecting to have autonomy to decide what and how to teach have discovered that those decisions have been taken out of their hands. The curriculum is rigidly prescribed, and the priority is on preparing students to take and pass standardized tests. Posner (2004) wrote that since the adoption of mandated testing programs, teacher competence is measured by students' scores and the pressure on teachers to raise the scores is enormous.

Under No Child Left Behind, schools in which students fail to make adequate yearly progress (AYP) for two consecutive years are designated in need of improvement and are required to develop plans for improvement. No one denies that schools in which students are not learning need to improve their programs. However, many people feel that labeling a school a failure on the basis of a single test is a mistake, and that no single test can accurately portray how well a school is performing (Klein, 2006).

One of the concerns about NCLB has been that the pressure it engenders to improve student performance would lead to widespread cheating in administering and scoring tests (Leithwood, 2001). That doesn't seem to have happened; however, there have been charges that some states have failed to test children with mental retardation and learning disabilities, and a recent report indicated that schools were not reporting test scores of nearly two million students from small racial subgroups (Davis, 2006).

Teachers in schools that lack instructional resources are especially likely to feel disgruntled when their schools are designated as failures. Many schools don't have funds with which to purchase the maps and charts, computer software, and supplemental books that help make lessons more meaningful for students and teachers' jobs somewhat more manageable. Schools with the greatest need for additional instructional resources—that is, those with concentrations of children from poor families—actually receive fewer resources than schools in more affluent areas, and the differences are substantial (Keller, 2003).

Teachers who are assigned to teach a subject for which they are not qualified often experience high stress and low satisfaction. If No Child Left Behind succeeds in ending the practice of assigning teachers to teach subjects they are not qualified to teach, it should help increase teacher job satisfaction.

Few conditions in schools arouse more teacher complaints than interruptions and distractions while they are trying to teach. Intercom announcements that interrupt instruction and required paperwork are two of the realities of teaching that cause frustration for teachers. Special education teachers in particular devote much of their own time to filling out forms documenting the needs of their students and the services provided for them. It has been estimated that special education teachers spend a half day each week on required paperwork. Most of these teachers understand the need for extensive record-keeping and view the extra work as a necessary, if unpleasant, part of the job. Nevertheless, excessive paperwork is probably a contributing factor to the high rate of attrition among special education teachers. Professional organizations representing special education teachers have appealed to the federal government to reduce the amount of paperwork teachers are responsible for, but those requests are opposed by parents who view the record-keeping as necessary to ensure that their children receive the services to which they are entitled (Goldstein, 2003).

JOB SATISFACTION AND TEACHER TURNOVER

Attrition is an important problem in teaching, as it is in many occupations. It has been estimated that about 13 percent of teachers leave the profession or change jobs every year (National Center for Education Statistics, 1998) and that about one-half of new teachers in urban schools leave within five years (Streisand & Toch, 1998).

Some districts have adopted new strategies to increase their teacher retention rates. Philadelphia Schools went from a 73 percent one-year retention rate for new teachers to 91 percent retention by spending more money on induction programs and coaching services (Phila. Makes Headway . . . , 2005). LaFourche Parish Schools in Louisiana lowered attrition from 56 to 7 percent after introducing a program that provided support for teachers. New teachers in that parish receive a warm welcome from the superintendent, followed by four days of training on effective classroom management and instructional practices. New teachers are made to feel they are part of the district "family" (Wong & Asquith, 2002).

Moving On

Recent entrants into teaching are less likely than earlier cohorts to plan for a life-long career in the classroom. These people expect to teach a few years and then move on to other jobs. However, dissatisfaction with the conditions of their work sometimes leads them to exit the profession even earlier than they had planned. It is important for administrators to identify the factors that contribute to teacher dissatisfaction and to work to eliminate as many as possible of those concerns in order to retain teachers who might otherwise exit early (Hardy, 2002).

As a group teachers are more satisfied with their jobs than people in most other occupations, but the conditions of their work, including the number of disruptive students in their classes, directly affect how they feel about their jobs. Some teachers leave the profession because they are discouraged by what they perceive as a lack of success in the classroom, and others decide they are not well suited temperamentally or intellectually for the work. Of course, some teachers leave the field for reasons that are unrelated to the work. Enrollment declines or changes in the family situation result in some teachers finding other work.

Inadequate salary is the reason given most often by individuals who leave teaching for other jobs, and some researchers have found that former teachers employed outside of the field of education do better economically than those who remain in the classroom (Metropolitan Life Insurance Company, 1985). Other reasons given for leaving teaching have to do with conditions in schools, including lack of input, too much paperwork, and dislike of the performance of nonteaching duties. There is some evidence that academically able teachers leave the field at a higher rate than their less-talented peers.

Organizational Correlates of Attrition

There has been little research on organizational features of schools that are related to higher levels of teacher attrition. If employees are able to develop feelings of belonging in the workplace, they are usually reluctant to leave. Some commercial firms do a better job than school districts in devising ways to retain employees, and school administrators might consider borrowing some of their ideas. Actions that have been used successfully in the private sector include creating websites where employees can register gripes about their work or obnoxious bosses. Even an action as simple as classifying e-mail messages so that employees are able to identify routine mail and delete it can make a job more pleasant. To encourage its employees to "have a life" outside of work a Cincinnati firm displays photographs of its employees engaged in their favorite weekend activities. The photos heighten feelings of belonging and have proven to be a potent recruiting device (Harris & Brannick, 1999).

Demographic Correlates of Attrition

Several demographic factors correlate with employee retention. Among those that have been shown to be related to attrition are length of service, age, level of skill, and education level. Workers who are younger, who have been with an employer a shorter length of time, and who have fewer skills are more likely than employees without those traits to leave their jobs. School districts that employ relatively large numbers of young teachers can expect to have higher-than-average turnover rates. However, teachers with higher levels of education are more, rather than less, likely to leave their jobs. That may be the result of increased awareness of job opportunities among teachers who hold advanced degrees.

In some districts, teachers who resign from their jobs are interviewed or asked to complete a questionnaire explaining their reasons for leaving. Although the validity of this information is debatable, it is an important source of data about an area of human behavior in which our knowledge is very limited. Unexplained increases in turnover may reveal previously unsuspected morale problems. An investigation is called for if turnover rates increase suddenly, particularly when the increase occurs among groups of teachers with normally low attrition.

Turnover generally refers to employees who leave a company or district altogether, but information about teacher transfers can also give clues about teacher motivation. Teachers transfer from one school to another in order to find more pleasant working conditions or greater convenience.

At the district level, a transfer has no effect on the overall composition of the teaching force, but at the school level it does. If an experienced teacher in a school is replaced by a less experienced one, the net result may be a decline in instructional effectiveness within the school. Principals, therefore, should be concerned with discovering the true reasons for teachers' requests for transfer and their decisions to leave the profession.

Not all attrition is to be deplored. Both from an individual point of view and from the point of view of the district, some is necessary and desirable. Individuals who discover that they have made the wrong career choice should be encouraged to seek other outlets for their talents.

SUMMARY

Motivation refers to conditions responsible for variations in the intensity, quality, direction, and duration of work-related behavior. Three theories cited to explain work motivation are expectancy theory (people are motivated by incentives), equity theory (people are motivated when a balance is maintained between the effort they and others put forth and the rewards received), and goal-setting theory (people are motivated to achieve goals). It is sometimes assumed that satisfaction leads to higher productivity, but the correlation is weak and may even go in the opposite direction. Career anchors refer to the meanings people derive from their work and include such things as influence or control, helping people, and recognition.

It is estimated that about 13 percent of all teachers change jobs or leave the profession every year. About one-half of new teachers in urban schools leave within five years. Programs that provide additional support for new teachers have been successful in reducing attrition among teachers in the districts that have tried them.

SUGGESTED ACTIVITIES

1. A consulting firm claims that 80 percent of employees could perform their jobs better if they chose to, 50 percent put forth only enough effort to keep from losing their jobs, and 10 percent would continue to work if they won a million dollars in the lottery. Do you think those figures are true of school employees? If you said *no*, what do you think the true figures are for teachers? What action might a principal take to reduce the percentage of teachers who work only hard enough to keep their jobs?

2. Consider the career anchors in Exhibit 5.1 and rate each factor on its importance for teachers. Rate each item as you think the majority of teachers would rate it, using the terms "Very important," "Somewhat important," and "Not important." For example, you might rate interesting work as very important to teachers and tangible rewards as somewhat important.

3. According to expectancy theory, employees are motivated when they believe that putting forth effort will lead to a reward. If no reward is offered, the theory says, they will not be motivated. If you were principal of a school and hoped to motivate teachers to prepare their students to do well on upcoming standardized achievement tests, what could you do to increase teachers' motivation? Is the action you propose to take consistent with expectancy theory?

4. Prepare a five-minute motivational talk for an orientation session with new teachers using one of the following quotations. (You can find these and other quotations at www.quoteland.com.)

   "I cannot believe that the purpose of life is to be happy. I think the purpose of life is to be useful, to be responsible, to be compassionate. . . . " (Leo Rosten)

   "Motivation is what gets you started. Habit is what keeps you going." (Jim Ryun)

   "I have not failed; I have just found 10,000 ways that don't work." (Thomas A. Edison)

ONLINE RESOURCES

Public Education Network (www.publiceducation.org)

> The network's mission is to "build public demand and mobilize resources for quality public education for all children."

Teacher Exchange Program (www.fulbrightexchanges.org)

> This site describes the Fulbright Teacher Exchange program by which American and foreign teachers can swap assignments for a semester or a year. Administrator exchanges are also offered.

Teachers' Resources (www.teachers.net)

> This site has lesson plans in a variety of subjects, classified advertisements, job listings, and chatboards for teachers.

Job Satisfaction among Teachers (nces.ed.gov/pubs97/web/97471.asp)

> Reports results of a 1997 National Center for Education Statistics survey of teachers' satisfaction with features of their jobs.

School Facilities and Teacher Satisfaction (www.edfacilities.org/pubs/teachersurvey.pdf)

> Findings from a survey by the National Clearinghouse for Educational Facilities of teachers' satisfaction with the facilities in which they teach. The survey was conducted in Washington D.C. and Chicago.

MetLife Survey (www.edweek.org/agentk-12/job-seeker-resources/2006/10/18/08metlife.h26.html)

> MetLife periodically conducts surveys of teachers' attitudes. This 2006 study found that teachers' satisfaction with their careers has increased over the past 20 years.

Workforce (www.workforce.com/index.html)

> This site provides information on topics having to do with motivation, including employee incentives, compensation plans, and satisfaction. The site is oriented to business users, but much of the material can be applied in educational settings. Free membership includes an e-mail newsletter.

CASE STUDIES

Case No. 1

Victor Sanchez is principal of Robin Hood Elementary School. Each year he gives a talk before new teachers in the district. His talk is entitled "How to Succeed on the Job." In it he tells teachers that they will be successful if they remember three rules:

1. Work hard at the right things.
2. Ask for help when you need it.
3. Develop a good attitude.

The teachers always have questions after his talk—What are the right things? How do I know when to ask for help? What is a good attitude, and how do I acquire it?

Questions

1. Do you agree with Sanchez that following his three "rules" will lead to success as a teacher?
2. Would you add other rules to his list or delete any of his three rules?
3. How would you answer the questions that teachers raise? (What are the "right" things? How to know when you need help? What is a "good" attitude?)

Case No. 2

Norine Schmidt teaches third grade at Drum Street Elementary School. This is her first year in the classroom. At the end of the first month of school, she asks to see the human resources director, Millie DuBois. "I'm going to have to quit my job," Ms. Schmidt says. She appears to be close to tears. Ms. DuBois asks what's wrong, and Ms. Schmidt explains:

"The principal is driving me crazy. Ms. Hawk. That's her name. That's a good name, too. She watches me like a hawk. She comes in my room when I'm teaching and tells me the window shades should all be at the same height—halfway up. She goes around and adjusts them all. She says the blackboard is dirty and I should wash it. Then she comes back a few minutes later with a bucket of water and starts washing the blackboard while I'm trying to teach. I say, 'You don't have to do that, Ms. Hawk. I'll take care of it. Right now I'm trying to teach a lesson.' She says, 'You need to keep the blackboard clean. When parents come in, the room should be clean and the blackboard freshly washed.'

"She comes back to my room after school and walks up and down, picking up scraps of paper and directing me to have my kids clean out their desks. 'I'll do that tomorrow,' I promise, but she ignores me. She says, 'Their desks are a mess. And while you're at it, straighten up your desk too. It's not much better than the kids' desks.'"

Ms. DuBois laughs. "That sounds like Ms. Hawk," she says.

"It's not funny," Ms. Schmidt says. "It's driving me crazy. I'm not the neatest person in the world, but my room's not that bad."

"You just have to get used to her," Ms. DuBois says. "She's a good principal and she will back you up if you have problems with parents. Just go along with her. After awhile she'll ease off."

"Can you transfer me to another school?"

"That's a drastic step, isn't it?" Ms. DuBois asks.

"I told you she's driving me crazy."

"I don't think it's a good idea to transfer schools in the middle of the year. You need to learn how to deal with problems. If you transfer, you'll still have problems. They may be different, but they'll still be problems."

"If you won't transfer me, then I'll submit my resignation and you can hire someone else to teach my class."

"I'd like you to take a day or two to think this over. I really believe you ought to talk to Ms. Hawk before you make a final decision. Tell her how you feel and that you want to work with her but her style makes it difficult for you."

"I'll think about it."

Questions

1. Does Ms. Schmidt have a legitimate complaint? Was Ms. Hawk out of line coming into Ms. Schmidt's classroom during a lesson?
2. Do you agree with Ms. DuBois's advice to Ms. Schmidt? Explain. Is any further action called for on Ms. DuBois's part? What would you advise Ms. DuBois to do?
3. What do you think Ms. Schmidt should do at this point?
4. Two values are in conflict in this scenario. What are they? Which value should prevail, in your opinion?

REFERENCES

Davis, M. R. (2006, May 3). Spellings addresses testing, NCLB issues. *Education Week,* pp. 27, 29.

Freemantle, D. (2001). *The stimulus factor.* London: Prentice-Hall.

Goldstein, L. (2003, May 28). Disabled by paperwork? *Education Week,* pp. 1, 23.

Hardy, L. (2002, April). Who will teach our children? *American School Board Journal, 189,* 18–23.

Harris, J., & Brannick, J. (1999). *Finding and keeping great employees.* New York: AMACOM.

Keller, B. (2003, May 28). Average teacher pay skews school budgets. *Education Week,* 3.

Kelley, C. (1998, May). The Kentucky school-based performance award program: School-level effects. *Educational Policy, 12,* 305–324.

Klein, A. (2006, May 3). Public dissatisfied over key NCLB provisions, report says. *Education Week,* p. 8.

Leithwood, K. (2001). School leadership and educational accountability: Toward a distributed perspective. In T. J. Kowalski and G. Perreault (Eds.), *21st century challenges for school administrators* (pp. 11–25). Lanham, MD: Scarecrow Press.

Locke, E. A., & Latham, G. P. (1984). *Goal setting: A motivational technique that works!* Englewood Cliffs, NJ: Prentice Hall.

Metropolitan Life Insurance Company. (1985). *Former teachers in America.* New York: Author.

National Center for Education Statistics. (1998). *The condition of education, 1998.* Washington, DC: U.S. Department of Education.

Phila. makes headway on recruitment, retention. (2005, April 27). *Education Week,* p. 11.

Pinder, C. C. (1984). *Work motivation: Theory, issues, and applications.* Dallas: Scott, Foresman.

Posner, D. (2004, June). What's wrong with teaching to the test? *Phi Delta Kappan, 85,* 749–751.

Ritchie, S., & Martin, P. (1999). *Motivation management.* Brookfield, VT: Gower.

Schein, E. (1990). *Career anchors.* San Diego: University Associates.

Streisand, B., & Toch, T. (1998, September 4). Many millions of kids, and too few teachers. *U.S. News & World Report.* [Online.] Available: www.usnews.com/usnews/issue/9809124 teac.htm.

Wong, H. K., & Asquith, C. (2002, December). Supporting new teachers. *American School Board Journal, 189,* 22–24.

CHAPTER

6   INDUCTION

People who are hired to fill a job they have not previously held have many questions about the work and the organization that will employ them. For those who are entering a field for the first time, the questions focus on job duties and expectations, income, opportunities for advancement, fellow workers, and one's superiors. Some of these questions are answered in the interview or in orientation sessions, but many are not. Unfortunately, most employers provide little information to help employees feel comfortable in their new work setting. What the new employee learns is usually acquired from other employees, varies in accuracy, and reflects the attitudes of those employees toward the employing organization.

PLAN OF THE CHAPTER

The following topics are discussed in this chapter: (1) from student to teacher, (2) purposes and types of induction, (3) mentors for beginning teachers, (4) administrative leadership for induction, and (5) induction for administrators.

FROM STUDENT TO TEACHER

Most teachers have had some teaching experience prior to their first job in the classroom. They've studied child psychology, instructional methods, and classroom organization in preparation for a teaching career, and they've observed many teachers at work. Yet despite this exposure, most beginners feel inadequate during their first few days and weeks on the job.

Becoming a teacher involves a role transition from student to teacher. Young teachers identify with the students they teach—after all, many are not much older than their students—and they feel awkward asserting authority and issuing directives. Some are afraid of appearing arbitrary or dictatorial and try to downplay the authoritarian aspects of the job. One teacher wrote of her first days in the classroom, "I identified emotionally with the students rather than the teachers. . . . I ricocheted between being a drill sergeant and Mary Poppins" (Metzger, 2002, p. 77). As a result of uncertainty such as this, which is common among beginning teachers, students are unclear about what is expected of them. They are quick to sense a teacher's vulnerability and take advantage of it.

Beginning teachers lack the adaptability that experienced colleagues have acquired over time. Veteran teachers sense students' confusion and boredom and make midcourse adjustments in their instruction to recapture attention or increase students' understanding. However, some beginning teachers hesitate to abandon a lesson plan, even if it is not working, afraid that the class will fall into chaos. Experienced teachers know that instructional strategies must be revised as a lesson progresses. This ability to observe and read students and use that information to make moment-to-moment adjustments to a lesson is a skill that comes from experience, which is acquired over time.

Functions of Induction

Induction programs are meant to help beginning teachers feel comfortable in their roles and help them acquire advanced instructional skills quickly. Unfortunately, many schools offer no induction program, or, if one is offered, it is deficient in the kinds of support teachers want and need. First-year teachers in these schools are left on their own with little help from the administration or their colleagues. Such schools have been charged with indifference to the needs of new teachers (Moir, 2005).

Induction serves several functions. It sets new teachers on a path leading to increased competence as professionals and initiates novices into a community of learners. Well-planned induction helps beginning teachers become participants in an ongoing interactive dialogue about teaching. It enhances teachers' job satisfaction and feelings of success and ultimately results in improved teacher retention. Sound induction programs are not cheap, but the high attrition that is typical of first-year teachers in districts without induction programs is also costly (National Commission on Teaching and America's Future, 2005). To appreciate the importance of induction and to gain insight into the elements of a well-designed induction program, it is helpful to understand what happens in the early years of teaching.

The New Teacher

The first years of teaching have been described as "intense and formative" (Feiman-Nemser, 2001) and a time of transition during which these young adults are learning who they are and what they wish to become (Schempp, Sparkes, & Templin, 1999). This is the period during which beginning teachers learn what behaviors are appropriate to their work and become aware of the unwritten values, norms, and operating procedures that guide interactions among the staff members in schools (Smylie, 1995). A teacher's first few years in the classroom are a critical period, when his or her identity is formed, skills are acquired, and far-reaching decisions about the future are made.

Beginning teachers have preformed impressions about the work of teaching gained from years of experience as students with a variety of teachers. From these mental images of teaching that they bring to the job, new teachers begin the work of creating professional identities. This is one of the critical tasks of the early years of teaching. The professional identity is forged from the teacher's own experiences in school, the ideas and experiences encountered during preservice preparation, and the experience of teaching itself (Feiman-Nemser, 2001).

The creation of a professional identity is only one of many challenges that new teachers face. Feiman-Nemser (2001) has identified four other tasks that also occupy the attention of young teachers: (1) to gain local knowledge of the students, the curriculum, and the school context; (2) to learn to teach responsively; (3) to develop a beginning repertoire of teaching strategies; and (4) to create a classroom learning community. Induction programs can be designed to help beginning teachers accomplish these tasks.

Learning about Students, the Curriculum, and the School Context. New teachers bring with them to the classroom information about child development from classes they've taken in teacher preparation programs, but what is true on average of all children in an age cohort is seldom true of any one child. The new teacher must learn to look at each child as an individual whose development fits the norm in some ways and departs from it in other ways. She or he learns that a child whose parents are divorced sees the world differently from one whose family is intact, that a child who has lived abroad for much of his or her life has a unique perspective, and that one who is well liked by classmates experiences a different reality from one who is ignored by peers. In short, new teachers must come to understand how students' life experiences shape and mold them.

Learning about one's students is only part of the knowledge new teachers acquire in their first few months on the job. They must also learn about the curriculum and the school context. Knowledge of curriculum entails awareness of the content that teachers are expected to cover, the number and types of state-mandated tests students will take, and the consequences of those tests for the students. In some districts teachers administer achievement tests and thus need to be familiar with testing procedures, and all teachers are expected to review test results and use the information to improve instruction.

New teachers begin to learn about context the moment they set foot in a school. School context refers to the community and the expectations held for teachers by parents and administrators. A school that was attended by the parents and grandparents of the current generation of children is markedly different from a school in an upwardly mobile community with few ties to the past. Parents in the first school may be skeptical of newer teaching methods and instructional materials. They may not be convinced of the need to change the way schools operate, whereas in the more mobile community, parents expect teachers to try new approaches.

Responsive teaching requires that a teacher be able to observe and understand the silent signals that indicate whether students understand the material, how interested they are in the lesson, and how well prepared they are to advance to the next level of comprehension. Beginning teachers have two problems in this area. One is their lack of familiarity with students' body language, and the other is their limited repertoire of teaching strategies.

Inexperienced teachers bring with them a limited repertoire of instructional strategies that they acquired during student teaching and from observing other teachers. They rapidly expand this repertoire through a process of trial and error, trying new ideas and retaining those that work while refining or discarding those that do not. Young teachers who are fortunate enough to teach in schools in which experimentation is encouraged and failure is not penalized will risk trying out new ideas, but if failure is looked down on, these teachers will play it safe and try only approaches that seem guaranteed to work. The result is that teaching is less varied and hence less likely to capture students' interest (Feiman-Nemser, 2001).

Survival. Beginning teachers are concerned about survival. They fear loss of control and thus move quickly to reestablish their authority when it is threatened by a disruptive student, but they may fail to spot signs quickly that indicate a student is confused. Indicators of lack of comprehension are more subtle than disruptive actions, but being able to understand them and act in response to them is no less important than acting quickly to end disruptive behavior.

A critical element of teaching is the ability to respond in useful ways to unexpected events. When a lesson doesn't go as planned or when instruction is interrupted, a teacher must be able to make adjustments to redirect the lesson or bring the group back on task. This is a learned skill that requires hard work on the part of beginning teachers.

The twin skills of interpreting student cues and responding appropriately have to be exercised together. Either one alone doesn't advance student learning. A teacher who understands students' cues but lacks a strategy to address the needs expressed thereby has limited success, as does the teacher with a broad knowledge of teaching strategies who is not able to tell when a particular strategy is called for. Teachers set a tone in their classrooms that may either add to or detract from student learning. A tone that encourages and demonstrates respect for other people's views creates a classroom climate that welcomes student success.

PURPOSES AND TYPES OF INDUCTION

The definition of *induction* used in this book is a planned program designed to facilitate the process by which new teachers in a school acquire the social and technical knowledge and skills they need to perform effectively in their work roles and interpersonal relationships (Smylie, 1995). Several distinct types of induction programs are in use in the schools: orientation programs, performance improvement programs, state-mandated assistance and assessment programs, and mentor programs.

These programs serve several purposes. They help to improve teacher effectiveness, encourage promising new teachers to remain in teaching by offering support and assistance, promote the professional and personal well-being of new teachers, communicate district and school cultures to beginning teachers, and help to meet state and federal mandates.

Orientation Programs

Orientation is the most common type of induction program in schools, but its impact on new teachers' instructional practices and professional commitments is minimal. Orientation sessions are brief and are designed to convey a large amount of information in a short time. Sessions often start by introducing members of the staff and critical central office personnel who explain their jobs and the kinds of assistance they can provide. Procedures for referring children for special attention are reviewed, and policies pertaining to grading, report cards, bell schedules, parent conferences, resource centers, computer use, and fire drills are discussed.

Participants in orientation sessions are at risk of being overwhelmed by information. They receive so much information, especially in the first few days of school, that they can recall only a fraction of it. Presentations are of more value if a handbook is available that summarizes important points and contains contact telephone numbers and e-mail addresses. A well-designed orientation program can help new teachers understand the expectations that are held for them and introduce them to members of their grade-level team or department. During orientation, some time may be reserved for department or grade-level planning.

Not all beginning teachers experience identical problems, but their experiences are similar enough that an orientation program can be developed around the issues with which they are most likely to need help. A good place to start is by asking what beginning teachers need help with. First-year teachers often have concerns about getting ready for the opening of school, dealing with parents, grading fairly, and covering the required curriculum.

Performance Improvement Programs

Performance improvement programs are offered for both new and returning teachers, and emphasize instructional and classroom management strategies that have been shown to increase student achievement. A topic that has received increased attention in performance improvement programs in recent years is how to assess student learning. Presenters explain the content of state-mandated achievement tests and offer suggestions on designing classroom tests that yield information on students' progress in learning that material. Teachers can use the information gleaned from these tests to determine which topics students have mastered, which ones may need to be reinforced, and which ones need to be retaught.

A number of topics of interest to teachers are suitable for a performance improvement workshop, for example, what to do about students who don't do their homework (Darling-Hammond & Hill-Lynch, 2006), adapting grading policies for students with disabilities (Munk & Bursuck, 2003), and managing classrooms effectively (Marzano & Marzano, 2003).

A common complaint of young teachers goes like this: "Most of my students are attentive and well behaved, but I have this one boy. . . ." Another begins, "I spend so much time trying to get students to settle down and stop talking and get ready to work. . . ." Or, "My students insult one another, call one another names, threaten one another. . . ." An experienced teacher who runs an orderly and child-centered classroom might be asked to talk about one of these issues with new teachers and share practices she or he has found to be effective.

Performance improvement programs are most effective when the sessions are scheduled at intervals over a semester or a year. Mastering new teaching strategies takes time, and few teachers derive lasting benefits from a one-shot, two- or three-hour workshop. Combining didactic instruction with small-group, open-ended sessions with specialists is an effective way to help new teachers achieve better results.

State-Mandated Induction Programs

In some states, beginning teachers are required to demonstrate that they possess certain teaching competencies in order to receive a permanent teaching certificate. In most state-mandated induction programs, an assessment or assistance team is designated to work with one or more beginning teachers. Usually, the team includes among its members one principal and one experienced classroom teacher. Some programs provide training for the team members, although the training is often brief and may be limited to use of a particular classroom observation instrument. Team members observe the beginning teacher and may give feedback on the teacher's performance along with recommendations on corrective actions. Four examples of state-mandated induction programs are as follows:

California Beginning Teacher Support and Assessment (BTSA) (www.btsa .ca.gov)

Connecticut Beginning Educator Support and Training (BEST) (www.state .ct.us.sde.dtl/s-a)

Louisiana Teacher Assistance and Assessment Program (LaTAAP) (www.doe .state.la.us/lde/uploads/2116.pdf). New teachers in Louisiana are assigned a mentor teacher who works with them for a full year to help prepare them for assessment.

Washington State Teacher Assistance Program (TAP) (www.k12.wa.us/ ProfDev/tap/default.aspx). This program provides grant funds for local districts to prepare mentors to work with beginning teachers.

MENTORS FOR BEGINNING TEACHERS

Some people equate induction with mentoring although the two are distinct and a district may offer induction with or without mentoring. Teachers have always mentored younger colleagues informally, but in recent years districts have moved to create formal mentoring programs. Rather than hope that experienced teachers will step in to help beginners, administrators are designating teachers for that role and offering training sessions to equip them with the skills they need to perform effectively. Many districts now either pay a salary supplement to mentors or allow them released time. In some cases, mentors work with other teachers half the day and teach classes the other half. Some districts use recently retired teachers as mentors.

Mentors go by a variety of names, including buddy teacher, support teacher, cooperating teacher, and teacher advisor, but regardless of the title, the duties are similar. Mentors help new teachers set up classrooms and prepare lesson plans; they suggest student activities and offer tips on managing classrooms and responding to parent inquiries. Mentors are available to answer the questions raised by new teachers. Many of these questions concern school policies and procedures, including questions about grades and initiating student referrals.

Teachers respond more readily to mentors than to principals and supervisors. This may be partially because teacher colleagues are more accessible than administrators, but it is also related to teachers' concerns that administrators may interpret the teachers' asking for help as evidence of lack of competence. Among the qualities that teachers look for in mentors are teaching experience, sensitivity, approachability, and a positive outlook. A longer list of desirable qualities of mentors appears in Exhibit 6.1.

Mentoring is credited with a number of beneficial results. They include helping teachers to adopt more effective instructional strategies, resulting in increased student achievement; creation of a more cohesive spirit among teachers; reducing the isolation of teachers; and lowering attrition (Brewster & Railsback, 2001).

Reducing Attrition

Research on the relationship of mentoring to teacher attrition rates shows that teachers in schools with mentoring programs are less likely to leave their jobs, as compared with teachers in schools without such programs. However, differences in the rates of attrition among mentored and nonmentored teachers are generally small and tend to narrow over time (Ingersoll & Kralik, 2004).

Teachers leave their jobs for a variety of reasons. Historically, male teachers have had higher attrition rates than females. Schools in which a majority of students are of a different racial or ethnic background than the teachers also have high

---

EXHIBIT 6.1

QUALITIES OF EFFECTIVE MENTORS IDENTIFIED BY MENTORS AND BEGINNING TEACHERS

PROFESSIONAL QUALITIES

Familiarity with school and district policies

Expertise in subject area or grade level

Knowledge of school's culture

Knowledge of "how things get done"

PERSONAL QUALITIES

Enthusiastic

Positive outlook

Patient and caring

Tactful

Accessible

TUTORIAL QUALITIES

Excellent teacher

Able to provide emotional support

Respectful of teacher's autonomy

Committed to providing time for advisee

---

attrition rates, and schools in which teachers say they receive little support from the principal lose proportionately more teachers than schools with more supportive administrators. Induction programs can be designed to address problems such as these.

Mentoring Minority Teachers

Teachers who are in a minority in a school may face special adjustment problems related to their status. Some minority teachers report that they are viewed by parents and even by other teachers as representatives of their group. Their values are sometimes taken to be typical of the values held by the group as a whole rather than as expressions of their individual attitudes and beliefs. Minority teachers are sometimes surprised to find that others expect them to know how other members of their group feel about a variety of educational and social issues (Brock & Grady, 2001).

Minority teachers also report that they are occasionally called on to give assistance when a majority teacher encounters a problem with a minority child.

They note that they do not mind helping other teachers, but they feel put on the spot when these requests involve assisting with discipline problems that have arisen as a result of a teacher's failing to state clear expectations for his or her students (Brock & Grady, 2001). Induction programs can be designed to include opportunities for both majority and minority teachers to explore issues that arise in the course of working together.

Starting a Mentoring Program

Teachers in schools that decide to start a formal mentoring program should be actively involved in its design. They will need to consider several critical questions as they prepare to implement a program. Among these questions are the following:

> *Who mentors?* In some programs, mentors are selected from teachers who work in the school, whereas in others retired teachers are recruited, either to serve as mentors or as substitutes for teacher–mentors. Both approaches have advantages. Retired teachers have more time, whereas employed teachers are more likely to be well informed about current programs and recent developments in teaching.

> *How many mentors?* When mentoring programs emerged in the 1970s, each beginning teacher was assigned one mentor. As teaching becomes more specialized, new teachers may work with two or more mentors, each with a particular specialty.

> *Who participates?* Some districts require all first-year teachers to participate, whereas in other localities all new teachers, including those with previous experience, take part. Required participation is the norm; few districts that are serious about improving teacher effectiveness allow voluntary participation.

> *How much time?* The time devoted to mentoring varies across the school year. Demands on a mentor's time are heavy during the first month or two of school but lessen as the year proceeds. A minimum of 50 hours of face-to-face interaction during the school year is a reasonable goal if teachers have a planning period that can be used for mentoring. In schools without planning time, it may be necessary to schedule conferences before or after school. E-mail is a convenient way for teachers and mentors to stay in touch when time for face-to-face meetings is limited.

> *Confidentiality of communications?* Beginning teachers should be told in advance whether information they give a mentor may be shared with an administrator. Some teachers will only agree to serve as mentors if they are assured that they will not be asked to evaluate their protégés or to share information about them. However, in some districts, mentors are expected to offer evaluative comments about their protégés. If that is the plan, all teachers should be told in advance.

Written policies? In districts with negotiated agreements, it is important that the union support the mentoring program. It is often wise to prepare a written policy statement that describes the purpose of the program and provides assurances that all provisions of the negotiated agreement will be upheld.

Training provided? Training to help prospective mentors acquire the skills they need to be effective with other teachers is a key element of successful programs. Brief, superficial training is not likely to have much impact. Training sessions should be designed to help mentors identify problems commonly encountered by beginning teachers and suggest possible solutions. Mentors should plan to spend more time listening than talking. They may also need to be reminded to maintain a nondirective stance and to show respect for the autonomy of the teachers with whom they work. The North Carolina Department of Public Instruction has an online handbook for mentors that can be used as a resource guide (www.ncpublicschools.org/mentoring_novice_teachers/mentoren.htm).

Change school culture? When mentoring is introduced into schools without a culture that values collegial support, it is seldom successful. Existing beliefs and practices should be studied to determine if they make teaching easier or more difficult for beginners. Practices that work against new teachers' success in the classroom should be discouraged.

ADMINISTRATIVE LEADERSHIP FOR INDUCTION

Principals play a key role in the success of induction programs in their schools. They act as facilitators by leading discussion groups or arranging for space, materials, and speakers. Principals also help facilitate induction by assigning mentors to new teachers and scheduling classes so that mentors and their charges have common planning periods. Principals who are committed to continuous learning serve as models for teachers in their schools and encourage new teachers to take advantage of the opportunities provided by induction (Payne & Wolfson, 2000).

One of the problematic aspects of programs that use mentors is helping experienced teachers to overcome a reluctance to comment on their colleagues' work. One author (Zahorik, 1987) made the following observation:

> Teachers must come not to fear exposing their classroom practices. They must see that knowledge of their classroom behavior by others as well as by themselves is essential to improvement. . . . Changing teachers' views of teaching is obviously a difficult and lengthy process, but it seems to be an unavoidable first step to developing collegiality, improving instruction, and making teaching satisfying work (p. 395).

Principals can help by encouraging all teachers to be more open in their teaching and by reassuring those who are observed by colleagues that they will not be evaluated on the basis of collegial observations.

Induction programs are subject to failure when unreasonably high expectations are held for them. They cannot be expected to overcome problems related to resource scarcity or policy limitations. Induction does not remove the need for ongoing professional development activities aimed at raising or maintaining the quality of the instructional program, and it does not take the place of performance evaluation.

Principals should be aware of the danger that induction may make poor teachers feel good about doing a poor job. Other potential problems arise when teachers without supervisory training or experience attempt to assist beginning teachers in improving their instructional practices or when narrowly defined instructional models are prescribed for all teachers, leading to standardized practice.

Induction is not a substitute for instructional leadership. Clearly defined performance expectations are essential for effective instruction, and induction programs cannot take the place of that ingredient. Principals are sometimes surprised to hear teachers report that performance expectations are not clear because they seem clear to them. What is needed is continuous reinforcement of behavioral expectations as employees learn new roles.

Recommendations for Principals

Following are suggested ways by which principals can help ensure the success of first-year teachers:

1. Do not overload new teachers or give them only the classrooms, materials, and students that other teachers reject (Patterson, 2005).
2. Limit extra duties for beginning teachers to allow them time to plan instruction (McCann, Johannessen, & Ricca, 2005).
3. Make performance evaluation a learning experience by providing feedback on ways of improving teaching and helping the new teachers connect with sources of support (Wayne, Youngs, & Fleischman, 2005).
4. Plan induction sessions that deal with topics of interest to beginning teachers timed to the school calendar.
5. Schedule a session early in the year on how to evaluate students' work and assign grades.
6. Plan a session on what to expect from parents and how to obtain their support.

INDUCTION FOR ADMINISTRATORS

Many teachers who consider becoming principals decide after investigating the job that they prefer something less stressful and without so many sticky problems. They conclude that principals are underpaid, considering the time they spend at work, and that their freedom of action is limited by laws, board policies, and parental vigilance. They become convinced that the negatives of being a principal outweigh the positives, and so they choose to remain in the classroom, leaving districts scrambling to fill administrative vacancies.

Traditionally, principals have been recruited from the ranks of assistant principals, but even that source of supply has shrunk as more assistants opt to stay where they are and let someone else assume ultimate responsibility for the school. They are willing to forgo the slightly higher salary and increased visibility that goes with the job of principal in order to limit their work-related stress.

There is a question whether being an assistant principal is really the best way to prepare for the principalship. Many assistants are so overwhelmed with the duties for which they are responsible—handling discipline referrals; supervising transportation; and making appearances at football and basketball games, school dances, and parent teacher association (PTA) meetings—that they have only limited opportunities to learn other aspects of the job. Some districts have recognized this problem and initiated programs to "grow" administrative leaders (Hix, Wall, & Frieler, 2003). These programs invite teachers who are considering switching careers to try out a variety of administrative tasks to find out what the job is like and decide whether they might like it.

Teachers in these programs have the title of aspiring administrator, administrative intern, or teaching assistant principal and spend as much as half of each day helping with student discipline, chairing various district or building committees, mentoring new teachers, coordinating student teachers, offering professional development workshops, and participating in peer evaluation programs. By the time they have had some experience with all of these activities, they understand the principal's job pretty well and know whether it's a role they would enjoy (Burdette & Schertzer, 2005). However, even with excellent preservice preparation, the job of being a principal can be daunting.

Learning the Job

Two areas that first-year principals find particularly challenging are learning what is expected of them in the role of principal and acquiring the technical skills to perform competently. These areas are related, but they are not identical. Conflicting role expectations are a persistent problem for principals. Teachers expect one thing, whereas many parents expect something different. Sometimes central office personnel hold a third set of expectations. The principal can't please all of these parties and must search for a solution that at least partly satisfies all constituents. New principals are tempted to agree with the first person who seeks to influence them, but when they do, they quickly discover that other members of their role set prefer different actions. Learning to negotiate a satisfactory response to varied expectations is essential for survival in the job, and until a new principal is able to do that, he or she is likely to be wracked by stress.

Learning the technical skills needed on the job is partly a matter of mastering the contents of policy manuals and master contracts. These documents spell out how recurring problems are dealt with and provide answers to frequently asked questions. If a principal faces a dilemma that is not covered, he or she has to try to find someone who has encountered the problem in the past. For a first-year principal every problem is new, but somewhere in the district there is probably an administrator who has dealt with a similar dilemma who would be willing to share what he or she learned. Finding that person requires some searching, which is a good reason why new principals should start on the day they begin the job to line up a list of individuals they can turn to for advice when they face a critical decision.

In districts that offer induction programs for principals, the process of locating advisors is easier. If the district assigns mentors to new principals, the mentor is usually the first contact, and if the mentor is not able to answer the question, he or she can usually suggest someone who can. A well-designed induction program helps new principals quickly acquire much of the knowledge they need to meet the challenges of the job. Although induction is only one aspect of a comprehensive professional development program, it is an important component.

Elements of Induction

Induction for principals should include an orientation session for all principals who are new to the district. First-year principals should be assigned individual mentors who can answer their questions and who are accessible on a regular basis. Arrangements should be made to set aside time for the new principal to meet face to face with the mentor away from possible interruptions to discuss professional issues. A support team consisting of the mentor and a central office administrator and perhaps one or two others should be appointed early in the year to observe the new principal and evaluate his or her performance. The mentor probably should not be asked to evaluate the principal because that is likely to hinder the trust and open communication that is an essential part of mentoring.

Features of some induction programs that appeal to first-year principals include shadowing a practicing principal (possibly the mentor) and making site visits to other schools. Shadowing allows the new principal to watch an experienced administrator at work and gives the newcomer a chance to discuss the rationale for the principal's decisions. Site visits should be as unstructured as possible and allow the visitor a chance to roam the building, observing and chatting with teachers and other staff members.

Orientation

Orientation helps new principals learn a lot about the job in a short time. A sound orientation program acquaints new administrators with district policies and procedures and reviews significant legislation, both state and federal. Exhibit 6.2 lists topics that might be included in an orientation session for new principals. To cover

EXHIBIT 6.2
TOPICS TO BE COVERED IN AN ORIENTATION
SESSION FOR FIRST-YEAR PRINCIPALS

District organizational structure
District strategic plan
Professional development programs for teachers
School curriculum and testing program
School improvement process
Special education laws and regulations
Parent and community relations
Media communications
Budgeting
Facilities management
Sexual harassment policy
Student discipline policy
Recruiting and hiring employees
Staff supervision and evaluation
Administering the master contract
Employee misconduct
Nonrenewal and termination
Calendar of events

all of the material shown in the exhibit would require several sessions spaced over a period of weeks or months.

Simply reviewing district policies may not be sufficient to ensure that new principals acquire the skills they need to be effective. Although most first-year principals have had some administrative experience, some will have had more experience than others, and induction programs should be designed to take these differences into account. For individuals with minimal administrative experience, a longer and more intensive induction experience may be needed.

The Massachusetts Department of Education has prepared a list of recommended objectives for an induction program for first-year principals and assistant principals. Following are some of the objectives from that list. These are ambitious goals, and some of them will require that participants have an opportunity to practice the skills and receive supportive feedback from an experienced administrator.

1. Learn to create and sustain a school culture that focuses on high achievement and helps teachers to work together
2. Expand and refine knowledge related to supervision and evaluation of staff
3. Learn how to provide instructional leadership for teachers by serving as a knowledgeable resource
4. Develop the ability to collaborate with teachers, parents, and community groups on matters of importance to the school
5. Become familiar with procedures for collecting student performance data and engaging staff in analyzing and using data to inform decisions about instruction
6. Acquire proficiency in developing and implementing a school performance improvement plan
7. Learn skills of working in a group to plan strategies for improving student learning
8. Become familiar with budget planning and management
9. Understand and use conflict resolution and problem-solving strategies

Learning about Leadership

No one is a born leader; leadership is a skill that must be learned. However, some people are born with traits that predispose them to leadership. Presumably all principals have leadership qualities or they wouldn't have been selected for the job. Well-designed induction programs for administrators can sharpen and direct the leadership skills an individual possesses. Some skills that are characteristic of good leaders are as follows:

Ability to Create a Vision. Good leaders are not content with the status quo and are able to project a vision of an alternative future that inspires followers. The vision needn't be original; it may have been borrowed. What is important is that the leader is able to inspire followers to help realize the vision.

Acceptance of Responsibility. President Harry S. Truman had a sign on his desk that read "The buck stops here." He understood that, as president, he was ultimately responsible for both the successes and the failures of his administration. Good leaders accept responsibility for the performance of their organizations. When things go wrong, they accept the blame, and when things go right, they share the praise.

Willingness to Learn from Critics. Leaders are often criticized when something goes wrong in an organization. A leader must be able to accept criticism without lashing out or losing heart and use it to improve the organization's performance. Being able to explain and defend one's decisions are characteristic of good leaders.

Persistence. Good leaders stay with a project until it is completed. People with fleeting interests seldom make good leaders because when their interest lags, they abandon what they are working on and move on. Being able to stay with a job until it is done is especially critical when new ventures encounter difficulties.

SUMMARY

The first years of teaching are intense and formative. Many new teachers find the transition from student to teacher to be difficult. Well-planned induction programs can help ease this transition by initiating new teachers into a school community, thus increasing their comfort in the new role. They can also equip these teachers with skills they need to be successful in the classroom. The most common type of induction is orientation, which is heavy on information. Other types include performance improvement programs and state-mandated programs. Mentors are popular with new teachers who are attracted by the opportunity to interact with a person whom they hope has answers for the problems they encounter.

Questions to be considered in starting a mentor program include how to select mentors, how to decide who participates, and how much time to devote to mentoring activities. Confidentiality of communications between mentors and their protégés should also be addressed in planning mentor programs. Principals can help ensure new teachers' success by limiting their workloads and planning induction workshops around issues of immediate concern. Induction for administrators takes the form of internships, also known by other names, in which prospective administrators have an opportunity to deal with real-life administrative issues.

SUGGESTED ACTIVITIES

1. Pick a topic from Exhibit 6.2 and prepare a five-minute talk for a group of new principals to be presented at the opening of the school year.

2. Choose an occupation with which you are unfamiliar from the *Dictionary of Occupational Titles* (www.oalj.dol.gov/libdot.htm), preferably one outside the field of education. Suppose you have been offered a job in that field. Compose a list of 5 to 10 questions you would like to have answered before deciding whether to accept the position.

3. Interview a teacher about his or her experiences during the first year in the classroom and prepare a talk on your findings. How would this person characterize the first year? (A year of growth and discovery or a year of disappointment and despair?) Did the school offer an induction program for new teachers? If so, what was good about it? What was missing? What problems did the new teacher encounter in the first year with which he or she would have liked help?

4. Locate information about No Child Left Behind on the Internet and prepare a five-minute talk to inform new teachers about the law's important features and how to comply with them.

ONLINE RESOURCES

National Education Association (www.neafoundation.org/publications/mentoring.htm)

This publication is based on proceedings of a symposium on teacher mentoring sponsored by the National Education Association's Foundation for Improvement of Education in 1999. It contains a number of suggestions on designing effective mentoring programs.

LearnNC (www.learnnc.org)

Sponsored by the School of Education at the University of North Carolina at Chapel Hill, this site provides an abundance of ideas and resources for beginning teachers. Among them are lesson plans, articles, references, lists of online courses, teaching websites, and information about field trips in North Carolina.

Scholastic (http://teacher.scholastic.com/newteacher)

This site contains ideas, activities, and support for first-year teachers. Lesson plans, classroom organizers, assessment resources, and a teacher store are found here.

Howard County Public Schools (www.howardk12.md/us/sdc/newteacher.html)

This site features an outline of new teacher orientation sessions offered by Howard County (Maryland) Schools.

Alliance for Excellent Education (www.all4ed.org)

The complete text of a report entitled "Tapping the Potential: Retaining and Developing High-Quality New Teachers" is available at the Alliance website.

CASE STUDIES

Case No. 1

You are the new principal of Plateau Elementary School. The faculty is divided into two camps—a large group of older teachers who have taught at the school for 20 or more years and a smaller group of younger teachers who have arrived within the past two years.

In a meeting with young teachers, you've learned that several older teachers in your school discourage young teachers from asking questions or making comments at faculty meetings. They tell them, "We'll get out earlier if you don't say anything." Two of the young teachers have told you that they would like to have commented about some items on recent meeting agendas but remained silent out of fear they would be ridiculed by older teachers. You have a faculty meeting scheduled later today.

Question

1. Which of the following responses will you give the young teachers who have just met with you? Give reasons for your choice.

   a. Thank you for coming.

   b. I'll put this on the agenda for today's faculty meeting.

  c. Give me the names of the teachers who told you to keep quiet.

  d. No one wants to prolong faculty meetings. Next time you have a question, see me after the meeting.

  e. This is something you should work out with the other teachers.

2. Which of the possible responses do you think is weakest? Explain why you think so.

Case No. 2

"Ann asked me to bring this to you." Jonathan handed an envelope to Ms. Stanley, the school secretary.

"Ann who?" Ms. Stanley asked.

"My teacher."

"You mean Ms. Szymendera, don't you?"

"That's her. She asked us to call her Ann," Jonathan replied.

Ms. Stanley ripped open the envelope and peeked inside. It contained unsold tickets for the upcoming spaghetti supper and cash receipts from tickets that had been sold. "Fine. Thanks." She frowned. "Why does Ms. Szymendera want you to call her Ann?"

"Because no one can pronounce her name."

"Don't you think you could learn it?" Ms. Stanley asked.

Jonathan shrugged. "She just said to call her Ann."

"I think you'd better call her Ms. Szymendera," Ms. Stanley replied.

"Yes, ma'am. But she insists we call her Ann in class."

Later Ms. Stanley spoke to Brad Post, the principal. She said, "I thought you ought to know. Jonathan Brady told me that Ms. Szymendera asked her students to call her Ann. It's probably none of my business, but that seems awfully familiar. I know she's new and not much older than her students, but still. . . ." Her voice trailed off.

Post looked up from his computer. "Why does she want them to call her by her first name?"

"The students have trouble with Szymendera."

Post smiled and jotted a quick note on his legal pad. "Ask her to stop by my office after school. I'll speak to her about it."

Questions

1. What are some arguments for and against teachers' inviting students to use their first names?

2. If you were Brad Post, what would you say to Ms. Szymendera when you meet with her?

REFERENCES

Brewster, C., & Railsback, J. (2001, May). Supporting beginning teachers: How administrators, teachers and policymakers can help new teachers succeed. Portland, OR: Northwest Regional Educational Laboratory. [Online.] Available: www.nwrel.org/request/may01/textonly.html.

Brock, B. L., & Grady, M. L. (2001). *From first-year to first-rate* (2nd ed.). Thousand Oaks, CA: Corwin.

Burdette, M., & Schertzer, K. (2005, May). Cultivating leaders from within. *Educational Leadership, 62,* 40–42.

Darling-Hammond, L., & Hill-Lynch, Olivia. (2006, February). If they'd only do their work! *Educational Leadership, 63,* 8–13.

Feiman-Nemser, S. (2001, December). From preparation to practice: Designing a continuum to strengthen and sustain teaching. *Teachers College Record, 103,* 1013–1055.

Hix, B., Wall, S., & Frieler, J. (2003, February). From the ground up: Growing your own principals. *Principal Leadership, 3,* 22–25.

Ingersoll, R., & Kralik, Jeffrey M. (2004, February). The impact of mentoring on teacher retention: What the research says. Retrieved from www.ecs.org/clearinghouse/50/36/5036.htm.

Marzano, R. J., & Marzano, J. S. (2003, September). The key to classroom management. *Educational Leadership, 61,* 6–13.

McCann, T. M., Johannessen, L. R., & Ricca, B. (2005, May). Responding to new teachers' concerns. *Educational Leadership, 62,* 30–34.

Metzger, M. (2002, September). Learning to discipline. *Phi Delta Kappan, 84,* 77–83.

Moir, E. (2005, December 7). New-teacher support: Improving retention and quality simultaneously. *Education Week,* p. 36.

Munk, D. D., & Bursuck, W. D. (2003). Grading students with disabilities. *Educational Leadership, 61,* 38–43.

National Commission on Teaching and America's Future. (2005). *Induction into learning communities.* Washington DC: Author.

Patterson, M. (2005, May). Hazed! *Educational Leadership, 62,* 20–23.

Payne, D., & Wolfson, T. (2000, October). Teacher professional development—The principals' critical role. *NASSP Bulletin, 84,* 13–21.

Schempp, P., Sparkes, A., & Templin, T. (1999). Identity and induction: Establishing the self in the first years of teaching. In R. Lipka & T. Brinthaupt (Eds.), *The role of self in teacher development* (pp. 142–161). Albany: State University of New York Press.

Smylie, M. (1995). Teacher learning in the workplace: Implications for school reform. In T. Guskey and M. Huberman (Eds.), *Professional development in education* (pp. 92–113). New York: Teachers College Press.

Wayne, A. J., Youngs, P., & Fleischman, S. (2005, May). Improving teacher induction. *Educational Leadership, 62,* 76–78.

Zahorik, J. A. (1987). Teachers' collegial interaction: An exploratory study. *Elementary School Journal, 87,* 385–396.

PROFESSIONAL DEVELOPMENT FOR EDUCATIONAL PERSONNEL

All personnel functions have a direct or an indirect impact on school effectiveness, but none has a greater potential effect than professional development and training. Professional development provides opportunities for teachers and other professional and support personnel to acquire new skills and attitudes that can lead to the changes in behavior that result in increased student achievement.

However, despite its promise, professional development often fails to achieve the results that planners hope for and expect. This chapter examines some of the reasons that professional development is less successful than it might be and reviews how these programs are changing in response to shifting expectations and the emergence of new organizational forms in schools.

PLAN OF THE CHAPTER

The following topics are discussed in this chapter: (1) functions of professional development, (2) characteristics of effective professional development, (3) planning for professional development, and (4) professional development for administrators and support personnel.

FUNCTIONS OF PROFESSIONAL DEVELOPMENT

In this book, *professional development* is defined as any activity or process intended to maintain or improve skills, attitudes, understandings, or performance of professional and support personnel in present or future roles. Professional development activities are intended to increase the capacity of the entire faculty of a school to strengthen student performance (Youngs & King, 2002). Thus, professional development is best viewed from a systemic perspective, taking into account the cumulative strengths and weaknesses of the total staff for the purpose of developing plans for improving the knowledge and skills of instructional staff members as a group.

Professional development serves four important functions: (1) implementing curriculum change, (2) improving instructional practices, (3) enabling teacher growth, and (4) changing organizational climate. The first three of these functions are described in this chapter; organizational climate is covered in Chapter 10.

Implementing Curriculum Change

When a school system adopts new curricula, workshop leaders have the task of helping teachers prepare to teach the new content to their students. Presenters explain reasons for the change, address teachers' concerns, share appropriate materials and ideas, and offer demonstration lessons. They may also suggest ways of assessing student mastery of the revised content. If the new curriculum is a departure from previous ones, the presenters may also coach teachers in order to ensure a smooth transition.

Students learn more from teachers who have actually worked with a new curriculum before they teach it, according to the results of a study in California. Researchers compared the results of two types of professional development sessions for 559 teachers preparing to introduce a new math curriculum. Some of the teachers took part in one-day workshops, and others were involved in longer-lasting sessions in which they actually worked with the new curriculum units. The results showed that students of teachers who had worked with the new curriculum scored higher on state math exams compared to students taught by the teachers who spent less time preparing and who did not have a chance to handle the curriculum units (Viadero, 2005).

Improving Instructional Practices

The accepted measure of instructional quality is student performance, which is strongly influenced by teacher expertise. One study found that 40 percent of the difference in student test scores was attributable to teacher skills (Viadero, 2005). Given that finding, professional development activities that focus on adding to teachers' instructional repertoires hold promise for increasing student achievement. Combining professional development with thoughtful attention to teacher selection can lead to dramatic improvements (Simmons, 2005).

Enabling Teacher Growth

Professional development has long been viewed as a means by which teachers are able to "keep up" with new developments in their fields. Since the passage of No Child Left Behind, professional development is seen as a way to help school districts comply with the law's requirement that all students be taught by "highly qualified" teachers.

Highly qualified teachers hold bachelor's degrees, are fully certified or licensed by the state in the subject or at the grade level they teach, and demonstrate knowledge of their subject field. Knowledge of subject is shown by completion of a college major or course credits equivalent to a major, passing a state-developed test, or holding a graduate degree in the field.

For current teachers, one other avenue is available to meet the highly qualified standard—High Objective Uniform State Standard of Evaluation or HOUSSE, which offers current teachers a means by which to demonstrate their knowledge of a subject without having to take additional training or pass a test. The federal government requires that state-developed HOUSSE programs meet several criteria, including these:

- HOUSSE requirements must be aligned with challenging state academic content and be developed in consultation with teachers, principals, and subject specialists.
- Requirements must be applied uniformly to all teachers in a given subject field or at a specified grade level.
- Requirements may take into consideration the length of time an individual has taught, but experience may not be used as the sole criterion for subject matter competence.
- Requirements may involve multiple objective measures of teacher competence.

CHARACTERISTICS OF EFFECTIVE PROFESSIONAL DEVELOPMENT

There is little agreement about which features of professional development are most important. Guskey (2003) reported that he had examined 13 lists that claimed to identify characteristics of effective professional development programs and found that the various lists had few items in common. Elements of one list were contradicted by those of other lists. Of course, discrepant findings from research are not unusual. In this case they may have resulted from the use of different definitions of *effectiveness* or from differences in the way variables were measured. Whatever the cause, one would be wise not to take any single report as the final word on effectiveness of professional development.

Recent research has shown that programs that involve teachers in collaborative activities and in which all teachers in a school, department, or grade level are involved, are more likely to produce observable changes in instruction than programs that involve only a few members. This seems to be especially true when teachers are learning about new technology (Desimone, Porter, Garet, Yoon, & Birman, 2002). However, some researchers have found that technical skills are best learned, not as distinct topics of study, but with consideration given simultaneously to teachers' knowledge, experience, and beliefs (Lieberman, 1999).

Activities that emulate what takes place in classrooms are the surest way to have an impact on teaching practice. In these activities teachers take on the role of learner and experience how an explanation or demonstration by a skilled facilitator enhances their understanding of new material. Facilitators model for teachers the techniques that research and experience have shown to be effective. They pose open-ended questions about content and provide opportunities for teachers to work on activities that allow them to think as scientists, mathematicians, historians, or authors (Cutler & Ruopp, 1999).

Teachers acquire knowledge about teaching from a variety of sources, of which professional development is only one. Reading, coursework, conversations with colleagues, and work with students are other sources from which teachers gain new insights, expand their knowledge, and add to their repertoire of skills. One writer distinguishes "inside" and "outside" knowledge. *Outside knowledge* comes from consultants, conferences, and books, whereas *inside knowledge* is learning that is gained from conversations with and observations of colleagues and from one's own experience in the classroom. Teachers tend to view outside knowledge as abstract and theoretical. It is advisable for planners to maintain a balance between the amount of inside and outside knowledge presented and to seek to blend information from these sources into a meaningful configuration to increase teacher interest and comprehension (Lieberman, 1999).

NCLB Requirements

No Child Left Behind establishes standards for professional development activities for teachers. The law advocates plans that are high quality, research based, and classroom focused and that help to increase teachers' knowledge of their subjects. NCLB also requires that professional development programs be "regularly evaluated" for their impact on teaching practices and student academic achievement. (The evaluation of professional development activities is discussed at length later in this chapter.) As noted previously, research on the effects of professional development on teachers' classroom practice is often inconclusive or contradictory, and there is little agreement about which specific features of these programs are key to their effectiveness.

Preparing for Change

Professional development programs seldom have any lasting effect on teachers' classroom practice unless the workshop is supplemented by efforts to prepare teachers to adopt the new approach and combined with support and assistance for those attempting to make the change. Teachers are inclined to continue to teach the way they have taught in the past unless they see a reason to change and believe they will gain something by changing.

Advance preparation for change starts with an awareness of the need for change. When the current way of doing things doesn't lead to the desired results, people begin to search for a better way. When most everyone agrees on the need for change, a new approach is likely to be welcomed.

Congruence and Ease of Adoption

Successful adoption of new ways of teaching requires that teachers understand the new approach and take time to practice it. Teachers prefer strategies that are congruent with their teaching philosophies and that are not too difficult to implement—that is, that do not take undue amounts of time and effort to master. Teachers seldom adopt new methods that take a great amount of time to learn or that they regard as being in conflict with their closely held beliefs. Consider a teacher who prefers to use the discovery method for teaching science. In this approach, the instructor organizes learning materials and guides students through a series of experiences that are designed to lead students to new insights about the topic under consideration. If this teacher were asked to adopt a curriculum that transmitted knowledge to students through reading and listening to lectures, it is unlikely that teacher would welcome the change.

Most teachers would like to find methods and materials that produce better results than those they are using, and they are inclined to try innovations that promise to do that. For staff developers, the implications of those facts are clear. They should select strategies that have been shown to be effective in increasing student learning and should plan workshops to include clear explanations and demonstrations showing how the techniques work.

PLANNING FOR PROFESSIONAL DEVELOPMENT

Three features of high-quality professional development programs are important. They are (1) sustained rather than sporadic, (2) intensive rather than disconnected, and (3) classroom focused rather than theory centered. A sustained program is one in which a series of workshop sessions, rather than one or two, are offered over a period of time. Intensive activities engage learners in observing, listening, processing, reacting, and practicing as opposed to simply listening. Classroom-focused activities feature ideas with immediate application to teaching. Traditionally, much professional development for teachers has consisted of brief one-time workshops that lacked intensity and were not immediately applicable to classroom practice.

Planning for professional development should take into account the results of research on teacher learning and on teacher adoption of new instructional methods. Some of the findings of this research that are useful for planning are as follows:

1. Increasing the amount of time devoted to professional development results in more change in teachers' classroom practices and more student learning.
2. Presenting academic content that teachers are expected to cover is more effective than limiting the focus to teaching techniques.
3. Encouraging teachers to adapt their instruction to students' thought processes helps increase student achievement.

4. When teachers engage in professional development in intact teams that include administrators, the results are more effective and longer-lasting than when individuals from several schools come together.
5. Aligning professional development to a school or district mission and goals produces better results than more generic approaches to training.

Centralized versus Decentralized Programs

Planners of professional development must consider whether to offer centralized or decentralized workshops. There are advantages and disadvantages to both practices. Centralized offerings are designed to involve large numbers of teachers from all or most of the schools in the district, whereas decentralized plans are developed for teachers in a single school based on the needs and interests of those teachers.

Goodlad (1983, p. 36) claimed that "the individual school is the most viable unit for effecting educational improvement." Proponents of that position argue that, by directly involving teachers in decisions about content and format, decentralized programs generate interest and commitment and lead to more collaboration between teachers and administrators. Another advantage cited by supporters of the decentralized approach is that such programs are more relevant than centralized offerings to the needs and interests of teachers in each school.

However, decentralized programs also have potential disadvantages. One of the main drawbacks is the heavy demand they make on the time of the principals and teachers who are involved in planning and presenting training workshops. Most principals feel they already have too little time for instructional leadership responsibilities, and adding more duties further complicates that problem. School-based programs are also somewhat less efficient than centralized operations because some duplication is unavoidable.

Cost of Professional Development

A Maryland district that has dedicated a substantial amount of its resources to professional development has seen students' test scores rise and the gap between various ethnic and racial groups narrow. Montgomery County (Maryland) sets aside about 3 percent of its annual budget for recruitment and development of staff (Gewertz, 2005). Some features of Montgomery County's professional development programs include the following:

- Partnerships with local universities help the universities tailor their preparation programs to identified needs of Montgomery County schools.
- Principals are given greater freedom to make teacher selection decisions.
- Teachers and other staff members are involved in the selection process.
- Administrators are trained to identify and support good teachers.
- Every school has a full-time staff-development teacher.
- Every teacher is required to prepare an individual improvement plan.

The National Staff Development Council (NSDC) recommends that 10 percent of school budgets and 25 percent of teacher time be devoted to professional development (Kelleher, 2003). School districts with limited financial resources for professional development must choose between in-depth programs for a few staff members and less intensive activities for a greater number. Most districts choose the second option, even though research suggests that more intensive programs have greater impact on teachers' instructional practices (Desimone et al., 2002). Collective participation (that is, all or most of the teachers from a single school participating in the same activity) enables teachers to discuss problems that arise in implementing new strategies and allows them to share workable adaptations with one another (Birman, Desimone, Porter, & Garet, 2000).

Time and Pacing

Finding time for professional development is a challenge. Workshops may be scheduled early in the day before classes start or after the school day ends, on days set aside for that purpose, during regularly scheduled department or faculty meetings, during times when substitute teachers are able to take over classes, or during the summer. All of these plans have advantages and disadvantages. Freeing teachers from teaching duties during the school day is desirable, but it is also the most costly. Summer workshops allow teachers to focus on their own learning without the distractions that are present during the school year, but teachers like to reserve their summers for their families. Summer training is also expensive.

The least desirable time for scheduling workshops is at the end of a school day, when teachers are likely to be tired and preoccupied with other responsibilities. Some teachers like early morning sessions, but those with small children may complain about the difficulty of getting their children dressed, fed, and off to school or daycare an hour or two early on training days.

Some school districts start classes late once a week and use that time for professional development (Standerfer, 2005). A month's schedule of early morning sessions might include one devoted to curriculum exploration within departments, one for sharing and demonstrating instructional strategies, and a third for practice in analyzing student test results to determine what areas and skills are in need of improvement. The key to success with a plan such as this is to keep it flexible. No single approach fits all teachers, and allowing for varied content and formats produces better results.

Many districts dismiss students one day a month to allow for uninterrupted training time for teachers. The disadvantage is that students lose instruction and some parents complain about having to make other arrangements for child care on those days. Reserving time for teacher workshops during the week before classes start works well for many districts. Distractions are at a minimum at that time, and teachers are mentally prepared to think about instruction. That time also avoids loss of instructional time that results from scheduling teacher training during the school year.

Use of teachers' personal time for development is the least costly option for the district, but it is also the least feasible. Some teachers are willing to use their own time to work on advanced degrees, but few willingly participate in professional development activities on their own time.

Design of the Program

In designing professional development activities, planners need to consider six factors: objectives, content, teachers' opinions, delivery, pacing, and participants.

Objectives. The outcomes of professional development for teachers can be changes in knowledge, behavior, or attitudes for individuals or groups. A single activity may have objectives of several types, but the more different outcomes the planners envision, the more complex the venture becomes and the harder it is to ensure that the desired results will be obtained.

Objectives may be stated either as individual or group outcomes. Here is an example of an individual objective: "All participants will demonstrate familiarity with five techniques for teaching thinking skills to students in the grade level or subject they teach and will commit themselves to try all five techniques in their classes within one month." A group objective could be stated in the following way: "Participants will collectively identify methods of increasing time on task that have worked in their own classes and will agree to try at least two new methods in their classes and discuss the results with colleagues within one month." Exhibit 7.1 summarizes examples of the three types of objectives for both individuals and groups.

Content. The content of professional development programs usually comes from one of two areas—subject matter knowledge or pedagogical knowledge. A number of educators believe that the key to raising student achievement is ensuring that teachers have a sophisticated understanding of the subject they teach and are well informed about how students learn (Birman et al., 2000).

However, not everyone agrees. Those who do not share the belief that lack of knowledge of content is a greater problem than lack of pedagogical knowledge have received support from a recent survey of principals conducted in New York State (Torff, 2005). Responses from 242 principals, about half from high-performing and half from low-performing schools, showed that administrators in both types of schools regarded deficiencies in teachers' pedagogical knowledge as the more common problem.

Researchers asked principals to rate the frequency with which teachers whom they considered to be weak displayed each of five deficiencies (lack of content knowledge, poor lesson-planning skills, poor lesson-implementation skills, inability to establish rapport with students, and ineffective classroom management skills). The last four items were treated as examples of pedagogical

EXHIBIT 7.1

INDIVIDUAL AND GROUP OBJECTIVES OF PROFESSIONAL DEVELOPMENT

INDIVIDUALS	GROUPS
Behaviors	
Learn and use new teaching strategies	Agree to adopt a sharing format for department- or grade-level meetings
Meet individually with children on watch lists, offering support and encouragement	Agree to coordinate instruction on critical content
Attitudes	
Greater willingness to invite parents to discuss child's progress	Faculty change their thinking, see benefits from accepting children from schools that failed to make AYP
Increased feelings of comfort in using computers for instruction	Science teachers reach out, invite teachers from other schools to join them in a nature walk
Knowledge	
Develop individual plans to increase knowledge of subject	Department members agree to take a class together to update their knowledge of subject
Agree to research and locate three new Internet sites suitable for use with their students in the next month	Grade-level teachers hear a specialist on working with children with learning disabilities

knowledge. Principals in both types of schools rated inadequacies in the four pedagogical skill areas as more common problems among teachers in their schools than lack of content knowledge.

Those who subscribe to the belief that teachers need more content knowledge suggest that teachers with a thorough grounding in their subject are better prepared to diagnose students' difficulties with the material and plan instruction accordingly. They believe that subject matter knowledge helps teachers answer such critical questions as: Which concepts are most important for students to understand? What beliefs, conceptions, or misconceptions do students hold about the subject? and What instructional activities or techniques will increase children's curiosity about the subject matter (Solomon & Morocco, 1999)?

The adoption of mandated curriculum standards has created a need to better prepare teachers to plan instruction covering the content on required achievement tests. Well-planned professional development activities can help teachers to teach mandated content without unduly narrowing the curriculum. Professional publications contain many articles on this topic. Among the ideas covered in these articles are suggestions on integrating content from different fields, such as social studies and science (Drake, 2001); how to cover the standards without sacrificing creativity (Scherer, 2001); and deciding what knowledge is most worthwhile for students to learn (Raywid, 2002).

Teachers' Opinions.   A survey instrument on which teachers can register their views about a preferred format for professional development and indicate topics about which they would like more information is shown in Exhibit 7.2.

Delivery.   Content may be delivered in several ways. The most common method is through workshops. Other methods include observation of other teachers, visits to schools, individual or collaborative reading and research, university courses, peer coaching, and computer-based or online instruction. Learning may be enhanced by combining two or three of these methods. Teachers who hear about a new idea in a workshop and then observe a teacher using it in a classroom are better prepared to adopt and use the strategy than those who hear about it but do not get to see it in action or practice using it.

Computer-based instruction and online courses have the advantage of being highly flexible. Teachers may study early or late, on weekends or holidays, at any time that is convenient. Collaborative reading and research are also flexible, but because two or more people are involved, some coordination is required.

Programs are available through online learning communities for teachers who wish to increase their knowledge of content or to master new instructional strategies. A potential drawback to the use of online instruction is that some teachers do not have access to a speedy Internet connection, and they can quickly become frustrated with long waits to download material or post online messages for the instructor or other students. However, as the cost of broadband connections decrease, more people will subscribe, and delays should diminish.

Pacing.   Pacing refers to the speed with which new material is introduced. A slow pace may lead to boredom, whereas a pace that is too fast risks participant confusion or information overload. It is sometimes necessary to cover a large amount of material in a short time, in which case a faster pace is called for. To maintain a fast pace without loss of comprehension, presenters should reinforce instruction with advance organizers or backup materials. An example of an advance organizer is an overview of the content when instruction starts; handouts that summarize the main points of a presentation are examples of backup materials. Demonstrations and hands-on practice are other ways of improving comprehension and retention.

EXHIBIT 7.2

SURVEY OF TEACHERS' OPINIONS ON DEVELOPMENT

Directions: The information you provide will be used in planning for staff development activities in the district. Please answer all questions thoughtfully and truthfully.

1. How many years (total) teaching experience do you have?
2. What grade level(s) do you teach?
3. What subject(s) do you teach?
4. What is the highest degree that you hold?
5. When did you last take a college course in your subject specialty?
6. With which of the following groups would you prefer to attend a staff development workshop?
   - ❏ Teachers from your own school
   - ❏ Teachers from other schools in this district
   - ❏ Teachers from other districts
   - ❏ Mixed groups, including teachers and administrators from this district
   - ❏ Mixed groups, including teachers and administrators from other districts
7. What is your preference of day and time for professional development sessions?
8. From the following list, select the three workshops you would be most interested in attending.
   - ❏ Time on task
   - ❏ Classroom organization and management
   - ❏ Classroom climate
   - ❏ Learning styles
   - ❏ Teacher-made tests
   - ❏ Higher-order thinking
   - ❏ Using technology in the classroom
   - ❏ Effects of teacher expectations on student achievement
   - ❏ Using student achievement data for instructional decisions
   - ❏ Curriculum revision
   - ❏ Lesson design
   - ❏ Teaching students with special needs
   - ❏ Preparing an individualized educational plan
   - ❏ Teaching gifted children
   - ❏ Site-based management
   - ❏ Assessing student performance
   - ❏ Working with parents and the community
9. Can you suggest presenters for any of the topics on the list? (If so, list the name of the topic and the presenter.)
10. Would you be willing to serve as a workshop leader presenting a topic in which you have received previous training? (If yes, give your name and school and the topic you can present.)

Participants. Professional development programs are more effective when planners consider the backgrounds and needs of participants. Beginning teachers have different needs from those with more experience, and teachers who teach students with special needs seek content that is geared to their situation.

Information about participants that will help in planning professional development activities include: length of teaching experience, subjects taught, types of students, and type and extent of graduate work. It also helps to know something about the schools in which participants teach. What is the school's mission? What are the greatest challenges faced by teachers? Does the school's curriculum differ from that of other schools? Do the teachers have consistent views about instruction, or are their beliefs widely divergent? Is the principal seen as the instructional leader, or does someone other than the principal assume that role? Are teachers generally receptive to new ideas, or do they tend to rely on tried-and-proven methods? Answers to these questions will help planners to structure workshops that will be more relevant to teachers' beliefs and concerns.

Evaluation and Follow-Up

The best indicator of the effectiveness of a professional development program is found in classrooms of participants several months after the workshop ends. If teachers who took part have adopted the ideas and strategies they learned, the project can be regarded as a success. The ultimate measure of a program's effectiveness, of course, is student performance. If students who are taught by teachers who received the training show greater gains on standardized measures of achievement, as compared to students of teachers who did not have the training, with extraneous factors held constant, then the professional development program has demonstrated its value.

Teachers who participate in workshops generally give favorable ratings on evaluation forms. However, enthusiasm alone is unlikely to lead to behavior change in classrooms. Teachers need ongoing support, in the form of technical advice and feedback, in order to adopt and use new methods of teaching. The more complex the innovation teachers are expected to learn, the more important it is to provide advice and support.

An effective method of evaluating professional development ideally should consist of four phases, as shown in Exhibit 7.3. The most widely used evaluation technique is to ask for teachers' reactions to the workshop itself, using a survey instrument to register their satisfaction with the presenters and the content. The evaluation items may be closed or open ended. An example of an open-ended form appears in Guskey (2000). In that example, workshop participants are asked to complete five sentence stems ("I learned . . . ," "Most helpful . . . ," "Least helpful . . . ," "I would like to learn . . . ," and "Appreciations, Concerns, Suggestions"). The next phase in the evaluation of professional development activities is to determine how much teachers actually learned about the material presented

EXHIBIT 7.3

INFORMATION TO BE COLLECTED IN A COMPREHENSIVE EVALUATION OF PROFESSIONAL DEVELOPMENT PROGRAMS

OUTCOME	ITEMS
Teacher Reactions	Convenience of time and day of session
	Convenience of the location
	Comfort of the room
	Ability of presenters to make concepts clear and to maintain interest
	Presenters' knowledge of subject
	Appropriateness of the content for teachers' own schools or classrooms
	Probability of using strategies presented in the workshop
	Estimated need for feedback and follow-up
Teacher Knowledge	Teachers' estimates of their knowledge of subject before and after attending session
	Pre- and posttest to measure knowledge gain
	Desire to learn more about the subject
Behavior Change	Teachers' estimate of frequency of use of new strategy one month after attending session
	Data from classroom observers showing frequency of use
	Teachers' estimates of difficulty of use (time involved, student understanding and receptivity)
	Teachers' estimates of likelihood they will continue to use strategy
Student Learning	Results of experimental research on student gains in classes with teachers using new techniques, compared to students in classes with teachers using old techniques
	Students' estimates of amount they learn when teachers use new versus old techniques
	Data from classroom observers on student interest and participation in classes using new versus old techniques

during the workshop. This effort may take place at the end of the workshop or at a later date, or both. Teachers will not be able to implement material they have not learned. The third stage in the evaluation process is to determine to what extent teachers are using the strategies they studied. This information is best collected from classroom observations. The final and most difficult stage of evaluation is measuring the effect of the new practices on student learning. The only way to accurately measure this effect is by means of an experimental research design.

PROFESSIONAL DEVELOPMENT FOR ADMINISTRATORS AND SUPPORT PERSONNEL

Administrators are key players in bringing about improved instruction in schools, but many districts either offer no professional development for principals or present hastily planned workshops that most participants find uninspiring. Workshops that can help administrators to understand and facilitate change should be a central feature of district strategy for improving the quality of teaching.

Principals have difficulty finding time for professional development. Most have very little time that is not committed. Between faculty meetings, parent conferences, central office sessions, athletic contests, and community events, they feel overburdened and mentally fragmented. Even if they are able to squeeze in a few hours for their personal needs, their sense of responsibility sometimes prevents them from relaxing and giving full attention to professional growth. During workshop breaks, they race to a phone to check on their school, hoping that a disaster hasn't occurred in their absence. They're ready to dash back to the school if they sense that their assistance is required.

Principals who take advantage of professional development opportunities for themselves report that they do so because it helps them to grow and learn or helps them avoid burnout. One principal commented, "It's very important to me to continue to learn. It's self-satisfying, it makes me feel good about myself." Another stated, "[I] need energy from outside, otherwise I'd be burned out or bored out" (Hallinger & Greenblatt, 1989, p. 71).

The School Leadership Program, authorized by No Child Left Behind, provides support to assist high-need school districts in recruiting and retaining principals and assistant principals. This program also is intended to help provide professional development for building administrators (*K–12 principals guide . . . ,* 2003). The creation of the School Leadership Program is evidence of a growing awareness of the importance of providing high-quality professional development opportunities for school administrators and an acknowledgment of the fact that few such programs are currently available.

The NSDC recently identified desirable features of professional development activities for school leaders, and not surprisingly the characteristics identified by the council are similar to those recommended for professional development programs for teachers. They include ample time (longer rather than shorter), embedding (direct tie-ins to the jobs practitioners perform), planned activities (well thought out rather than hastily assembled), and instructionally oriented content (focusing on ways by which by which practitioners can help improve student achievement) (Peterson, 2002).

Some states and cities have leadership academies for principals and superintendents that incorporate some or all of the desirable features identified by the NSDC. Two examples of such programs are the Gheens Academy in Louisville (www.jefferson.k12.ky.us/Departments/Gheens) and the Mayerson Academy in Cincinnati (www.mayersonacademy.org). These academies offer workshops, mentoring, and/or individual assistance for aspiring or experienced principals (Peterson, 2002).

Conferences and workshops sponsored by professional groups, such as the National Association of Elementary School Principals (NAESP) and the National Association of Secondary School Principals (NASSP), offer rich opportunities for professional growth for principals. A recent summer academy sponsored by NAESP focused on standards for leaders of learning communities, including setting high expectations, developing content and instruction that ensure student achievement, using multiple sources of data as diagnostic tools, and actively engaging the community (www.naesp.org.npa.summer2003.htm).

Periodic surveys of principals' and supervisors' needs can help those responsible for professional development to provide sessions that will help principals and supervisors to feel better prepared to deal with the dual responsibilities of school management and instructional leadership. Perennial issues of concern to both groups include evaluation of teaching performance, supervision of teachers, and conducting postobservation conferences.

A newly emerging form of professional development for principals involves peer conversations aimed at helping principals to perform more effectively in their leadership roles. Small groups of administrators use structured protocols to look at their work and that of their students. A moderator convenes the group, explains the rules, and helps keep the conversation on the topic. The rules help prevent one or two participants from monopolizing the conversation by requiring that speakers take turns and listen attentively when others are speaking. Time is allowed for presenting work, listening without commenting, and giving and receiving feedback (Mohr, 1998).

SUMMARY

Professional development for teachers has four functions: to implement curriculum change, improve instructional practices, enable teacher growth, and change the organizational climate. NCLB initiated the HOUSSE program for the purpose of verifying the subject matter knowledge of current teachers. Effective professional development programs are sustained, intensive, and classroom focused. Centralized programs are offered for all or nearly all teachers in a district, whereas decentralized programs are tailored to the needs of a single school. Finding time for professional development activities is a problem. Using the week before the opening of school for professional development has many advantages and few disadvantages. Professional development for administrators has suffered from lack of attention. Principals are pulled in many different directions and often feel they cannot spare time for professional development activities.

SUGGESTED ACTIVITIES

1. Reread the description of the Torff (2005) study in this chapter and answer this question: Can you suggest an alternative interpretation of the results of this study? If you were to design a follow-up study to this one, what changes would you make to the original design? Explain how your changes would strengthen the research design.

2. A learning community is a group of people with similar interests, a desire to learn, and a willingness to share their ideas and opinions. Most people belong to several learning communities, although they may not think of them as such. Groups that function as learning communities include Alcoholics Anonymous chapters, bowling leagues, bridge clubs, fraternities and sororities, and child care cooperatives. Online learning communities have proliferated since the advent of the Internet. To what learning communities do you belong? What is the value of those groups to you?

3. Plan a three-hour in-service session for principals on a topic of your choice. Prepare an outline of the activities to be included and the handouts, tapes, films, or transparencies that will be used.

ONLINE RESOURCES

McGraw-Hill (www.mheducation.com)

McGraw-Hill offers online instruction for teachers of mathematics (two levels) and reading (three levels). University credit is available.

Scholastic (http://teacher.scholastic.com)

This site has sample lesson plans, online activities, and teaching strategies, as well as products available from Scholastic and other vendors.

(www.scholastic.com/administrator)

The administrator page has suggestions for staff development and parent involvement as well as lists of best practices and schools of distinction.

Education Week (www.edweek-chat.org)

Education Week offers online conversations on topics of interest to educators, including technology, teacher recruitment, achievement standards, and assessment. Participants can submit questions in advance or while the program is in progress. Transcripts are available.

National Staff Development Council (www.nsdc.org)

The NSDC's website has a wealth of information about professional development. It includes descriptions of prize-winning professional development programs and an explanation of the organization's standards for high-quality professional development offerings.

Pearson Education (www.pearsondigital.com)

> This site gives descriptions of digital products suitable for use with students in grades K–8.

North Central Regional Educational Laboratory (www.ncrel.org/sdrs/areas/pd0cont.htm)

> Critical issues in professional development are highlighted on this site. Examples include finding more time, professional development in technology, and evaluating growth and development. There are links to related sites that show how other schools and districts have addressed these problems.

Principals' Center for the Garden State (www.tcnj.edu/~princtr)

> This site describes Dodge Foundation fellowships for full-time public school principals in New Jersey that support nontraditional and imaginative professional development and personal renewal activities. Individual and team projects are considered.

Broad Foundation (www.broadfoundation.org)

> The foundation sponsors summer and two-year residencies to prepare leaders for senior management positions in urban schools.

New Leaders for New Schools (www.nlns.org/NLWeb/Program.jsp)

> This organization is dedicated to improving academic achievement of all children by recruiting, training, and supporting the next generation of leaders for urban schools.

Franklin Institute (www.fi.edu)

> The Franklin Institute's website offers a variety of information on science topics suitable for classroom instruction.

Educational Technology Clearinghouse (http://etc.usf.edu)

> This site has extensive instructional resources for teachers, including materials appropriate for use with art, foreign language, health, language arts, mathematics, physical education, science, and social studies.

Eisenhower National Clearinghouse (www.goenc.com)

> This site describes itself as the "largest, most comprehensive resource for K–12 math and science educators."

CASE STUDIES

Case No. 1

Juanita Diaz is describing a program she observed at a recent national conference. This was an in-service activity designed to help teachers assess the incidence of bullying in a school and take action to reduce its frequency and severity. She is speaking to fellow eighth-grade teachers at Bayside Middle School.

"The facilitator asked a group of teachers to make three lists. On List A they wrote the names of students who were victims of bullying. List B included the names of students who bullied others, and List C was for students whose names appeared on both of the other lists."

"Wait a minute." Joyce Berlin was speaking. "Is she saying that some kids are both—bullies and victims of bullies?"

"That's right."

"That's interesting."

Ms. Diaz continued. "Next she asked the teachers to list beside each name on List A an action they could take that would help that student be less likely to be a victim of bullying."

"What kinds of things did the teachers write?" Roberta Tompkins asked.

"One wrote that she would take a few minutes every day to make a positive pronouncement about a boy in her class on whom the other boys teased. She planned to say something favorable so other students would begin to appreciate his positive qualities. Another teacher planned to help a girl in her class buy better-fitting and more stylish clothes. The facilitator said that this technique had been tried in a dozen middle schools and that after six weeks the frequency of bullying had dropped by about half."

"That's impressive," Ms. Berlin said.

"I wonder if the bullies simply started picking on other kids?" Ms. Tompkins asked.

"There were a few cases where that happened, but overall there was much less bullying than before."

"Sounds like a workshop that would be beneficial for Bayside," Ms. Berlin said. "I have several kids in my class who are victims of bullies. I'd like to do something to stop it."

"What did the facilitator do with List B?" Ms. Tompkins asked.

"These were kids who were identified as bullies," Ms. Diaz said. "Teachers were asked to think of one or two things that might help these kids feel more accepted. For example, assigning a boy a task that would give him status in the classroom."

"I don't agree with that," Bessie Grant said. "That's rewarding him for being a bully. I think kids like that should be punished. Give them fair warning that if they keep doing it they will be suspended."

"We've tried punishment and it doesn't work," Ms. Berlin said. "I think it's time to try a different approach."

"I think you'll find out. . . . It only gets worse," Ms. Grant said. "Let's be realistic. The thing that gets these kids' attention is knowing they'll be punished."

"What about the third list?" Ms. Tompkins asked.

"She says that once these kids are no longer victims they will stop bullying others. She asked teachers to keep track of those kids to see if they continued bullying and, if so, how much."

Questions

1. Juanita Diaz described a program that she thought Bayside teachers might want to adopt. What other things might she have done to increase teachers' knowledge of and interest in the program?

2. Bessie Grant is skeptical about the program. What advice would you have for a trainer who encounters resistance or hostility to her ideas?
3. There may be other teachers in the school who share Ms. Grant's skepticism. What do you think about adopting a program in a school knowing that some teachers will not buy into it? Would you offer it anyway? Explain.
4. What actions might the administration of Bayside take prior to offering the program that would prepare teachers to evaluate the program's merits and demerits objectively?

Case No. 2

Mary Holcomb, assistant superintendent for instruction, is speaking with a group of principals regarding a proposed change in the professional development program for the district. Under the proposal each teacher would prepare an individual growth plan subject to approval by his or her principal to be carried out over the course of a year. Activities on the growth plan would be keyed to areas identified in the teacher's evaluation as being in need of strengthening.

> **MEYER LANE** (High School Principal): So, does this mean that there wouldn't be any more staff development sessions for the whole faculty?
>
> **MS. HOLCOMB:** Not necessarily, but there probably would be fewer of those and more individual activities.
>
> **ROSE SASH** (Middle School Principal): Can you give me an example of an activity a teacher might engage in for her growth plan?
>
> **MS. HOLCOMB:** Read three books on a topic, take a university class, observe classrooms in half-a-dozen schools and write up what you learn, interview experts on a particular topic. Those are some examples.
>
> **MS. SASH:** Sounds like there would be a lot of record-keeping.
>
> **MS. HOLCOMB:** Teachers would prepare a portfolio showing what they've done and you would review it at the end of the year.
>
> **JOYCE MERRITT** (Elementary School Principal): I think there's value in bringing the entire faculty of a school together for a workshop. Teachers reinforce one another when they work together, and when individuals work alone they don't get as much out of it.
>
> **LANE:** Don't take this the wrong way, but I'm concerned about the time involved in this program. I don't see how I can take on any more things than I'm doing, and it sounds like this would require a lot of time. What would you suggest I leave undone?
>
> **MS. HOLCOMB:** Now, Meyer, you know I'm not going to answer that question. You're saying that this plan would require more time than you'd be able to devote to it?

LANE: That's right. Of course, if you decide to go this way, I'll do the best I can. As good as this approach may be, if I'm not able to spend as much time on it as I need to, the program's going to suffer.

MS. HOLCOMB: How do the rest of you feel? Fred, what about you?

FRED BARRON (Middle School Principal): I agree with Meyer. This plan would require a lot of my time. We should devote more time to professional development than we do, but it has to come from somewhere. The idea of a growth plan is good, and I'm wondering if we could compromise and have some programs that all teachers would take part in and supplement that with a few days, maybe two or three days, of individually planned activities.

MS. HOLCOMB: That's a possibility.

MS. SASH: How about letting department heads work with teachers to develop growth plans and not require the principal to meet individually with every teacher?

MS. MERRITT: I don't have department heads in my school.

MS. HOLCOMB: Department heads might object that that's not in their job descriptions.

LANE: I might say the same thing.

MS. HOLCOMB: Let's see where we are. We seem to agree that growth plans will involve more time than you're able to give. Some of you see value in the idea but are concerned about implementation. I share that concern. I know you all already have plenty on your plates, but I guess I was thinking that the growth plan would be part of the evaluation process. We should be helping teachers find ways to strengthen areas of weakness, and I was hoping we could formalize that process. Maybe we need to start with evaluation and see what can be done there.

Questions

1. What are your views concerning an individualized professional development program as compared to offerings for large groups of teachers? What are the most important differences in how these two models are implemented?

2. What are your views concerning the alternatives proposed by members of this group? One alternative was to combine elements of the two programs so that teachers would take part in some group workshops and would also have a few individual activities. Another suggestion was to ask department heads to work with teachers to develop growth plans.

3. If you had been in Mary Holcomb's place leading this meeting with principals, what, if anything, would you have done differently? Did you feel that Ms. Holcomb prepared adequately for the discussion?

4. Given the results of this session, what do you predict about the prospects that the proposed growth plan will be adopted by the district? Has this

meeting helped or harmed the chances of this proposal being approved? Explain.

5. What next steps could Holcomb take in order to advance this proposal?

REFERENCES

Birman, B., Desimone, L., Porter, A., & Garet, M. (2000, May). Designing professional development that works. *Educational Leadership, 57,* 28–32.

Cutler, A., & Ruopp, F. (1999). From expert to novice: The transformation from teacher to learner. In M. Solomon (Ed.), *The diagnostic teacher* (pp. 133–161). New York: Teachers College Press.

Desimone, L. M., Porter, A. C., Garet, M. S., Yoon, K. S., & Birman, B. F. (2002, Summer). Effects of professional development on teachers' instruction: Results from a three-year longitudinal study. *Educational Evaluation and Policy Analysis, 24,* 81–112.

Drake, S. M. (2001, September). Castles, kings . . . and standards. *Educational Leadership, 59,* 38–42.

Gewertz, C. (2005, August 10). Staff investment pays dividends in Maryland district. *Education Week,* pp. 1, 16.

Goodlad, J. (1983). The school as workplace. In G. Griffin (Ed.), *Staff development* (pp. 36–61). Chicago: University of Chicago Press.

Guskey, T. R. (2003, June). What makes professional development effective? *Phi Delta Kappan, 84,* 748–750.

Guskey, T. R. (2000). *Evaluating professional development.* Thousand Oaks, CA: Corwin Press, Inc.

Hallinger, P., & Greenblatt, R. (1989, Fall). Principals' pursuit of professional growth: The influence of beliefs, experiences, and district context. *Journal of Staff Development, 10,* 68–74.

K–12 principals guide to No Child Left Behind. (2003). Alexandria, VA: National Association of Elementary School Principals. Reston, VA: National Association of Secondary School Principals.

Kelleher, J. (2003, June). A model for assessment-driven professional development. *Phi Delta Kappan, 84,* 751–756.

Lieberman, A. (1999). *Teachers—Transforming their world and their work.* New York: Teachers College Press.

Mohr, N. (1998, April). Creating effective study groups for principals. *Educational Leadership, 55,* 41–44.

Peterson, K. (2002, April). The professional development of principals: Innovations and opportunities. *Educational Administration Quarterly, 38,* 213–232.

Raywid, M. A. (2002, February). Accountability: What's worth measuring? *Phi Delta Kappan, 83,* 433–436.

Scherer, M. (2001, September). How and why standards can improve student achievement: A conversation with Robert J. Marzano. *Educational Leadership, 59,* 14–18.

Simmons, J. (2005, October 26). High-performance schools. *Education Week,* pp. 56, 46–47.

Solomon, M., & Morocco, C. (1999). The diagnostic teacher. In M. Solomon (Ed.), *The diagnostic teacher* (pp. 231–246). New York: Teachers College Press.

Standerfer, L. (2005, December). Staff development: Finding the right fit. *Principal Leadership, 6,* 16–20.

Torff, B. (2005, December). Getting it wrong on threats to teacher quality. *Phi Delta Kappan, 87,* 302–305.

Viadero, D. (2005, July 27). Pressure builds for effective staff training. *Education Week,* pp. 1, 18–19.

Youngs, P., & King, M. B. (2002). Principal leadership for professional development to build school capacity. *Educational Administration Quarterly, 38,* 643–670.

8 EVALUATING EMPLOYEE PERFORMANCE

Performance evaluation is a fact of life in most work settings, and even though it may be carried out in a routine and perfunctory manner, few individuals approach the experience with indifference. The reason for evaluating teachers is to help them improve their effectiveness. However, relatively few teachers believe that evaluation actually helps them to do a better job. The problem, they say, is that evaluation causes stress and makes it more difficult to change.

PLAN OF THE CHAPTER

This chapter deals with the following topics: (1) purposes of performance evaluation, (2) models of teacher evaluation, (3) characteristics of successful evaluation programs, (4) state-mandated evaluation systems, (5) evaluation of principals, and (6) legal considerations in personnel evaluation.

PURPOSES OF PERFORMANCE EVALUATION

This chapter examines two types of performance evaluation. On the one hand, summative evaluation refers to assessments carried out for accountability purposes. Summative evaluations are usually conducted annually or semiannually, and the results are used to support personnel decisions, such as whether to grant tenure, to terminate or transfer a teacher, or place an individual on a career ladder. Formative evaluation, on the other hand, serves a developmental purpose. Formative evaluation should be a continuous process, with the feedback from classroom observations presented in a way that helps individuals improve their teaching effectiveness. The two types of evaluation are distinct and work best when they are kept separate.

Formative evaluation depends on the establishment of a bond of trust between the employee and the evaluator. The trust is necessary to help teachers accept suggested improvements in their teaching. Summative evaluation, however, requires a judgment about the employee that carries with it the possibility of adverse action. Because of the high stakes involved, summative evaluation seldom lends itself to improving teaching performance.

MODELS OF TEACHER EVALUATION

Evaluation consumes a good deal of time and energy in schools, but as presently practiced, it often fails to improve teachers' instructional practices. Some critics claim that principals strive to comply with policies specifying the number and timing of classroom observations and follow-up conferences but pay less attention to whether evaluation makes a difference in terms of changing the way teachers teach. Further, the critics suggest that teachers conform to principals' expectations in order to receive satisfactory ratings, without regard to whether the feedback they receive leads to personal growth (Ponticell & Zepeda, 2004).

There are several models of teacher evaluation in use in schools. The assumptions about teaching and about the purpose for evaluating it vary from model to model. The models reviewed in this chapter include the remediation model, goal-setting model, portfolio model, student achievement model, and peer assistance and review model. Exhibit 8.1 summarizes the major features of each of these models.

Remediation Model

The remediation model is primarily a formative type but sometimes serves a quasi-summative purpose. The assumption behind the model is that individuals can become effective teachers by mastering a limited number of teaching behaviors identified in the research literature as related to improved student learning. It is the evaluator's job to offer guidance to help upgrade the teacher's skills. The object of the remediation model is to bring all teachers to a minimal level of competence. In extreme cases, a teacher with major problems may be given a mandate to demonstrate improvement or face termination. The remediation model uses a conjunctive approach to evaluation. That is, all teachers must attain a rating of "satisfactory" on all of the evaluative criteria. Exhibit 8.2 gives examples of evaluation criteria that might be used with the remediation model. Data for the evaluation are gathered from classroom observations.

The remediation model works best with teachers who have correctable problems, who are motivated, and who have the ability to profit from instruction. Classroom management is an example of a problem for which teachers can usually be helped by the remediation approach. The model is most successful when

EXHIBIT 8.1

COMPARISON OF EVALUATION MODELS

REMEDIATION MODEL

Type:	Formative, quasi-summative
Purpose:	Correct identified weaknesses.
Objective:	Bring all teachers to a minimum level of performance.
Assumption:	It is possible to specify effective teaching behaviors and teach them.
Method:	Assess, provide feedback, and reassess.
Works best with:	Teachers with correctable teaching problems.
Evaluator skills:	Ability to provide clear, specific directions.
Possible problems:	Heavy demands on evaluator's time; offers no challenge to more competent teachers; deemphasizes variety in teaching.

GOAL-SETTING MODEL

Type:	Formative
Purpose:	Involve teachers and administrators in choosing individualized evaluation criteria.
Objective:	Increase teacher autonomy and commitment.
Assumption:	Teachers are professionals and able to assess their own developmental needs.
Method:	Teacher prepares annual goals statement; principal reviews, approves, or amends it and evaluates teachers' attainment.
Works best with:	Experienced, motivated teachers.
Evaluator skills:	Ability to help teachers write relevant performance objectives and guide teachers into productive channels; ability to evaluate on individualized criteria.
Possible problems:	Weak or overly ambitious goals; lack of consensus on what constitutes attainment of objective.

PORTFOLIO MODEL

Type:	Summative
Purpose:	Base teacher evaluation on documented evidence of effective performance.
Objective:	Encourage teachers to cooperate in formulating high standards of practice.
Assumption:	Teachers can organize and present evidence demonstrating effective teaching.
Method:	Teachers maintain a file of handouts, tests, reports, student evaluations, documentation of teaching practices, and other information and submit it to the evaluator.
Works best with:	Experienced teachers in a variety of areas; especially well suited for teachers of art, music, and vocational subjects.

(continued)

EXHIBIT 8.1   CONTINUED

Evaluator skills:	Ability to synthesize a profusion of details into a meaningful assessment of an individual's performance.
Possible problems:	Teachers: Time required to prepare portfolio; temptation to impress with flashy packaging.
	Administrators: Amount of time required to review portfolios; need to equate evidence from many different sources.

STUDENT ACHIEVEMENT MODEL

Type:	Summative
Purpose:	Base teacher evaluation on amount of student learning.
Objective:	Determine amount of learning attributable to teacher's effort.
Assumption:	Each teacher contributes to students' accumulating knowledge.
Method:	Use pre- and posttests to measure student growth each year.
Works best with:	Teachers of subjects that have well-defined cognitive outcomes.
Evaluator skills:	Able to interpret and understand the limitations of achievement tests; able to take into account uncontrolled factors.
Possible problems:	Inflexible application of procedure results in loss of credibility; method does not identify teacher behaviors that affect learning.

PEER ASSISTANCE AND REVIEW MODEL

Type:	Formative
Purpose:	Make evaluation more meaningful and effective by assigning mentor teachers to evaluate colleagues and help them improve.
Objective:	Improve the process of evaluation and make more assistance available; enhance professionalism among teachers.
Assumption:	Mentor teachers can devote more time to teacher evaluation than the principal; the result is more intensive and extensive evaluations.
Method:	Experienced teachers are given released time to observe classes of colleagues, provide feedback, and help develop improvement plans for those needing improvement.
Works best with:	Teachers who are genuinely interested in improving their effectiveness and who are comfortable being evaluated by a colleague.
Evaluator skills:	Ability to build rapport with colleagues; ability to identify areas needing improvement and offer specific suggestions for improvement.
Possible problems:	Some union opposition persists although the National Education Association (NEA) and the American Federation of Teachers (AFT) have expressed support; some teachers may resent being evaluated by other teachers; some administrators are reluctant to relinquish responsibility for teacher evaluation.

EXHIBIT 8.2

SAMPLE EVALUATION CRITERIA FOR REMEDIATION MODEL

Teacher displays high expectations for student achievement and expresses confidence in students' abilities to learn.

Teacher develops instructional activities that increase student understanding of the subject matter.

Teacher maintains a businesslike atmosphere without being humorless or repressive.

Teacher provides a safe, orderly, and attractive environment.

Teacher uses preventive techniques to minimize disruption and maintain learner involvement.

Teacher uses a variety of instructional activities and materials.

Teacher develops instructional activities that encourage self-motivation, critical thinking, and problem solving.

Teacher asks questions that most students are able to answer correctly.

Teacher's instructional activities conform to the school's curriculum goals.

Teacher adjusts the pace and difficulty level of instruction to increase student comprehension.

Teacher checks students' understanding and reviews or reteaches content as needed.

Teacher uses formal and informal assessment strategies to evaluate learners' progress.

Teacher is fair and impartial in dealings with students, including those of other races and nationalities.

specific corrective techniques can be prescribed and when support is provided to help teachers expand their skills. The remediation model involves the steps shown in Exhibit 8.3.

Goal-Setting Model

The goal-setting model is a formative model designed for experienced teachers who are able to identify their own developmental needs. Each teacher identifies goals expressed as targets for personal growth and development. These goals may relate to a common schoolwide theme or emphasis. Near the beginning of the year teachers meet one on one with the evaluator, usually the principal, to review and clarify the goals. Once the two agree on the relevance and value of the goals the teacher has chosen and have identified ways of measuring progress toward achieving them, the teacher begins working toward carrying out the plan.

Once a plan has been agreed to by both parties, it becomes a contract between the teacher and the principal. In most schools the principal meets with the teacher

EXHIBIT 8.3
STEPS IN CARRYING OUT REMEDIAL EVALUATION

Step 1. Evaluator schedules an optional preevaluation conference with the teacher to explain evaluation procedures and answer the teacher's questions.

Step 2. Evaluator observes classroom, recording behaviors on a checklist or observation instrument.

Step 3. Evaluator reviews data and prepares notes or written observation report.

Step 4. Evaluator meets with the teacher in a follow-up conference to clarify the teacher's intent in the lesson, fill in missing information, and encourage the teacher to reflect on the lesson. The evaluator also points out strengths and weaknesses and suggests steps the teacher might take to correct observed problems or shore up strengths. (Steps 2–4 may be repeated several times during the year.)

Step 5. Evaluator prepares an annual evaluation report on each teacher, drawing on the observation reports and information from other sources. For teachers with performance deficiencies, this report may include a plan of assistance, identifying goals and available resources, and establishing benchmarks for tracking progress.

Step 6. Evaluator shares the annual evaluation report with the teacher and hears the teacher's comments. Evaluator may revise the plan of assistance based on the teacher's suggestions.

once or twice during the year to check on progress and, if necessary, to adjust the goals the teacher has selected.

A potential problem with goal-setting plans arises from disparities in the complexity of teacher-selected goals. Some teachers choose goals that require little or no effort, whereas others identify objectives so ambitious that they exceed the time and energy available to accomplish them. Both cases require the evaluator to exercise critical judgment in reviewing teachers' proposed plans.

State-developed curriculum frameworks that identify what students are expected to learn in each grade level may be used as guides for teachers' performance goals. If, for example, frameworks specify that all students should be able to multiply 2 two-digit numbers (48×35), that objective might be one that all teachers in the target grade level adopt. The major strength of the goal-setting approach is its flexibility and the fact that it gives teachers autonomy in identifying and achieving their professional growth needs. Goal-setting requires considerably more teacher input than the remedial model.

Portfolio Model

A portfolio is a collection of documents and artifacts gathered by a teacher for the purpose of demonstrating his or her instructional effectiveness. A portfolio might include lesson plans; a videotape of a class; records of student learning; and comments from students, parents, and professionals. Teachers who are evaluated by this summative model are expected to show that they have reflected on their teaching and incorporated emerging insights into their practice. Teachers who seek certification by the National Board for Professional Teaching Standards submit a portfolio that includes videotapes of a lesson or a counseling session. Teachers are also asked to include samples of their students' work.

Portfolio evaluation appeals to teachers because it gives them more control of the evaluation process, but many teachers find that collecting the information they need to assemble a file is onerous. The process is somewhat less burdensome if specific guidelines are available showing what to include and what to omit. In most portfolio plans, teachers receive a checklist or outline of the materials they are expected to include in the portfolio. Items on the list might include the following (Painter, 2001; Wolf, 1996):

- Samples of completed student work
- Grade distributions
- Student evaluations
- Resumé
- Educational philosophy and teaching goals
- Professional activities
- Letters of recommendation
- Formal evaluations
- Lesson plans
- Sample tests
- Sample handouts
- Parent comments
- Teaching license or certificate
- Professional development activities
- Documentation of teaching practices, including videotapes of class sessions
- Awards or commendations
- Teacher-developed websites
- Curriculum guidelines
- Published articles

The resumé contains information about the teacher's educational background, professional experience, and professional leadership activities. Leadership activities include serving as an officer for a professional association or taking part in regional or statewide service activities such as serving on accreditation teams. District leadership activities that are included on the resumé include chairing committees for staff development or textbook selection. Activities for the school, such as serving as a mentor to another teacher or serving as grade-level chair or department head, are also featured.

Portfolios have two major advantages over conventional methods of evaluation. First, they involve teachers proactively in gathering, organizing, and evaluating the material that composes the portfolio. Although most educators agree that teachers should be active participants in their own evaluation, most acknowledge that it seldom happens. Portfolios give teachers an opportunity to be active in their own evaluation. A second advantage of portfolios is that they offer a more comprehensive picture of a teacher's approach to the craft of teaching as compared to conventional means of evaluation. Even the most conscientious principals seldom observe a teacher more than three or four times in the course of a year, and although those brief glimpses of the teacher yield useful data, the picture they present is far from complete. Portfolios help fill in the gaps. The main disadvantage of portfolios is the time required in preparing and evaluating them (McNelly, 2002). A principal who must read and evaluate a portfolio for every teacher in the school may find that it is necessary to put aside other important tasks.

Principals use a compensatory approach when evaluating teachers' portfolios, in contrast to the conjunctive approach used with the remediation model of evaluation. In a compensatory approach, a low rating in one area can be offset by a higher rating in another. For example, a teacher who gives only true–false tests in her classes might balance a low rating on that measure with higher ratings on a videotaped lesson in which students discuss the reasoning processes that led to the correct answer choices on the test.

The online journal *Practical Assessment, Research and Evaluation* contains an article with suggestions for implementing portfolio programs. Among the recommendations are these: Start slowly, involve teachers in developing the program, and use portfolios in conjunction with other sources of information to evaluate teaching. The complete article is available online at http://pareonline.net/getvn.asp?v=4&n=1.

Student Achievement Model

This summative approach to evaluating teaching performance establishes a more exacting standard of teaching effectiveness than the approaches previously described. Under the student achievement model, teachers are evaluated on their ability to increase student mastery of challenging subject matter. The evaluation is based on analysis of evidence of student growth attributable to the teacher being evaluated.

A potential problem with this model is the difficulty of showing that students' learning gains can be attributed to a particular teacher. Because learning is influenced by many factors, including previous teachers, no foolproof way exists to measure how much of a child's knowledge was contributed by a given teacher.

Most teachers are uneasy about being evaluated on the basis of student achievement. They argue that such systems are inequitable because teachers with smaller classes, more highly motivated students, or more up-to-date materials and equipment have an advantage over other teachers. Some districts try to soften teachers' opposition by reviewing a wider range of student outcomes, such as citizenship, class participation, and original scholarship, and by allowing teachers themselves to decide which indicators they wish to present for evaluation purposes. Teachers may decide, for example, to include results from teacher-made tests in place of standardized achievement test results (Peterson, Wahlquist, Bone, Thompson, & Chatterton, 2001).

Peer Assistance and Review Model

Several large districts are experimenting with peer review as a method of formative evaluation of teachers. Chicago schools, as well as those in Toledo, Cincinnati, Columbus, Rochester (New York), Minneapolis, and Montgomery County (Maryland) have all adopted peer review systems (Keller, 2006). Experienced teachers who have been successful in the classroom and who are highly regarded by their colleagues are released from teaching duties for a period of time and assigned to observe and evaluate other teachers, including those who are new to the profession and those who have been identified as needing assistance. The two main drawbacks to peer review, according to those experienced in its use, are teacher opposition to being evaluated by another teacher and principals' reluctance to give up the responsibility for evaluation.

CHARACTERISTICS OF SUCCESSFUL EVALUATION PROGRAMS

The goal of teacher evaluation is to ensure that all students are taught by well-qualified teachers. Information collected as part of the evaluation process is used to identify areas in which individuals are proficient as well as those in which they need improvement. In a successful program, teacher evaluation is coordinated with the district and school missions, and evaluation of teachers is integrated in a seamless web with professional development programs and curriculum development activities so that knowledge gained from one area informs the others.

In a successful evaluation program, teachers are informed in advance about the steps involved and are told on which criteria their performance will be judged. Successful formative evaluation supports teacher growth and development by providing feedback on their strengths and suggesting ways of addressing identified deficiencies.

Successful summative evaluation programs are guided by written policies that identify the purposes of the program, explain the procedures to be followed, list the criteria to be used, and spell out appeal procedures. These policies also address privacy concerns by limiting access to evaluation reports to those with a legitimate need to know. With policies in place teachers are aware of what to expect and are not surprised by unexpected events. Evaluators possess the skills and authority they need to perform their duties equitably and reliably.

Differentiated Approaches

In most districts, evaluation of first- and second-year teachers differs in intensity and focus from evaluation of experienced teachers. Beginning teachers need feedback on the basic processes of teaching, including lesson planning and classroom management. Observations at this stage are usually diagnostic in nature and are intended to help beginners lay foundations for later growth. A secondary purpose of evaluation for these teachers is to identify those who may be at risk of early termination and to provide support and assistance to help them improve.

For experienced teachers who have consistently been effective over time, evaluation is aimed at encouraging professional growth and development. The emphasis is on finding opportunities for these teachers to explore new interests, try out new strategies, or take on new leadership responsibilities. The teacher and evaluator usually jointly develop a long-range plan of professional growth activities, which might call for the teacher to work toward an advanced degree or seek National Board certification. The plan might include granting leave to allow the teacher to conduct research on a topic related to his or her subject field.

Evaluating Evaluation Systems

The process of evaluating an evaluation system should begin by determining what type of evaluation the system is intended to perform. If the evaluation plan is intended primarily to assist in making personnel decisions, the evaluation of it should consider how well it performs that function. Are the recommendations clear-cut and free of ambiguity, and do they result in actions that are sound and defensible? If not, the plan may need an overhaul, or those who administer it may need to be better trained in its use.

A summative evaluation system should specify the criteria on which all teachers must demonstrate satisfactory performance. Because of the high stakes, summative evaluation systems should be both reliable and credible. Reliability refers to the objectivity of a measure and the consistency of the results obtained when it is applied. Credibility is the quality of being believable or making sense in a particular context.

Evaluation systems are sometimes subverted for uses for which they were not intended. The most potentially damaging example of misdirected evaluation is making summative judgments using data gathered for formative purposes. With formative evaluation, the question is whether teachers have made changes leading to greater effectiveness as a result of having received formative feedback. If evaluators can point to specific instances of increased teaching effectiveness, it is fair to conclude that the program is achieving its goal. If no such evidence is available, then there is a question as to the program's effectiveness. Feedback alone is seldom sufficient to bring about marked improvement in performance. It needs to be coupled with support and assistance from an experienced teacher or supervisor.

Conducting Classroom Observations

Principals rely on classroom observations to gather data for evaluation purposes. Although some information is obtained in other ways (e.g., teacher attendance records, parent and student comments, and comments from other teachers or department heads), by far the most widely used source of data for teacher evaluation is that gathered by principals during classroom visits.

In some districts classroom observations are very structured, whereas in others they are more open. In districts with collective bargaining agreements principals are required to comply closely with the terms of the agreement in carrying out observations. Contracts frequently specify the number of classroom observations required during the year as well as the minimum length of each observation. It is also common for the contract to require that the principal schedule a follow-up conference with the teacher shortly after the observation.

What does a principal look for during a classroom observation? Typically, observers seek to determine whether the teacher has identified instructional objectives and whether those objectives address mandated content. Observers are also interested in the extent to which students participate in the lesson by asking or answering questions, volunteering opinions, or demonstrating processes; how well-prepared the teacher is; evidence of effective classroom management; and whether and in what ways the teacher uses technology in presenting the lesson.

Observing a class requires the observer to make evaluative judgments about the lesson and the way in which it was presented. For example, on the question of student participation, the observer watches to see whether students volunteer to participate because they are interested in the topic or because they are called on by the teacher. The observer will also want to note whether participation is limited to a few students and whether the teacher makes an effort to involve students who are reluctant to volunteer.

Stevens (2001) has developed a comprehensive list of items on which observers can evaluate a teacher while visiting a classroom. The behaviors on his list include stating the purpose of the lesson, arousing student interest in the topic, using a variety of instructional methods, providing for individual differences, and summarizing the material. Other items from Stevens's list include classroom appearance and the teacher's handling of student discipline, along with the teacher's appearance, enthusiasm, and knowledge of subject.

Many principals find that it is difficult to keep track of so many details. To make the task more manageable, they adopt an instructional model as a guide to the observation. The model helps by narrowing the list of behaviors they watch for while also giving them a mental picture of how and when certain behaviors should be enacted.

STATE-MANDATED EVALUATION SYSTEMS

Most states require regular evaluation of teachers. Statutes and administrative regulations specify who is responsible for developing and carrying out the evaluation. Some states require a minimum number of classroom observations and establish the performance standards by which teachers are evaluated. Following are descriptions of several state-mandated evaluation procedures.

Iowa. Iowa law establishes eight standards for evaluating teachers:

1. Enhances students' academic performance
2. Demonstrates knowledge of subject
3. Demonstrates competence in planning and preparing for instruction
4. Uses instructional strategies that meet the various needs of student
5. Uses a variety of methods to monitor student learning
6. Demonstrates competence in classroom management
7. Shows evidence of continuing professional growth
8. Carries out professional responsibilities established by the district

Tennessee. In June 2004, the Tennessee State Board of Education adopted an elaborate framework to guide teacher evaluation efforts in schools. The framework is organized around six domains:

1. Planning
2. Teaching strategies
3. Assessment and evaluation
4. Learning environment
5. Professional growth
6. Communication

Each domain has one or more related performance indicators. For example, one indicator under Domain 4 (Learning environment) reads, "Manages classroom resources effectively." Domain 3 (Assessment and evaluation) includes this indicator: "Uses appropriate evaluation and assessments to determine student mastery of content and make instructional decisions." An indicator under Domain 5 (Professional growth) reads, "Collaborates with colleagues and appropriate others." The framework also identifies data sources from which information for evaluation may be obtained. They include teacher conferences, classroom observations, and school records.

Oregon. Oregon law gives district superintendents responsibility for conducting or arranging for teacher evaluations. It requires that all probationary teachers be observed at least twice and that the evaluation be based on the results of those observations "and other relevant information developed by the district." The statute identifies two purposes of teacher evaluation: To aid the teacher in achieving continuing professional growth and to assess the teacher's performance of teaching responsibilities.

Oregon school boards are responsible for developing a teacher evaluation process in consultation with school administrators and with teachers. The law specifies that the evaluation process must include these elements:

- Job descriptions and performance standards;
- A preevaluation interview at which performance goals are established;
- An evaluation based on written criteria that include the performance goals;
- A postevaluation conference; and, if needed,
- A written program of assistance for improvement.

Pennsylvania. The Pennsylvania Department of Education requires that teachers be evaluated twice a year using a form provided by the department. The evaluation consists of ratings in four categories as follows:

Category I—Planning and preparation. This category covers knowledge of content; Pennsylvania academic standards; students; and resources, materials, and technology. The category also evaluates teachers on their abilities to select instructional goals, design coherent instruction, and assess student learning.

Category II—Classroom environment. This category covers teachers' interactions with students, the establishment of a learning environment, and interactions among students.

Category III—Instructional delivery. This category incorporates reviews of communication, questioning and discussion techniques, engaging students in learning, providing feedback, and demonstrating flexibility and responsiveness.

Category IV—Professionalism. This category includes maintaining clear and accurate records, communication with families and students, and contributions to the school and the district.

EVALUATION OF PRINCIPALS

Principals are key players in creating effective schools. They provide vital leadership by setting priorities, motivating staff, promoting good teaching, and involving parents and community leaders in school programs (Cross & Rice, 2000). In spite of the importance of the role, however, evaluation of principals doesn't get much attention. Most principals are evaluated once a year, with a few evaluated every other year. Regardless of the frequency, principals report that evaluation has little impact on their performance.

Principals are usually evaluated by a central office administrator using a model similar to the remedial model used with teachers. The evaluator rates principals on performance criteria similar to those shown in Exhibit 8.4, using a conjunctive approach (that is, a principal must receive at least a "satisfactory" rating on all items). An alternative approach to evaluating administrators that has gained favor in recent years is the 360-degree model.

360-Degree Feedback

The 360-degree feedback approach to evaluation is used to give leaders formative feedback on their performance as seen through the eyes of others who are familiar

EXHIBIT 8.4
PERFORMANCE CRITERIA FOR PRINCIPALS

VISION

Principal works with teachers to develop a shared vision and mission statement for the school.

SCHOOL IMPROVEMENT

Principal provides leadership to develop a school environment that supports learning.

Principal encourages teachers' adoption and use of engaging and effective instructional practices.

Principal monitors achievement data to improve student performance.

HUMAN RESOURCES LEADERSHIP

Principal selects staff members with input from other staff.

Principal supports the growth and development of all staff members.

Principal evaluates the performance of all staff members and works with them to improve the school's performance.

MANAGEMENT OF FACILITIES AND FINANCES

Principal directs the activities of support staff in maintaining facilities and supervising the expenditures of funds in accordance with applicable laws and policies.

COMMUNITY RELATIONS

Principal informs the community about school programs and develops community support for the school.

ETHICAL BEHAVIOR

Principal demonstrates honesty, integrity, and fair dealing with all people.

SAFETY AND SECURITY

Principal leads efforts to maintain a safe, secure learning environment in the school.

Ratings: Needing improvement; Adequate; More than adequate

with their work, including colleagues, superiors, and subordinates. Principals are rated by teachers and central office staff members. This formative evaluation process is used to help individuals sharpen their performance in areas identified as needing improvement. It is not intended to support decisions about salary, promotion, or termination. A strength of 360-degree feedback is that the data obtained are more reliable and comprehensive than evaluations prepared by one person (Dyer,

EXHIBIT 8.5
360-DEGREE FEEDBACK MODEL FOR
EVALUATING ADMINISTRATORS

Purpose:	Collect formative evaluation data on leader from multiple sources.
Objective:	Provide perspectives on leader's effectiveness from members of role set.
Assumption:	Evaluation data from several sources is more reliable and comprehensive than judgments of a single evaluator.
Method:	Multiple raters complete survey instruments rating leader's effectiveness on specific criteria; coach helps leader interpret data and develop an action plan for improvement.
Works best with:	Individuals who have held a leadership position for one year or more; a job description spells out leader's duties clearly.
Evaluator skills:	Able to evaluate another person objectively and without bias (no axes to grind); willing to provide feedback to the leader for purposes of improvement.
Possible problems:	Rater fatigue (evaluators who must rate a number of subordinates grow tired); data overload (more data than one person can absorb and use); lack of qualified coaches (a sound action plan is key to success of this strategy; coaches help leader develop a plan).

2001). If most of the teachers in a school rate a principal as having poor communication skills, that is evidence that a problem exists. The principal, working with a knowledgeable coach, could then develop an action plan to help correct that weakness. If the problem had been cited by a single evaluator, the principal might have been inclined to reject the comment as one person's opinion.

Survey fatigue is a potential problem with 360-degree feedback programs. Because some raters might be asked to evaluate a number of other individuals, the quality of the data declines as the evaluator tires. The success of these programs hinges on the availability of knowledgeable coaches to help leaders prepare action plans for improvement. If coaches are not available or are in short supply, the program may fail. The 360-degree feedback model is described in Exhibit 8.5.

LEGAL CONSIDERATIONS IN
PERSONNEL EVALUATION

Teacher evaluation decisions provoke more legal challenges than any other decisions in schools. To protect teachers' rights to procedural fairness, most states adopt detailed rules for personnel evaluations. In some states, teachers must be notified in advance about the criteria on which they will be evaluated, and they must be given notice about the date and time of observations.

Negotiated contracts may also contain provisions on evaluations, such as specifying how many observations are required and who will do them. If a teacher's performance is rated unsatisfactory, the contract may require that he or she be informed about the specific areas in which improvement is needed. A deadline for completion of the evaluation process may also be specified.

Legal challenges to evaluation decisions most often take the form of questions about the criteria used to rate teaching. Basing a teacher's evaluation on criteria for which no direct links to student learning have been established is likely to invite a legal challenge. Two examples of criteria that are questionable are appearance, or grooming, and personal lifestyle. In reviewing termination decisions, courts consider whether the terminated teacher was given an opportunity to correct the problem and whether he or she received assistance making the necessary improvements.

Limiting Legal Challenges

Challenges to evaluation practices and decisions can be minimized if principals are thoughtful, fair minded, and flexible in carrying out evaluations. Some suggestions for principals that will help schools avoid unnecessary legal challenges to evaluation practices follow.

1. *Heed the rules.* Adhere closely to administrative regulations and statutory requirements pertaining to the frequency and timing of performance evaluations.
2. *Avoid surprises.* Inform teachers in advance about the criteria on which they will be evaluated and, if possible, notify them when to expect a classroom visit.
3. *Be flexible.* Allow teachers to reschedule an observation if the time chosen for the visit is inconvenient.
4. *Talk about the lesson.* Discuss the observation with the teacher after the visit, allowing the teacher to explain the instructional objectives and the reasons for his or her choice of teaching strategies.
5. *Avoid nitpicking.* Focus on the important elements of the observation and overlook minor faults.
6. *Ground your comments.* Be prepared to cite incidents from the lesson to explain how you arrived at particular ratings.
7. *Be fair.* Balance negative comments with attention to positive aspects of the lesson.
8. *Offer assistance.* Let the teacher know that you are willing to help develop an individualized plan for improvement.
9. *Be circumspect.* Do not say anything to imply that a teacher will be recommended for a continuing contract if there is a possibility that will not happen.
10. *Anticipate legal action.* Be aware that your words may be repeated in court and speak accordingly.

SUMMARY

Formative evaluation serves a developmental function—to help employees improve their performance. Summative evaluation is used to gather data for decisions on retention, promotion, and salary. Five models of teacher evaluation are in use in schools—goal-setting model, peer assistance and review model, portfolio model, student achievement model, and remediation model. The first two involve formative evaluation, and the next two are summative in nature. Remediation is used for both formative and quasi-summative purposes.

In a successful instructional program, teacher evaluation is coordinated with district and school missions and integrated with professional development and curriculum development activities, so that these endeavors reinforce one another and contribute to improving instruction. Sound evaluation programs allow for flexible implementation, so beginning teachers are evaluated using criteria suitable for that stage, whereas experienced teachers are evaluated on criteria more appropriate for their level of expertise. Classroom observations are at the heart of some teacher evaluation models. A principal who is responsible for observations needs to know what to look for while viewing a lesson in progress. Keeping track of the many details observed during a lesson can be difficult, but the task is simplified if the observer relies on an instructional model as a guide. Most states require teachers to be evaluated, and some states have established statutory evaluative criteria.

Principals are key players in creating effective schools and providing leadership to set priorities, motivate staff, promote good teaching, and involve parents. A relatively new approach to evaluation of principals is the 360-degree feedback model, by which school leaders are evaluated on a variety of criteria by a number of individuals, including teachers, district office supervisors, and parents. Teacher evaluation often leads to legal challenges. These challenges can be minimized if principals are fair, flexible, adhere to policies, and avoid surprises.

SUGGESTED ACTIVITIES

1. In a 360-degree evaluation plan, teachers in a school evaluate the principal. Look at the following criteria listed and decide whether teachers would be able knowledgeably to rate their principal on each criterion.

   a. Principal works to improve the instructional program of the school

   b. Principal is receptive to teachers' suggestions

   c. Principal represents the school favorably with parents and other groups

   d. Principal manages the school budget responsibly and fairly

   e. Principal is respected by parents and others outside the school

   f. Principal hopes to move to a higher position in the system

g. Principal involves teachers in selecting new staff members

h. School has improved since this principal arrived

2. Most teachers associate evaluation with classroom observations. However, on some evaluative criteria, other methods of gathering data might be more useful than observations. Look at the criteria in Exhibit 8.2 and tell for which items you use these sources of information in evaluating a teacher (either in place of or in addition to classroom observation):

   a. Conversations with the teacher

   b. Information from students and parents

   c. Student achievement test results

3. One of the problems with portfolio evaluations is deciding how to use the information submitted in a portfolio by a teacher. Select three or four items from the list of items to be included in a teacher evaluation portfolio and be prepared to discuss what you might learn from each piece about a teacher's instructional effectiveness if you were the teacher's evaluator. (*Example:* Suppose a teacher includes examples of classroom tests in a portfolio. What could you learn about his or her teaching from examining these tests?)

4. A frequently heard complaint about summative evaluation plans is that they seldom lead to dismissal of incompetent teachers. Do you agree? If so, explain why you believe it is true. Do you believe the problem is lack of training for those who administer teacher evaluations, opposition from teacher unions contesting the dismissal of members, or courts that are inclined to support teachers' rights over administrators' efforts to improve school performance?

ONLINE RESOURCES

Teacher Evaluation Kit (www.wmich.edu/evalctr/ess/glossary/glossary/htm)

This site contains a glossary with definitions of a variety of terms related to evaluation of teachers, including technical terms (congruence analysis, conjunctive model, domain, indicator, critical incident) as well as acronyms (KSAs, BARs, BOS) and humorous names (dance of the lemons, turkey trot, and similar-to-me effect).

Annenberg Institute (www.annenberginstitute.org/tools/index.php)

This site has a section on using data for school improvement and links to sites with data collection tools that can be used for that purpose.

School Improvement in Maryland (www.mdk12.org)

This site has information on leading school improvement; analyzing and using data; and understanding standards, assessments, and AYP.

Tennessee Framework (http://state.tn.us/education/frameval)

The Framework for Evaluation and Professional Development is a statewide program used to evaluate all teachers. This site links to an extensive list of forms developed for the program.

CASE STUDIES

Case No. 1

Albert Knowles, principal of Brigham Young Elementary School, is meeting with Joy Malcolm to discuss her portfolio. Ms. Malcolm has taught at Brigham Young for five years. Other teachers regard her as conscientious and hard working, but they admit that her classroom is messy and that she is forgetful. Recently, she forgot a meeting with a parent and had to reschedule it. Knowles reprimanded her for that. Earlier in the year Knowles observed her class and commented on her lack of patience with students. Ms. Malcolm said that she is impatient when students don't think. "I'm not going to do their thinking for them," she said.

The following is a partial transcript of the conference:

KNOWLES: Thanks for staying late to meet with me.

MS. MALCOLM: Sure.

KNOWLES: I've looked over the materials you submitted with your portfolio.

MS. MALCOLM: And?

KNOWLES: Well, to be frank, I had a hard time figuring out why you included some items.

MS. MALCOLM: Like what?

KNOWLES: There was a photograph of you with some of the students and no explanation. And there were several student papers, stories about vacations and planting gardens, favorite pets, things like that. There was no explanation.

MS. MALCOLM: I didn't mean to include the photograph. Sorry about that. But you said you wanted examples of student work. That's what the papers are.

KNOWLES: OK, but I also wanted your thoughts about the assignment. What you hoped students would learn, what adjustments you made in your teaching after reviewing the work they turned in, your reflections.

MS. MALCOLM: That was in there.

KNOWLES: I didn't find it.

MS. MALCOLM: You didn't? Maybe I forgot to put it in.

KNOWLES: Joy, I hate to say this but my impression is that you put your portfolio together rather hurriedly. It really doesn't present your teaching in the best light.

MS. MALCOLM: Honestly, I don't see the point of having to gather a bunch of stuff to prove I'm a good teacher. You can come to my classroom and watch me teach, and you'll see I do a good job.

KNOWLES: I have watched you teach, and I don't have any major complaints. However, the district has decided that teachers will collect and present evidence to show their strengths as teachers. In my judgment, you haven't done that.

MS. MALCOLM: This portfolio business simply creates extra work. I'd rather put that time and effort into my teaching.

KNOWLES: Evaluating your teaching is part of being a good teacher. I can't agree that assembling a portfolio is a waste of time.

MS. MALCOLM: So what do you want me to do?

KNOWLES: I'm asking you to take your portfolio back and organize it in a way that I can see you've given some thought to it. Look at the guidelines I gave you and follow those.

MS. MALCOLM: And if say I don't want to do that?

KNOWLES: I hope you won't say that.

Questions

1. Ms. Malcolm feels that preparing a portfolio is a waste of time. Did Knowles offer an effective counterargument to her position? Explain.
2. What is the purpose of asking teachers to include student work in the portfolio and write a commentary explaining what the students were asked to do and what the teacher hoped they would learn from the assignment?
3. Suppose other teachers at Brigham Young feel as Ms. Malcolm does about preparing portfolios. What suggestions would you give Knowles for dealing with teachers' opposition?

Case No. 2

Sarah Jefferson is principal of Cave Rock Middle School. It is early April, and in a week or so Jefferson must submit end-of-year evaluation reports on all new teachers in the school to the human resources director, along with a recommendation for retention or nonrenewal.

Joyce Calvin is a new teacher at the school; it is her first year in the classroom. Two other teachers with classrooms nearby have told Jefferson that Ms. Calvin has difficulty managing her classes. Ms. Jefferson visited Ms. Calvin's classroom twice and both times found the students reasonably well behaved. She is reluctant to give Ms. Calvin an unsatisfactory rating for classroom management when she has not personally observed any problems.

Ms. Jefferson has spoken with Felicia Goode, who is the mentor teacher assigned to Calvin. She asked Ms. Goode about Ms. Calvin's classroom management, and after some prodding, Ms. Goode admitted that she had never been in Ms. Calvin's classroom. She said they had met to talk a couple of times after school but that their conversations hadn't touched on that subject.

Ms. Jefferson must soon decide how to evaluate Ms. Calvin on her classroom management skills.

Questions

1. What advice would you give Sarah Jefferson to help her solve her dilemma?
2. The problem goes beyond whether Ms. Calvin is able to manage students' behavior. What other problem did you notice? What action would you recommend to deal with that problem?
3. When a principal doesn't have enough information to rate a teacher in a critical area, what rule of thumb would you suggest he/she follow?
4. In general, how much weight should a principal give to information from other teachers? What factors might the principal want to consider in evaluating information obtained in this way?

REFERENCES

Cross, C. T., & Rice, R. C. (2000, December). The role of the principal as instructional leader in a standards-driven system. *NASSP Bulletin, 84,* 61–65.

Dyer, K. (2001, February). The power of 360-degree feedback. *Educational Leadership, 58,* 35–38.

Keller, B. (2006, January 25). Teacher to conduct peer reviews in Chicago. *Education Week,* p. 8.

McNelly, T. A. (2002, December). Evaluations that ensure growth: Teacher portfolios. *Principal Leadership, 3,* 55–60.

Painter, B. (2001, February). Using teaching portfolios. *Educational Leadership, 58,* 31–34.

Peterson, K., Wahlquist, C., Bone, K., Thompson, J., & Chatterton, K. (2001, February). Using more data sources to evaluate teachers. *Educational Leadership, 58,* 40–43.

Ponticell, J. A., & Zepeda, S. J. (2004, June). Confronting well-learned lessons in supervision and evaluation. *NASSP Bulletin, 88,* 43–59.

Stevens, Larry J. (2001). *An administrative handbook.* Lanham, MD: Scarecrow Press.

Wolf, K. (1996, March). Developing an effective teaching portfolio. *Educational Leadership, 53,* 34–37.

9 COMPENSATION AND REWARDS

Education is a labor-intensive enterprise. A larger share of school budgets is spent for personnel than for any other item. Estimates of the amount range from 60 to 85 percent. With such a major investment, it is important that school districts develop personnel compensation plans to ensure that the funds are spent wisely.

PLAN OF THE CHAPTER

This chapter deals with the following topics: (1) sound compensation plans, (2) reasons for low salaries, (3) single salary schedules, (4) forms of incentive pay, (5) containing costs, and (6) constructing a salary schedule.

SOUND COMPENSATION PLANS

Personnel costs absorb a substantial share of school district budgets, and a well-designed compensation plan is needed to ensure that the money is spent in accordance with the district's priorities. A compensation plan helps a district recruit and retain qualified employees by offering salaries and benefits that are competitive with those of other employers in the region. Many private employers pay higher salaries than schools, but school districts tend to offer more generous benefits, including more paid holidays and more generous sick leave and retirement policies.

Externally Competitive Salaries

A compensation plan that is externally competitive features salaries and benefits that attract enough qualified applicants to fill vacancies. A plan that is externally competitive offers equal or higher compensation than employees could make at other similar jobs in the area. Although salary is only one element of compensation, it is the feature that holds most interest for prospective employees.

Consider two school districts—A and B—located in the same region of the country. Suppose District A has a starting salary for teachers with no experience that is $3,000 more than the comparable figure for District B. District A's salary is externally competitive with District B's, but District B's salary is not externally competitive with respect to District A. District A is likely to have an abundant supply of applicants and should be able to pick and choose the teachers who fit its needs. District B, however, may face a shortage of qualified applicants and may have to make do with individuals who were turned down by District A. When starting salaries of two districts are similar, neither district has an advantage, and prospective employees will consider other factors, such as commuting time, in deciding where to work.

Suppose the two school districts described in the previous paragraph were located in different states, one with a state income tax and the other with no income tax. If District A were located in the state with an income tax, its competitive advantage over District B would shrink or perhaps even disappear. States without an income tax remind prospective applicants that their salaries are more attractive than they appear because there is no income tax. Two states in particular stand to benefit from that argument—Florida and Texas, neither of which has a state income tax (Keller, 2006a).

Competitors

School districts must compete for personnel with private employers who seek applicants with similar qualifications. A district seeking a physical education teacher may find that health clubs, recreation centers, rehabilitation agencies, and physical therapy practices are pursuing the same applicants. Schools trying to hire math teachers must compete with insurance companies, stock brokerages, and engineering firms. Hospitals, cafeterias, and food producers compete with schools to hire people with training in nutrition, and art teachers are recruited for jobs in advertising agencies, retail stores, and newspaper and book publishing. In short, schools compete with many organizations that need personnel with similar skills. When school districts offer lower salaries than other employers, they are at a disadvantage.

Salaries can be made more externally competitive by granting across-the-board increases or by providing targeted increases to selected subgroups of teachers. If the district is losing experienced teachers, the board may decide to increase salaries at the upper end of the scale, but if the district has problems attracting young teachers, it may raise the starting salary. Another approach to making salaries more externally competitive is to add steps to the salary schedule. Experience increments might be scheduled for 20 rather than 15 years. Experience increments average about 4 percent per year, so adding five additional steps to a 15-step scale, each providing a 4 percent increase, results in a top salary that is 21.7 percent higher, with compounding, than the 15-step maximum.

Increasing salaries to make them more competitive can be an expensive proposition. An increase of 1 percent for a teacher making $45,000 raises that person's salary to $45,450. A district that employs 500 teachers averaging $45,000 each would incur additional personnel costs of $225,000 by granting a 1 percent increase to teachers. That figure does not include the additional cost of fringe benefits.

Cost of Increases

The Southern Regional Education Board estimated that, to raise the salaries of all teachers in Texas by only 1 percent, would cost $91 million. A 1 percent increase for Delaware teachers was estimated to cost $3 million. Needless to say, a 1 percent raise would produce only a slight improvement in external competitiveness.

It is not unusual for a district to be able to compete with other districts at the low end of its salary scale but not be competitive at the high end. If the differences are large, such a district stands to lose experienced teachers. However, money is only one of several factors that experienced teachers consider when they think about changing jobs. Like other workers, teachers establish ties to a community over time and often are reluctant to cut them. They accumulate retirement benefits or seniority privileges that they might forfeit if they were to relocate. Teachers who have held their jobs for several years also acquire informal benefits, such as having a comfortable classroom or the chance to choose one's classes, that they might be reluctant to give up for a higher salary.

Internally Competitive Salaries

Departments within an organization compete with one another for personnel. In order to be effective, a department must be able to attract enough qualified employees to carry out its functions. If one department offers lower salaries than others, it lacks internal competitiveness and may not be able to recruit the workers it needs to accomplish its mission. Consider an example: A large supermarket hires a manager for each of its departments (produce, dairy, meat, grocery, bakery, deli, etc.). Some of these managers have more responsibility than others. The bakery employs only a few workers, whereas the grocery department has a large staff. If the salary plan is internally competitive, the salaries of the managers of those departments should reflect this difference in supervisory responsibilities.

Salaries are internally competitive when the compensation for different positions accurately reflects disparities in the level of responsibility and expertise required. In most school districts, principals are paid more than teachers because they have more responsibility. Principals of large schools earn more than those in smaller schools, and high school principals make more than elementary and middle school administrators because of differences in school size and the broader range of activities for which they are responsible. Middle and high school principals work more days per year than teachers (approximately 230 versus 200), and they also work longer hours. It is not unusual for a high school principal to arrive at school by 7:30 A.M. and leave 12 hours later, following a volleyball game or parent–teacher meeting. When principals' and teachers' salaries are compared on an hourly basis, principals' salaries lose much of their competitiveness.

Comparing Salaries

The American Federation of Teachers found that the average salary of public school teachers in the United States in 2003–2004 was $46,597, 2.2 percent above the previous year's figure. Teachers actually lost ground that year because inflation increased 2.7 percent. Beginning teachers with a bachelor's degree were paid $31,704 on average in 2003–2004 (www.aft.org/presscenter/releases/2005/100605.htm).

The Bureau of Labor Statistics reported that teachers in the United States whose salaries were in the top 10 percent of the distribution earned between $66,000 and $71,000 in 2004. Those with salaries in the lowest 10 percent earned between $27,000 and $31,000 (www.bls.gov/oco/ocos069.htm#earnings).

According to the National Education Association the state with highest average salary in 2002–2003 was California ($56,283), followed by Connecticut ($55,367) and New Jersey ($54,158). At the bottom of the range were South Dakota ($32,416), North Dakota ($33,869), and Mississippi ($34,555) (www.nea.org/neatodayextra/salaries.html).

The decade between 1992–1993 and 2002–2003 saw very small gains in teachers' salaries in constant dollars. The largest average increase during that decade was 18 percent in Georgia, but salaries actually decreased in 18 states. The largest loss was suffered by teachers in Alaska (−16.6 percent), followed by Connecticut, where teachers saw the buying power of their paychecks drop by 10.3 percent (www.nea.org/neatodayextra/salaries.html).

Table 9.1 shows how 2005 teachers' salaries compared with those of other professionals, using data from the U.S. Bureau of Labor Statistics. The factor column shows each salary as a multiple of the average teacher salary. For example, on average physicians earned almost three times what teachers earned in 2005, but reporters made only about nine-tenths of the average elementary school teacher's salary.

Table 9.1 shows that teachers were near the low end of the income distribution among professionals. The level of education required in an occupation correlates roughly with salary. With the possible exception of computer programmers and airline pilots, all of the occupations shown in Table 9.1 with average salaries higher than teaching require an advanced degree, and at least four of them (physician, dentist, veterinarian, and attorney) require a doctorate or

TABLE 9.1   Comparison of Average Elementary School Teachers' Salaries and Those of Other Professionals, 2005

	AVERAGE SALARY	FACTOR
Physician, surgeon	$138,910	2.96
Airline pilot	135,040	2.87
Dentist	133,680	2.84
Attorney	110,520	2.35
Architect	68,560	1.46
Veterinarian	77,710	1.65
Physical therapist	65,350	1.39
Accountant	58,020	1.23
Registered nurse	56,880	1.21
Librarian	49,110	1.05
Police officer	47,270	1.01
Elementary school teacher	46,990	1.00
Paralegal	43,510	.93
Social worker	42,720	.91
Reporter	40,370	.86

Source: U.S. Bureau of Labor Statistics (www.bls.gov/news.release/pdf/ocwage.pdf).

equivalent. Most states do not require teachers to have a master's degree, although some do.

Second Jobs

It has been estimated that about 4 percent of teachers (nearly 5 million people) hold second jobs. Other occupational groups with large percentages of moonlighters include farmers; sales workers; and a category that consists of writers, artists, entertainers, and athletes.

Teachers who hold second jobs earn about $2,400 from the second job, and those with summer jobs earn slightly less ($2,300). Men's earnings are higher than women's in both cases ($3,400 and $1,900, respectively, for men and women who hold another job during the school year; and $2,900 and $2,100 for summer jobs). Some experts believe that the number of people with second jobs is underreported.

People who work two jobs usually do so because the salary from the primary job is not adequate for their needs. Cost of living varies greatly from one region of the country to another. As a rule, the cost of living is higher in urban areas and along the coast. Housing prices are an important component of living expenses. It is not unusual for teachers to find that they cannot afford to live in the district where they teach because of the high cost of housing. The same holds true for other public employees such as police and firefighters.

REASONS FOR LOW SALARIES

To what can the disparity between teachers' salaries and the salaries of workers in other occupations with comparable educational requirements be attributed? In part, the decline in teachers' salaries during the 1970s was the market's response to an oversupply of teachers. However, even during periods of short supply, teachers make relatively lower salaries than members of most other comparable occupations.

Teachers work about 9 percent fewer days each year than other workers. However, teachers' salaries appear to be lower than expected, even allowing for the difference in days worked. One other factor that contributes to low salaries for teachers is the composition of the teaching force. As a general rule, professions in which women predominate have lower salaries than those with more men.

Daily Wages

Some critics believe that teachers' salaries are about right or may even be too high. One economist claims that one-third of teachers are paid too little and one-third are paid too much (Keller & Galley, 2003). Because teachers work fewer hours per year than other professionals, comparing annual salaries can be misleading. A more accurate comparison might be daily wages. Teachers are employed on average about 200 days per year, compared to about 230 days for other professional employees. Thus, a teacher earning $45,000 makes about $225 per day, whereas an architect making $65,000 earns slightly more than $280 daily. However, teachers claim that, counting the time they spend outside of school preparing tests and grading papers, they work more than 200 days.

Salary Equity

In addition to being externally and internally competitive, compensation should also be equitable, meaning that individuals with similar qualifications who perform jobs of equal worth under the same conditions should be paid about the same. Aside from adequacy, employees value equity more highly than any other feature of a compensation package. There is no widely accepted objective measure of equity because people's perceptions vary depending on their definitions of their own and others' contributions and rewards. Accurate judgments about equity are speculative when individuals do not have access to information about how much colleagues are paid.

Equal Pay Act.   Lack of salary equity is a source of morale problems and, in certain cases, is illegal. The Equal Pay Act of 1963 requires employers to refrain from discriminating against female employees by paying them less than males for performing the same or similar jobs. (See Chapter 11.) Since the act was passed, some progress has been made in closing the gender gap, but discrepancies remain. Women who work in occupations that are dominated by women, such as teaching and nursing, generally earn less than people in so-called "male" occupations, such as truck driving or electrical work. However, female employees have no redress under the law unless an employer pays a male more to do what is essentially the same job.

Few cases involving equal pay for teachers have been litigated under the Equal Pay Act because teachers' salaries are assumed to be gender neutral. However, figures from the National Center for Education Statistics showed that in 1999–2000 female teachers earned a base salary that was on average $1,600 less than that of men, holding education level and years of experience constant. The only explanation for such a discrepancy is that male teachers receive more credit for previous teaching experience than female teachers.

Weighted Student Funding. A movement is under way to change the way funds are allocated to schools. At present, schools with more senior staff members receive more money, and those with fewer experienced employees get less. Under weighted student funding, allocation decisions are based on student characteristics. Schools with high concentrations of students from poor families and those with disabilities or limited English proficiency would receive more money, and other schools would get relatively less. Decisions about how the money is to be spent are decentralized to the schools. Some urban districts already use the weighted student method of allocating funds. They include Houston, Seattle, Los Angeles, Chicago, Denver, Milwaukee, Oakland, and Baltimore. An ad hoc group consisting of former secretaries of education and former governors, among others, was formed recently to promote the plan among other districts (Hoff, 2006).

In some districts weighted student funding can have a profound impact on budgets. An example of how student weighted budgeting affects funding comes from Houston, where one well-funded school lost nearly $1 million, or 34 percent of its budget, under the plan, whereas another school gained about half that amount, or about 17 percent of its budget. (See Online Resources for more information.)

Fringe Benefits

Salaries are only part of total compensation, which includes benefits such as health insurance and retirement contributions. Three types of benefits are available:

Collateral benefits. These are direct and indirect forms of payment that are received without additional effort. Sick leave, medical insurance, and retirement contributions are examples of collateral benefits.

Nonsalary payments. Teachers who perform duties outside of their normal teaching responsibilities receive nonsalary payments. Coaching, sponsoring cheerleaders, and advising a yearbook staff are examples of jobs eligible for nonsalary payments.

Noneconomic benefits. Any feature of a job that does not involve money but that makes the job more attractive is a noneconomic benefit. Working with young people and having summers free are noneconomic benefits of teaching.

A survey of companies operating in Minnesota found that about 18 percent of the firms provided counseling services for their employees. Free parking, transportation assistance, job sharing, and wellness programs were other benefits offered by some employers. A number of firms had so-called cafeteria plans under which employees were able to choose the benefits they received. Exhibit 9.1 lists fringe benefits offered by school districts, along with the type and beneficiary of each benefit.

According to the Hoover Institution, teachers' retirement and medical insurance benefits cost school districts about 26 percent of employees' salaries, on average, whereas the fringe benefits paid to professional workers employed by private firms amount to about 17 percent of their salaries. Standard and Poor's estimated that employee benefits in school districts amounted to 18.1 percent of core spending (www.schoolmatters.com). Authors of a compensation study conducted for Montgomery County (Maryland) schools reported that fringe benefits for teachers in that county amounted to 25.7 percent of salaries, compared to 29.2 percent for all government employees and 27.2 percent for employees in private industry.

Pension programs for teachers in most states are expected to run out of money to pay pensions for retired teachers in the future unless benefits are reduced or additional funds are infused. It is estimated that public-sector pension funds, including teacher pensions, have only 89 percent of the money they need to meet long-term obligations (Hoff, 2005).

SINGLE SALARY SCHEDULES

The single salary schedule was proposed in the early 1920s as a way of removing teaching jobs from political patronage. After it was adopted by several cities, the single salary schedule took hold nationwide, supported by teachers who saw it as a way to professionalize teaching. Teachers liked the idea that men and women would be paid the same and that elementary teachers would make as much as high school teachers. They also approved of basing salaries on objective criteria rather than political connections. However, critics argued that the single salary plan ignored the law of supply and demand and suggested that administrators may have proposed the idea in order to avoid having to evaluate teachers for salary purposes.

Districts that use the single salary schedule sometimes provide a fixed dollar increment at each step. The increment represents a proportionally larger adjustment for teachers near the bottom of the scale as compared to those near

EXHIBIT 9.1

EXAMPLES OF EMPLOYEE BENEFITS GROUPED BY TYPE

BENEFIT	BENEFICIARY	TYPE
Health insurance*	Employee and family	Collateral
Dental insurance*	Employee and family	Collateral
Term life insurance	Designated	Collateral
Sick leave	Employee	Collateral
Retirement contribution*	Employee	Collateral
Tax sheltered annuity*	Employee	Collateral
Leaves of absence		Collateral
Family leave	Employee and family	
Maternity leave	Employee	
Illness	Employee and family	
Military service	Employee	
Sabbatical	Employee	Noneconomic
Tenure	Employee	Noneconomic
Supplemental income	Employee	Nonsalary payment
Coach, club sponsor, summer school instructor, etc.		
Holidays and vacations	Employee	Collateral
Automatic deduction for professional dues	Employee	Collateral
Travel to professional meetings	Employee	Collateral
Tuition refund	Employee	Nonsalary payment
Reduction on apartment rent	Employee	Nonsalary payment
Allowance for child care	Employee	Nonsalary payment
Allowance for expenses of seeking National Board Certification	Employee	Nonsalary payment
Reimbursement for Praxis test cost	Employee	Nonsalary payment

*Employee may be required to share cost.

the top. To provide step increments that are proportionally equal, many districts use indexed schedules in which the dollar amounts vary but the rate of increase is fixed.

In most districts with single salary schedules, regular increases are provided for the first 12 or 15 years a teacher is employed, although a recent survey by the

American Federation of Teachers (1999) found that the number of steps in salary scales in the 100 largest city school districts in the United States ranged from 8 to 45. After a person reaches the top of the scale, longevity increases are granted about once every five years. Practically speaking, however, teachers in the United States reach the peak of their earning power within 15 years of entering the field. This is in contrast to most other occupations, in which salaries continue to rise throughout most of one's working life.

Because attrition is highest among teachers within the first few years of entering the profession, it stands to reason that giving proportionally more generous raises to beginning teachers should improve retention. However, the evidence for that conclusion is not strong. That suggests that factors other than salary are involved in teachers' decisions to transfer schools or leave the profession.

Some economists argue that, because the salary curve for teachers is so steep, a disproportionate share of salary funds goes to experienced teachers and, thus, is not available to attract younger, less experienced but more talented teachers. Those who express this opinion believe that there is relatively little difference in the effectiveness of a teacher with many years experience in the classroom and one who is new to the job. If one accepts the economists' premise, then it makes sense to pay higher salaries to beginning teachers and offer less lucrative rewards to more experienced individuals because the loss of experienced employees would not result in lower productivity. If experienced teachers are no more effective than beginners in the classroom, there is no justifiable reason for paying higher salaries based on experience (Ballou & Podgursky, 2002). Few educators would accept the proposition that experienced teachers are no more productive than those without experience, but they would probably agree that there is a point at which additional experience adds little in the way of increased productivity. The question is, at what point does that transition occur?

Motivating Employees

It is generally acknowledged that the single salary schedule lacks motivational power. None of the three motivational theories described in Chapter 5 would predict that a single salary plan would motivate teachers to work harder or longer. According to equity theory, the single salary plan should have a demotivating effect on teachers. The other two theories (expectancy and goal setting) would predict no effect on motivation from the single salary schedule.

The single salary schedule continues to have staunch supporters, but bit by bit the plan is giving way to concerted efforts to make salaries more responsive to teacher performance and working conditions in schools. No one wants schools staffed solely by teachers whose only motivation is money, yet it is a fact that money is a motivator, even for teachers. Individuals who teach in schools where jobs are more difficult and safety less certain expect to be rewarded for their courage and dedication.

FORMS OF INCENTIVE PAY

There is growing interest in developing compensation plans that reward outstanding teachers and teachers who accept assignments in hard-to-staff schools. Opinion polls show strong public support for both ideas. A majority of teachers support paying more for teaching in hard-to-staff schools but fewer of them support higher salaries for a short supply of teachers in particular subjects.

Several states have adopted incentive plans. Maryland offers several incentives designed to attract and hold outstanding teachers. Individuals with National Board Certification receive a $2,000 increase in salary, and teachers accepting assignments in schools classified as hard to staff also get a $2,000 raise. Teacher preparation graduates with grade point averages of 3.5 or higher qualify for a $1,000 signing bonus, and teachers can earn a $1,500 tuition tax credit for graduate work taken to maintain their certification.

Florida announced recently that it will link teacher pay to student scores on state achievement tests. Paying teachers on the basis of student learning is not a new idea, and although it seems attractive, it has critics who charge that singling out a few individuals for extra pay creates morale problems and leads to lower productivity (Schlechty, 2005).

Pay-for-Performance

Teachers oppose pay-for-performance plans because they feel they cannot trust principals to evaluate their performance fairly. They fear that principals will reward their friends and penalize enemies. However, recent research suggests that principals may be better at identifying and rewarding effective teaching than commonly thought.

Researchers from Harvard and Brigham Young Universities compared principals' evaluations of teachers to differences in student test scores where gains could be attributed to specific teachers. Thirteen schools were involved in the study, all from midsize districts. The study found that principals consistently and correctly identified the 10 percent of teachers whose students gained the most and the 10 percent whose students gained the least (Tonn, 2006). If subsequent research supports these findings, teachers may have to change their opinions about principals' objectivity.

New Strategies.   Policy makers and district administrators have learned from past failures of pay-for-performance plans and are developing strategies to avoid the problems that plagued earlier efforts. They have involved teacher unions earlier, with the result that unions are more willing now than in the past to support pay-for-performance. Most of the newer plans use several sources of data to identify outstanding teachers in order to avoid relying exclusively on principals' evaluations. To lessen public opposition, officials notify the public early about the expected costs of the plans and ask voters to approve tax increases, if needed, to cover the additional expense. Planners realize that many teachers prefer to collaborate with rather than compete with fellow workers and so include provisions to reward entire schools or departments rather than individuals.

Pay-for-performance plans are more likely to succeed when planners are aware of factors that affect teachers' acceptance. Teachers are unlikely to put forth extra effort for meaningless rewards. Unless the incentives are significant, these plans are likely to fail (Guthrie & Springer, 2006).

Alternative Pay Plans

In the sections that follow, several alternative pay plans are described. The first section describes the ProComp Plan adopted recently in Denver (Colorado) public schools.

Denver ProComp Plan.   The Denver Professional Compensation (ProComp) Plan is a comprehensive incentive program developed jointly by the school district and Denver Classroom Teachers Association to tie teacher pay to the district's mission. The plan rewards teachers with bonuses and salary increases for raising student achievement scores and offers monetary rewards for teachers who agree to teach in hard-to-staff schools or accept difficult-to-fill positions. Under the plan, teachers earn salary increases by improving student achievement, receiving satisfactory performance evaluation scores, participating in activities leading to professional growth, and accepting assignments to schools or positions that are difficult to staff.

Rewards are stated as percentages of an indexed salary. Those who attain National Board certification or who complete a graduate degree receive 9 percent of the index salary. (If the index salary is $33,000, they earn $2,970.) Probationary teachers who are rated satisfactory on the annual professional evaluation receive 1 percent of the index ($330), and nonprobationary teachers receive 3 percent ($990). Teachers who are rated exemplary receive an additional 2 to 3 percent of the index. Teachers who take positions that are hard to fill or who agree to work in difficult-to-staff schools receive a 3 percent salary increase. Teachers who achieve two of their performance objectives receive a 1 percent raise. However, teachers who fail to achieve their objectives and who had previously received an increase may have their salary reduced by the amount of the earlier increase.

Douglas County Incentive Plan.   Teachers in Douglas County (Colorado) may earn either individual or group rewards under that district's incentive plan. An individual teacher who is rated outstanding as documented by a portfolio qualifies for a salary increase of $1,250, and a teacher who completes advanced coursework or a degree receives $1,000. For developing and applying instructional skills identified by the district as priorities, teachers may be paid up to $500 per skill. Teachers who earn National Board certification and those who are designated Master Teachers receive bonuses of $2,500 a year for five years. Teachers may also qualify for $750 by accepting additional responsibilities. Group rewards go to teachers who jointly develop and implement plans to impact student achievement.

EXHIBIT 9.2

EXAMPLES OF PROFESSIONAL GROWTH AND CAREER DEVELOPMENT PROGRAMS FOR TEACHERS

STATE OR CITY	PROGRAM NAME	FEATURES
Minnesota	Quality Compensation (Q-Comp)	State provides grants to districts to develop plans for multiple career paths including objective assessment system.
Rochester (New York)	Career-in-Teaching	Teachers advance through four career steps: intern, resident, professional, and lead. Teachers are evaluated by colleagues or an administrator named by the teacher. Teachers having difficulty may request help.
Utah	Career Ladder	Extended-year contracts for teachers who teach summer school or take part in curriculum development or professional development activities or work on improving facilities or securing relations with parents or raising productivity.

Houston Bonus Plan. Houston teachers can earn bonuses for gains in students' test scores under a plan adopted recently by the school board. Teachers whose students show above-average gains on achievement tests will receive a one-time bonus, ranging from $500 to $3,500 per teacher for the 2005–2006 school year (Keller, 2006b).

Career Plans

Some states and cities have developed career plans that allow teachers to move through a series of positions of increasing responsibility and rewards. Three of these are described in Exhibit 9.2.

CONTAINING COSTS

A sound compensation plan must provide for careful monitoring of compensation costs in order to ensure that all monies are expended legally and that they yield the maximum possible benefits for students. If salaries are excessive given local market conditions, the district will be paying more than it should for the services it receives, and if salaries are too low the most highly qualified prospects will be lost to other districts and the quality of services received for the dollars spent will be diminished.

TABLE 9.2   National Average Salaries and Salary Ranges of School
Administrators and Other Personnel, by Position, 2003–2004

POSITION	AVERAGE SALARY	RANGE
Superintendent	$125,609	($96,387–$174,805)
Director of instruction	84,866	($66,648–$96,429)
High school principal	86,160	($74,139–$92,252)
Elementary school principal	75,144	($69,096–$80,714)
Teacher	45,646	($43,904–$45,570)

Source: Salaries and Wages Paid Professional and Support Personnel in Public Schools 2003–2004. Arlington, VA:
Educational Research Service, 2004. Reprinted by permission.

Overtime Pay

Some school employees qualify for overtime pay if they work more than 40 hours
per week. Regulations governing overtime are issued by the Department of Labor.
Exempt employees—that is, those not eligible for overtime pay—include teachers,
administrators, psychologists, and supervisors. Noncertified employees, including
cafeteria workers, custodians, instructional aides, and clerical employees, must be
paid overtime if they work more than 40 hours in a week. Districts should review
personnel records to ensure that employees are correctly classified. A school district
can be sued for failing to pay overtime to employees who qualify (Soronen, 2004).

Administrators' Salaries

Table 9.2 shows average salaries and salary ranges earned by central office administrators in 2003–2004. District superintendents earned, on average, $125,609, with
a range of salaries from $96,000 to almost $175,000. Elementary school principals
received more than $75,000 on average, whereas the average salary of high school
principals was 14.6 percent higher ($86,000).

CONSTRUCTING A SALARY SCHEDULE

Salary schedules are usually developed by firms that specialize in employee compensation. The task is one that requires a considerable amount of expertise and a
great deal of data. The first decision to be made in developing a salary schedule is
the number of grades or levels to be included. Henderson (1985) defined *pay grades*
as convenient groupings of a wide variety of jobs that are similar in difficulty and
level of responsibility but with little else in common. The number of grades to be
incorporated into a schedule varies depending on the number of employee specialties and the extent to which the district administration wishes to be able to
make small distinctions in compensation.

Each grade is subdivided into 10 to 15 steps to provide for differences in experience and level of educational attainment. The difference between the lowest step in adjacent grades in school district salary schedules typically ranges from 2.5 to 4 percent, and there is obviously considerable overlap across grades.

The procedure used to establish salaries for dissimilar jobs is *job evaluation* (Landy, 1985). A job evaluation involves these steps:

1. Select the jobs to be evaluated and choose the evaluation factors. The factors should be skills or abilities that are required to varying degrees in all of the positions and for which salary differences can be justified. An example of a factor that is frequently used is education; people who hold jobs requiring higher levels of education receive higher salaries than those whose jobs require less education, other things being equal.

2. Collect information about the positions from a variety of sources, including interviews, job descriptions, and observations.

3. Using information collected in Step 2, rate the jobs being evaluated by assigning points for each criterion. Sum the points to obtain a total for each position. This activity is normally carried out independently by members of a committee who compare their ratings after they are completed and discuss differences until a consensus is reached.

4. Rank the positions by point totals agreed on in Step 3. Select a few key positions and assign salaries to those by investigating salaries for similar positions in nearby districts.

5. Assign salaries to the remainder of the positions by comparing the point totals for those positions to the point totals for the key positions.

Job evaluation should result in a salary schedule that is internally consistent and externally competitive. It is necessary to repeat the procedure about every 10 years because jobs change over time and their relative importance to the district shifts. As duties evolve and new specialties emerge, some positions must be moved up or down on the scale to preserve internal competitiveness.

SUMMARY

Compensation, including salaries and benefits, consumes between 60 and 85 percent of school budgets. A sound compensation plan is externally and internally competitive, adequate, equitable, and able to control costs. On average, teachers earn less than people in other professional occupations. In 2005 registered nurses were paid 21 percent more than elementary teachers, and physical therapists' salaries were 39 percent higher than teachers' salaries. Many teachers hold second jobs, from which they earn additional income of about $2,400 per year. The Equal

Pay Act requires employers to pay male and female employees equally for performing the same or similar jobs. The law has had little effect on teachers' salaries.

Some districts have adopted weighted student funding, which takes student characteristics into account in distributing funds to schools. Under this plan schools with more difficult-to-educate students receive a larger allocation.

Fringe benefits are of three types—collateral benefits such as sick leave, nonsalary payments such as coaching supplements, and noneconomic benefits such as free summers. Studies have shown that teachers' fringe benefits are more generous than those paid to employees in the private sector.

The single salary schedule was first proposed as a way to professionalize teaching and eliminate politics from salary decisions. It is now the most widely used salary plan in schools. Some economists have argued that the salary curve for teachers is too steep, resulting in unjustifiably high salaries for experienced teachers. In 2004, high school principals earned on average 88.7 percent more than elementary teachers, and elementary principals earned 64.6 percent more.

Incentive pay for teachers has become a popular way to reward teachers who take on difficult duties or who upgrade their skills by earning additional degrees or certifications. A number of states now offer salary bonuses of as much as $2,500 to teachers who earn National Board certification.

SUGGESTED ACTIVITIES

1. In trying to construct a salary schedule that is externally competitive, a school district must sometimes sacrifice internal equity. Discuss the relative importance of these two features. Under what conditions is it advisable to increase external competitiveness at the cost of internal equity? What problems may arise as a result?

2. Adding additional steps to existing salary schedules has been proposed as a way to make teaching more competitive with other occupations. However, that idea has little support among teachers. Why do you think teachers are not in favor of adding steps?

3. As discussed in this chapter, some school personnel hold two jobs during the academic year. What are the factors that contribute to teachers and other employees working at two jobs? What is the likely effect of a second job on teachers' effectiveness? What policy should districts adopt with regard to second jobs?

4. Some incentive plans offer bonuses for teachers who obtain National Board certification or who agree to teach in a hard-to-staff school. Other plans reward teachers for taking on added duties, such as chairing a committee or serving as head of a department. Suppose teachers in a district earn an average annual salary of $42,000. What size bonus would you recommend for teachers in each of the categories mentioned (board certification, hard-to-staff school, committee chair, department head)? Explain your reasoning.

5. If a school district awards bonuses of $1,500 to all teachers who agree to teach in schools with a high percentage of difficult-to-educate students, what effect will that

decision have on the external competitiveness of the district's salaries? What effect will it have on internal competitiveness of schools in the district? What effect will it have on salary equity in the district?

6. Look at the following list of optional fringe benefits and rank them from 1 to 6 (1 = most desirable, 6 = least desirable) according to your personal preferences. Give reasons for your rankings.

   a. Sick leave (five additional days above the five days all employees receive)

   b. Term life insurance (policy equal to annual salary)

   c. Travel allowance for attending professional meetings ($600/year)

   d. Tuition benefit (up to $300 per course for approved study, with a maximum of two courses per year)

   e. Personal leave (five days/year)

7. Read the following descriptions and answer the question that follows.

   a. Male custodians in Highland District are required to climb ladders to replace light-bulbs in the auditorium and gym and are paid $2,000 more per year than female custodians. Does this comply with the Equal Pay Act?

   b. Beginning teachers in Hammond Parish earn $32,800; a neighboring district, Marguiles Parish, pays beginning teachers $31,100. Is Marguiles Parish externally competitive?

   c. The English department head at Graceland High School receives a salary supplement of $5,000 per year. Her department has 13 teachers. In addition, she has two free periods per day. The head of the math department, which has 10 teachers, receives a supplement of $3,000 and one free period. Is this plan internally equitable?

   d. Teachers with five years' experience in West Liberty District are paid $38,000 per year plus 25 percent in fringe benefits. Sligh River teachers with the same amount of experience receive $36,000 and fringe benefits of 30 percent. Is the Sligh River salary externally competitive?

ONLINE RESOURCES

American Federation of Teachers (www.aft.org/research/salary/home.htm)

>   The AFT conducts salary surveys annually and publishes detailed results on its website. The surveys compare salaries paid beginning and experienced teachers by state and show the amount of increase in recent years.

Consortium for Policy Research in Education (www.wcer.wisc.edu/cpre/tcomp/)

>   This site describes research on teacher compensation being conducted by CPRE at the University of Wisconsin–Madison. The center publishes an online newsletter that seeks to facilitate communication among educators who are interested in issues related to teacher compensation.

St. Petersburg Times (www.sptimes.com/2006/04/16/Hillsborough/Do_teacher_rewards_pa.shtml)

Report on experiences of teachers in Hillsborough County (Florida) who took positions in hard-to-staff schools in return for monetary rewards (10 percent salary bonus + $4,500 for obtaining National Board certification).

Employee Benefit Research Institute (www.ebri.org/)

This site publishes information about administering employee fringe benefit programs in public and private organizations. Issue briefs on a variety of topics are accessible online.

100 Percent Solution (www.100percentsolution.org/fundthechld/index.cfm)

This site contains information about the weighted student approach to allocating school funds.

American Association of School Administrators
(www.aasa.org/publications/content.cfm?ItemNumber=1190)

This is an article written by a superintendent describing weighted student funding of schools.

CASE STUDIES

Case No. 1

Joel Hoffman, principal of Grant Road Middle School, is meeting with the director of human resources, Helen Nelson, and the director of instruction, Wilma Tessla. They are discussing details of a planned incentive program for teachers, which will be presented to the board for approval. Five schools are under consideration for participation in the program, and this group has been asked to recommend three schools to include. All of the schools have difficulty recruiting teachers. The schools are as follows:

Adams Elementary School. Located in an old building near downtown. School will be closed within three years. Percentage of single-parent families: 43. Enrollment: 300 in grades K–3. Average family income: $13,500. Percentage of students on free lunch: 75. Teacher attrition: Low.

Hoover Elementary School. Located in a section of the city known for frequent shootings. Building is 20 years old and will accommodate up to 900 students. Percentage of single-parent families: 79. Enrollment: 700 in grades K–5. Average family income: $9,800. Percentage of students on free lunch: 67. Teacher attrition: High.

Morgan Middle School. Located 20 miles from city center in a rural community. Building is about 60 years old but has been refurbished. Percentage of single-parent families: 28. Enrollment: 450 in grades 6–8. Average family income: $22,300. Percentage of students on free lunch: 12. Teacher attrition: Low (but likely to rise as older teachers retire).

Grady High School. Located in a recently annexed section of the city. Building is 25 years old and is in reasonably good condition. Percentage of single-parent families: 41. Enrollment: 1,200 students in grades 9–12. Average family income:

$15,200. Percentage of students on free lunch: 11. Teacher attrition: Highest in the district.

Mechanics' Center School. An alternate school located in a converted church near downtown. School will be moved to a new location next year. Percentage of single-parent families: 52. Enrollment: 180 in grades 4–8. Average family income: $28,600. Percentage of students on free lunch: 7. Teacher attrition: Moderate.

Questions

1. Which three schools would you recommend for the incentive program? Would you recommend the same bonus for all schools? If no, explain.
2. What evidence would you look for in determining whether the incentive program has been a success?
3. What other information about these schools would you like to have had before making your decision?
4. Would you recommend that the incentive be paid as a one-time bonus to teachers who accept a transfer to a qualifying school, or should the increases be permanent? Explain your reasoning.

Case No. 2

Members of an ad hoc committee have been asked to review supplemental payments to teachers who perform certain extracurricular duties. The current pay scale follows. The committee must decide whether to leave the payments unchanged or recommend changes.

High school yearbook	$1,850/year
Middle school yearbook	$1,500/year
Cheerleader coach (high school)	$1,500/year
Cheerleader coach (middle school)	0
Pep band	$500/year
Technology coordinator (elementary)	$500/year
Technology coordinator (high school)	$1,000/year
Director of drama productions (two per year)	$1,150
Head coach (football)	$2,700/year
Head coach (basketball)	$2,700/year
Head coach (track)	$2,400/year

Questions

1. Which payment do you think is too low? What should it be?
2. Which payment is too high? What should it be?
3. How do the payments compare to the amount of teacher time devoted to the activity?

REFERENCES

American Federation of Teachers, Department of Research. (1999). *Survey and analysis of teacher salary trends 1999*. [Online.] Available: www.aft.org/research/survey99/tables.

Ballou, D., & Podgursky, M. (2002, Fall). Returns to seniority among public school teachers. *Journal of Human Resources, 37*, 892–912.

Educational Research Service. (2004). *Salaries and wages paid professional and support personnel in public schools, 2003–2004*. Arlington, VA: Author.

Guthrie, J. W., & Springer, M. G. (2006, April 5). Teacher pay for performance: Another fad or a sound and lasting policy? *Education Week*, pp. 42, 52.

Henderson, R. (1985). *Compensation management* (4th ed.). Reston, VA: Reston Publishing.

Hoff, D. J. (2005, May 18). State facing fiscal strain of pensions. *Education Week*, pp. 1, 21.

Hoff, D. J. (2006, July 12). Call of "weighted" student funding gets bipartisan stamp of approval. *Education Week*, pp. 1, 30.

Keller, B. (2006a, May 17). Florida urges comparable teacher-compensation reporting. *Education Week*, p. 12.

Keller, B. (2006b, January 18). Test-tied bonuses to take effect in Houston. *Education Week*, pp. 5, 12.

Keller, B., & Galley, M. (2003, May 28). Economists: Scrap single salary schedule for teachers. *Education Week*, p. 12.

Landy, F. (1985). *Psychology of work behavior.* Homewood, IL: Dorsey

Schlechty, P. C. (2005). *Creating great schools.* San Francisco: Jossey-Bass.

Soronen, L. E. (2004, September). Who is eligible for overtime? *Principal Leadership, 5*, 56–60.

Tonn, J. L. (2006, March 1). Study backs principals as effective in evaluating teachers. *Education Week*, p. 7.

10 CREATING PRODUCTIVE WORK ENVIRONMENTS

In recent years there has been a reconsideration of what it means to be a teacher and a member of a learning community. As a result of this rethinking, student learning has emerged as the goal that guides the work of teachers and administrators, and with this change has come the realization that collaboration is essential to success, that without it the chances of success are slim. Policy makers are belatedly learning that the environment of a workplace has an impact on those who work there. In this chapter we examine some of the characteristics of schools that lead to feelings of satisfaction and accomplishment among both students and teachers.

PLAN OF THE CHAPTER

The following topics are examined in this chapter: (1) psychological success and work environments, (2) qualities of productive work environments, and (3) teacher stress and burnout.

PSYCHOLOGICAL SUCCESS AND WORK ENVIRONMENTS

Psychological success occurs when an individual performs competently at a task that he or she values. New workers in a job frequently find success elusive because of their lack of competence. They may even have doubts about the importance of the work, but over time, as their competence and confidence grow, they begin to derive feelings of success.

Conditions in schools may either help or hinder teachers' abilities to experience success in their work. Students' attitudes, administrators' interest and support, and even the appearance of one's classroom all contribute to or detract from teachers' success on the job.

Some conditions found in schools prevent employees from doing their best work, whereas others simply make it more difficult to do a good job. Many teachers manage to be effective in spite of large classes by taking work home on evenings and weekends, and they overcome the lack of materials and supplies by buying them from their own funds. Other employees cannot solve their problems as easily, however. A counselor who is assigned to an office in which his or her conversations with students can be overheard by others is unable to conduct confidential counseling sessions with students, and a teacher who cannot be confident of receiving support from the principal must avoid teaching topics that offend sensitive parents.

School administrators need to be aware of the conditions in a school that can help make it a good place to work. Some of these conditions may be things that a principal has little control over, but others are amenable to change.

QUALITIES OF PRODUCTIVE WORK ENVIRONMENTS

An extensive survey of principals and teachers conducted by the Southeastern Center for Teaching Quality (Jacobson, 2005) identified working conditions in schools that contributed to increased student achievement. According to teachers who responded to the survey, time for planning and teaching is a critical factor, and there is never enough of it. The study found a significant relationship between availability of time and student success. Two other factors that were positively associated in teachers' minds with student learning gains were professional development opportunities and the quality of facilities and resources.

Teachers and principals who responded to the survey did not always agree with one another in their responses. Principals were less likely than teachers to say that teachers were required to perform duties that interfered with their instructional responsibilities. Teachers more often agreed with that sentiment.

Following are eight characteristics of a work environment that seem to have the greatest effect on employee satisfaction and feelings of success. They include the factors identified in the Jacobson (2005) study. Seven of the eight factors are discussed in the sections that follow. Professional development is dealt with at length in Chapter 7.

1. Clear mission
2. Stimulating professional development opportunities
3. Supportive administrative leadership
4. Professional culture
5. Opportunity to use one's talents and skills
6. Comfortable, attractive, and well-equipped physical space
7. Adequate time to perform required duties
8. Adequate supply of materials and equipment

When one of these conditions is missing, teachers are less likely to be able to carry out their work successfully and hence are not as likely to experience psychological success.

Clear Mission

An indispensable ingredient for a productive school is a mission that is understood and accepted by all members of the staff. Teachers recognize the need for a mission that everyone can rally around, but they say it is difficult to "stay on the same page." Teachers all have instructional goals for their students, which may or may not fit neatly into their school's mission. Finding a theme or themes to bring people together is a challenge for everyone in the school (Huffman & Hipp, 2003).

Most school faculties agree that schools should enable children to grow and develop, but they don't always agree on how best to do that. In recent years, more attention has been given to academic learning than to the other aspects of children's development. Some believe the emphasis on academics has crowded out other worthwhile goals and that it is time to correct the imbalance. James P. Comer (2006) wrote that the standards movement

> focuses primarily on teaching subject matter, on achievement outcomes as measured by test scores, and on accountability sanctions; it does not stress development . . . [which] continues to receive inadequate attention (p. 59).

Among the outcomes that Comer believes today's schools neglect are physical, social, and moral development. However, teachers and administrators say that the pressure to achieve high test scores is so intense that they are forced to ignore other objectives. In the words of one scholar, teachers have learned to keep their heads down, focused on raising test scores (Fuller, 2006).

Some districts have begun to explore ways to devote more attention to neglected aspects of children's development. Rhode Island recently adopted regulations that will require all districts in that state to design new graduation requirements that use techniques other than tests to measure student learning (Archer, 2005). Some Rhode Island districts have adopted plans that require seniors to participate in a work setting before they graduate.

The pressure to raise test scores has resulted in gains in math and reading, but progress has slowed, even declined in some cases, and there it is a question whether continuing pressure on teachers and administrators to raise test scores further might be counterproductive. Some critics believe that continued progress may depend on making schools more pleasant places to work.

The achievement picture is confused by some states' practice of lowering the cutoff scores used to indicate proficiency in order to maintain the appearance of continuing gains. The result is that data from the states reflect a much rosier picture of student achievement that the federal government's reports (Fuller, 2006).

Those who believe that academic achievement is the primary focus of the schools' mission are not conceding. They are promoting a plan to require schools to permanently commit a larger share of resources for instruction. The movement is called the "65 percent solution"; the number refers to the amount of resources proponents want to require schools to invest in instruction.

At least one state has made the 65 percent requirement into law, and drives are underway in other states to adopt similar measures (Hoff, 2006). Opponents point out that spending 65 percent of school funds on instruction does not ensure that test scores will rise, and they say it may force districts to lay off librarians, nurses, and other workers who are not considered instructional personnel.

Many districts already commit 65 percent or more of their budgets to instruction. According to the website www.schoolmatters.com, an average of more than 68 percent of school budgets is spent on instruction, not including money for instructional staff support. When instructional staff support is included, the total rises to 72.5 percent.

Supportive Administrative Leadership

Supportive principals exhibit behavior that is friendly, open, and guided by norms of equality. They do not have hidden agendas, play favorites, or use the power of their office to punish employees who disagree with them. Supportive principals solicit suggestions for improvement from parents and teachers and are not threatened by comments from well-intentioned critics. They take seriously all concerns expressed by parents and staff.

Supportive principals express their expectations of staff clearly. This includes involving teachers and others in setting the school's priorities and establishing standards of performance for students and teachers. Supportive principals are able to exert influence throughout the district hierarchy to obtain the resources to help teachers and other staff members succeed (Henderson et al., 2005).

A recent study concluded that principals control only about 3 percent of their schools' budgets (Clover, Jones, Bailey, & Griffin, 2004). The other 97 percent of funds are committed or restricted. A principal who is successful in obtaining increased funding for the school is able to use those resources to produce results more in line with the priorities of the school.

Supportive leaders give employees the opportunity to decide how to organize and carry out their work. Research has shown that workers who control those decisions report higher job satisfaction and a stronger commitment to the job. In most cases, their performance also improves, although those changes are often shown indirectly by a decrease in the number of days of lost to sick leave and by lower turnover (Louis & Smith, 1990).

Principals show support for teachers by soliciting their opinions on important decisions, being optimistic, being available and accessible, and being direct and honest. Teachers are more likely to perceive a principal as supportive if he or she encourages teachers to try out new ideas and helps obtain resources for those trials. Providing funds to allow teachers to attend professional meetings is another way principals demonstrate support.

Teachers would like to be able to discuss problems and issues with their principals, including questions about their personal and professional growth and career prospects. However, opportunities for such conversations are limited. Some principals, recognizing the need for more interaction, schedule informal meetings with individuals or small groups several times a year to talk about whatever is on teachers' minds.

In order to be supportive, principals must sometimes go around the bureaucracy or "beat the system." When district administrators value following the rules more than getting a job done, that attitude is often conveyed through principals to teachers. Principals take a risk when they violate accepted norms of behavior, and some are understandably reluctant to do that. The result is that teachers are frustrated and principals are blamed. Richard Laine of the Wallace Foundation, said, "Leaders should not have to beat the system for their kids to succeed" ("Chat wrap-up," 2006).

Professional Culture

Teaching has traditionally been thought of as a solitary occupation in which adults interacted with children but seldom saw other adults. Teachers always welcomed the opportunity to work with their colleagues, but as schools were organized, cooperation was difficult. That is now changing. One of the positive outcomes of the standards movement has been the attention it has brought to the need for more cooperation among teachers. Examples of cooperation in schools are numerous. Team teaching is now common in schools, and in many classrooms two adults—a teacher and an aide—work side by side to plan and present instruction. Teachers regularly work cooperatively with specialists—for example, librarians, psychologists, speech therapists, nurses, home visitors, and subject specialists—to improve instruction, identify and solve developmental problems of children, and investigate and try to ameliorate family crises.

Teachers often describe the school in which they work in terms of how close teachers are and how willing they are to work together. Close knit faculties are sometimes referred to as communities. A sense of community exists within a group when six elements are present (Belenardo, 2001):

> Shared values
> Commitment
> A feeling of belonging
> Caring
> Interdependence
> Regular contact

Shared Values. Groups are held together by common interests and shared values. For members of a football team, winning is a common interest. The way they win—whether by a relentless onslaught against opponents or a slow but steady pace—reveals their values. In a school, some indicators of commonly held values are teachers' attitudes about homework, the use of calculators in math classes, and encouraging or discouraging students from seeking help from parents or older siblings when working on science projects.

Commitment. Showing up for meetings on time and staying late to work on special projects are examples of commitment. Other examples include working with another teacher who needs help with instructional planning, volunteering to work on an ad hoc committee, and spending one's own money, when necessary, for materials or equipment.

Feeling of Belonging. A person who is committed to a group may or may not belong to the group. People who aspire to membership adopt the group's values as a way of gaining acceptance. An example is college students who aspire to join a sorority or fraternity and who adopt clothing styles and even speech mannerisms favored by members of the organization they seek to join. But it is possible for a person to belong to a group without being committed to it. An example is a person who holds membership in a club but seldom attends meetings and never volunteers to serve on committees or hold office.

Caring. People demonstrate caring through respect. Workers who fail to receive respect from those with whom they work lose self-confidence and begin to feel ineffective. They feel marginalized and powerless. Lack of respect can result in teachers retreating to their classrooms to avoid interacting with co-workers (Bailey, 2000).

Interdependence. Workers are interdependent when they must rely on others in order to do their jobs. A waiter takes orders from customers and relays them to the cook, who prepares the food and arranges it on the plate. When the cook has completed those tasks, the waiter carries the food to the customer and provides utensils with which to eat it. The cook and waiter are interdependent. Teachers rely on other teachers in the earlier grades to teach prerequisite skills to their students, so every teacher is dependent to some extent on other teachers.

Regular Contact. In some communities, members are in intimate contact with one another most of the time. Think of a monastery or members of an infantry squad. The members live together, eat together, and study, worship, or patrol together every day. Most teachers are in regular contact with their colleagues, but that doesn't necessarily mean they see one another every day. They may see those in their department or grade level every day but encounter other teachers less often.

School cultures influence teachers' beliefs about cooperation and their willingness to work with other teachers on a common purpose. Recent research has identified three types of professional cultures in schools. *Veteran-oriented professional cultures* are typical of schools in which a group of veteran teachers have taught together for many years. In these schools, long-time teachers form a closely knit social group, and although they may be friendly toward new teachers, there is usually little effort made by the older teachers to offer assistance and support to beginners. Some experienced teachers in these schools are confident and competent in their work, whereas others indicate that they are tired and waiting for retirement. In schools with this type of culture, new teachers receive little support or encouragement (Kardos, Johnson, Peske, Kauffman, & Liu, 2001).

A second type of professional culture described by Kardos et al. (2001) was the *novice-oriented culture,* characterized by high proportions of young teachers. Teachers in these schools tended to be idealistic and hard working. Professional interaction was frequent but characterized by an absence of expertise. The wisdom born of experience common among teachers with years of experience was missing from novice-oriented schools. As was true in schools with veteran-oriented professional cultures, new teachers in novice-oriented schools received little assistance or support from their colleagues.

New teachers in schools with the third type of professional culture, in contrast to the first two types, did receive support and assistance from colleagues. This type of culture was labeled *integrated* by Kardos et al. (2001). Experienced teachers in schools with an integrated culture understood the importance of mentoring new teachers, but they also engaged in exchanges with their experienced colleagues. The atmosphere in integrated schools was characterized by conversations and deliberations among teachers at all levels of experience about many aspects of instruction and the school curriculum.

Principals can help develop an integrated culture in a school by creating opportunities for collaborative work. Exhibit 10.1 lists suggestions of how teachers can cooperate with one another. However, they may also need to provide guidance and train teachers in the skills that make for effective collaboration. Specifically, training in communication, team building, and conflict resolution may be needed for teachers to share with one another in beneficial ways (Rallis & Goldring, 2000). Most teachers are willing to share with colleagues what they are doing in their classrooms but prefer to speak with those whom they know well and for whom they feel an affinity. Few are willing to speak out in schoolwide faculty meetings unless group norms support such sharing.

Integrated cultures in schools enhance teachers' sense of professionalism. Talbert and McLaughlin (1996) described the advantages of and necessary conditions for maintaining these professional communities:

> Strong teacher communities foster a shared knowledge base or technical culture, shared commitment to meeting the needs of all students, and durable professional identities and commitments. Without opportunities to acquire new knowledge, to

---

EXHIBIT 10.1
EXAMPLES OF COOPERATION AMONG TEACHERS

Planning instruction together
Developing instructional materials jointly
Cooperating to develop tests
Observing one another's classrooms
Team teaching
Serving together on a committee to develop a curriculum
Planning and presenting a workshop for other teachers
Sharing readings and in-class activities
Mentoring a beginning teacher
Sharing ideas that work with a particular child
Offering suggestions on dealing with parents

---

reflect on practice, and to share successes and failures with colleagues, teachers are not likely to develop a sense of professional control and responsibility (p. 133).

Accepting a collaborative mode of operation in schools requires first adopting an attitude that improvement is necessary and desirable. If teachers have not fully accepted that value, the principal should make its adoption the first priority. After that, administrators can suggest activities that will permit teachers to work collaboratively for more effective instruction.

Using Talents and Skills

Few experiences are more important for employees' feelings of well-being than holding a job that allows them to fully use their talents. Young workers typically have lower levels of job satisfaction as compared to more experienced individuals. The reason is that entry-level jobs tend to be less challenging and offer fewer opportunities for workers to stretch themselves.

Employees who are required to stretch in order to meet challenging aspects of their jobs are generally happier in their work and more productive than those for whom the job is a familiar routine. Of course, mastery is partly a function of one's experience, and the longer an individual is in a job, the less likely it is that he or she continues to be challenged by it. For that reason, the opportunity to move into new positions or take on demanding new duties that force the employee to acquire new skills and knowledge are important for maintaining employee interest and involvement.

Some teachers find that the emphasis on a mandated curriculum and the drive to increase test scores limit their opportunities to use their creativity, knowledge, and skill and lead to a decrement in their job satisfaction. Principals who help teachers view mandated testing as a way of improving learning for all students can help minimize the negative effects of the legislated curriculum (Hargreaves & Fink, 2003).

Comfortable Facilities

Teachers are more productive when the school building and its surroundings are clean and attractive and repairs are made promptly to malfunctioning physical systems. A maintenance schedule that includes painting at regular intervals and improvements to run-down classrooms, workrooms, and restrooms sends a message to teachers that their work is valued.

It has been estimated that about 3.5 million children attend school in buildings that are in poor condition. Under No Child Left Behind, children in poor-performing schools have the option to transfer to better schools. But when the better schools are already overcrowded, as is the case with many, these children have no choice but to remain in low-performing schools. Today, no educator would seriously propose an educational program that did not include access to computers, yet because of the condition of electrical wiring in many older schools, children in those schools have only limited access to the Internet.

Principals can make a difference in schools by taking action to improve the appearance and comfort of physical facilities. Lucy Phillip, the principal of Groves High School in Savannah (Georgia), offered to buy paint for any teacher willing to paint his or her classroom. She arranged for repairs on broken air conditioners and replaced missing windows. She inspected custodians' work and ordered them to redo classrooms that were still dirty. She persuaded the district to supply additional seating for the school cafeteria so that no student would have to eat standing up (Krajewski, 2005).

Air quality is a topic of growing concern among those who work in buildings with windows that do not open. The air in these buildings can become suffused with fumes that irritate occupants' eyes, throats, and sinuses. Fumes are released by glue, carpets, cleaning chemicals, and insecticides, but finding the source and cleaning it up is not always easy. In a few cases, districts have been unable to pinpoint the cause of polluted air and were forced to close new buildings temporarily.

Adequate Time

Teachers' complaints that there are too few hours in the day to teach everything they are expected to cover seem to be well founded. Florian (1999) found that teachers' estimates of the total amount of time they would need to teach the required content in four subject areas (language arts, civics, math, and science) exceeded the time available in one year by almost 60 percent in grade 8, 25 percent in grade 12, and 17 percent in grade 5. Only in grade 2 were teachers confident they could cover the mandated content in the available time. The study assumed a school year of 180 days, with five hours per day available for instruction, for a total of 900 hours. The teachers in this study were from schools in four different states in the western United States and had an average of more than 18 years experience. Hence, their estimates should be reasonably accurate. Because some instructional time is lost to noninstructional activities, the discrepancy may be even greater than the figures suggest.

Teachers vary in the amount of time they devote to noninstructional activities such as collecting money, calling roll, or correcting disruptive students. The more time spent on these non-essential activities, the less students learn. Stallings (1984) described classroom strategies that teachers can use to reduce lost instructional time and improve student learning. She offered guidance on the allocation of time among various activities and discussed ways by which teachers' expectations of students can increase efficiency in the use of classroom time. Stallings also described a method by which teachers can monitor the time they are off-task in their classes.

A principal who seeks to help teachers solve the time dilemma might begin by asking teachers to discuss the questions in Exhibit 10.2. The answers may suggest ways that more time can be found for teaching important content. Teachers will not be able to give precise answers to these questions. That is not the point. However, the questions may help to make teachers aware of how time is used and where savings may be possible.

The question asking how teachers decide what to omit when they are not able to teach everything in the curriculum is critical. It is important to know how they

---

EXHIBIT 10.2

QUESTIONS TO HELP TEACHERS FIND MORE TIME FOR INSTRUCTION

1. How much time is spent each day reviewing or reteaching material that students have studied earlier this year or in a previous year?
2. How much time is spent each day collecting money from students?
3. How much time is spent each day correcting disruptive students?
4. How much time is spent each day on activities that are not essential or that could be performed at other times, without loss of instructional time?
5. How much time is spent each day by students getting ready to study (locating paper and pencil, sharpening pencils, etc.)?
6. How much time is spent each day listening to announcements or responding to requests from parents or the school office?
7. How much instructional time is lost each day as a result of disruptions from students arriving late?
8. How much time is spent each day moving students about the building?
9. How often do lesson props contribute to loss of instructional time?
10. When the amount of time allotted for instruction is not sufficient to cover all of the subject matter, how do you decide what to omit?
11. Would you be willing to loop with your students (that is, remain with the same group for two years)?

decide what to leave out. Some may simply go as far as they are able to in the allotted time and omit whatever they don't get to. But some thought should be given to rationalizing those decisions by considering the significance of the material being omitted and choosing to cover that which is most important for understanding and as preparation for future learning.

Teaching props are often helpful in improving student comprehension, but they may also cause more confusion or result in a loss of instructional time (Kennedy, 2006). Everyone has had the experience of trying to use an overhead projector or make a PowerPoint presentation when the equipment malfunctioned or discovering too late that there are too few handouts for the number of students. Those who have had those experiences know about the panic that ensues. Having to make last-minute adjustments adds to teachers' stress and often results in loss of instructional time. A professional development session on how to design or select visual aids would be useful in helping teachers to decide which aids are really worthwhile.

Teachers often respond to questions such as these by protesting that they cannot accomplish more in the time they have. However, they can be reminded that some teachers use quite a bit more time than others for noninstructional responsibilities. Saving just a few minutes each day can, over the course of a school year, add up to a significant gain in instructional time. Teachers who are asked to find ways of increasing the amount of time they devote to instruction often point out that some time is lost because of administrative actions, including intercom announcements and requests for information or due to early dismissal for athletic contests and pep rallies. The faculty may need to discuss whether those activities are important enough to devote instructional time to them.

Materials and Equipment

The Internet is a treasure trove of instructional resources. The problem for teachers is finding time to search for the many ideas and materials offered there. Teachers would like to find websites that provide reviews of and links to instructional resources. One of the richest instructional websites is MERLOT. (See Online Resources.) In this case the name does not refer to wine, although teachers who visit it may go away intoxicated with delight. The acronym stands for Multimedia Educational Resource for Learning and Online Teaching. Although it is designed primarily for use by higher education students and faculty, many of the activities are appropriate for students in middle and high school (Powers & Barnes, 2001).

Teachers are accustomed to working in what has been called "a culture of scarcity" in which the materials and equipment they need to do their jobs are in chronically short supply. It is not uncommon for teachers to use their own money to buy books, paper, pencils, and maps if their school has no funds for these necessities. However, even in schools with ample resources, teachers steeped in the culture of scarcity may be reluctant to ask for anything other than bare necessities.

TEACHER STRESS AND BURNOUT

Teachers have historically been attracted to the profession because of their desire to work with children, and that factor is still an important motivation for teachers. In the past 30 years, however, a number of changes in families and society have made it more difficult for teachers to reach students as effectively as they could in earlier times, with the result that some teachers feel their work is less rewarding. Today's teachers have less freedom to decide what to teach and how to teach it, and they feel more pressure from administrators and parents. Much of what they teach is prescribed, and teachers are held accountable for preparing students to pass standardized tests on the prescribed content. Teachers feel less like professionals who exercise their judgment and more like clerks who carry out directives from superiors (Provenzo & McCloskey, 1996).

Some teachers are better prepared, both by temperament and training, to deal with stress, but excessive and prolonged stress saps any teacher's energy and sharply reduces productivity. Stress also contributes to teacher attrition. According to one report, stress was cited more often by teachers who had decided to leave the field than either working conditions or low salaries (Darling-Hammond, 2001).

The stress experienced by teachers varies depending on the type of teaching position a person holds and the extent to which the individual is able to shrug off job-related stressors. Teachers with large classes and many disruptive students are likely to experience more stress than those with smaller classes and more well-behaved students. Yet, even in comparable teaching situations, two individuals may experience different levels of stress because of individual variations in the tolerance for stress. Thus, no action is likely to reduce stress for all teachers, although some actions have more promise for relieving stress than others.

Types of Stress

People experience four types of stress—time stress, situational stress, encounter stress, and anticipatory stress (Albrecht, 1979). Teachers are subject to stress of all four types. The more stress one experiences, the more likely it is that he or she will succumb to burnont.

Time Stress.   Time stress occurs when the time allotted for completing a task is insufficient. Teachers constantly feel pressured by lack of time, according to a study of working conditions in schools conducted by the Southeastern Center for Teaching Quality (Jacobson, 2005). Most teachers report they are not able to complete their work during the school day and must finish it at home.

Time stress is especially acute for special education teachers because of the extensive paperwork they must handle. It is estimated that special education teachers spend five or more hours per week doing paperwork. Recent efforts by professional organizations to reduce that load have been opposed by parents and district administrators, who believe it is necessary to document every decision affecting the instruction of children with disabilities (Goldstein, 2003).

Situational Stress. Situational stress is triggered by a perception of inability to cope with the demands of a situation. When a teacher experiences more demands than he or she is able to respond to, situational stress is occurring.

Teachers who have been adequately prepared for the job are less likely to experience extreme levels of situational stress. However, recent research has shown that a significant number of beginning teachers don't feel ready to cope with the demands of the job. In a national survey, only 61 percent of new teachers reported that they felt they had had adequate preparation for teaching. They reported that they were better prepared to maintain order and discipline in the classroom than to use newer instructional methods, implement state or district curricula, address the needs of students from diverse cultural backgrounds, or integrate educational technology (National Center for Education Statistics, 2000).

Any teacher who is assigned to teach a subject in which he or she lacks adequate background preparation is by definition unprepared. Adequate preparation to teach a high school subject is usually defined as a major or at least a minor in the subject area, but about one-third of high school mathematics teachers and one-fourth of English teachers do not have even a minor in the subject (Ingersoll, 2001). The additional work required to plan lessons in a subject with which one is unfamiliar adds to teachers' stress levels, to say nothing of the loss of learning experienced by students.

Situational stress may also be induced by poor hiring practices. When teachers are hired late, either shortly before classes start or later, they are more likely to feel unprepared for the job and thus experience situational stress. This is especially likely to be a problem for people who are new to the field. A study of hiring practices in four states determined that about 62 percent of new hires occurred within 30 days of the start of classes and that one-third of new teachers were hired after the school year was underway (Liu, 2003). Not all last-minute hires can be avoided because late resignations, budget problems, and enrollment surges may force a district to make last-minute offers. However, last-minute hires that result from lack of proper planning should be avoided.

Encounter Stress. Encounter stress occurs when an individual must deal with a person who is critical or hostile. People who serve the public on a regular basis, such as waitpersons and store clerks, must occasionally deal with individuals who are rude or thoughtless. They are usually able to ignore such behavior, but it is difficult for teachers to do that. Teachers are with their students every day, and when a student is hostile or disruptive, the teacher has few options. She or he may discipline the child or send him or her to the office to meet with the principal or assistant principal, but the child soon returns to the class.

Dealing with unhappy parents is especially stressful when the parents challenge teachers' professional judgment and competence. In many of these cases, teachers believe that parents have unrealistic views of their child's ability and are not able to accept the teacher's more objective opinion. Parents sometimes charge teachers with favoritism and may threaten to appeal the teachers' actions to the principal or the superintendent. Those threats increase teachers' stress.

Anticipatory Stress.   Everyone has had moments of anxiety before a big test or while waiting to give an important presentation. Those are examples of anticipatory stress. Teachers experience anticipatory stress before a classroom observation by the principal or when they are called in to meet with the principal following a parental complaint. In states that link teacher pay to student test scores, teachers have anticipatory stress while they wait to hear the results of the latest series of tests. Some teachers are so fearful that their students will not test well that they request transfers to grade levels at which students are not tested.

Stress and Burnout

Individuals under stress experience anxiety, fatigue, sensitivity to criticism, and hostility toward others. Stress also produces physiological effects, such as changes in skin conductance, heart rate, and blood pressure. Individuals are unlikely to be aware of physiological changes except when the level of stress is quite high. However, the physiological stress exacts a cumulative toll on mental and physical health over time.

When individuals are under stress for prolonged periods of time, they burn out. Burnout has been described as a form of alienation characterized by the feeling that one's work is meaningless and that one is powerless to bring about change. People who experience burnout often feel that they are alone and isolated. They find fault with others and miss work. When they do report for work, they may complain about their health. The symptoms of burnout are very similar to symptoms associated with depression—lack of energy, heightened anxiety, and sadness bordering on despair.

Factors in Burnout

Factors that contribute to teacher burnout are role ambiguity (having a job in which duties are not clearly spelled out); responsibility/authority imbalance (having insufficient authority to carry out the responsibilities one has been assigned); a workload that is either too heavy or too light; inability to obtain information needed to carry out one's responsibilities; and job insecurity. Interactions with superiors can also lead to stress for some teachers. Teachers who receive no performance feedback from principals and who feel that they are unable to influence the administrators' decisions about their work are more likely to experience stress.

Principals can help alleviate stress and remove the conditions that lead to burnout among teachers by taking some commonsense precautions. Some of these actions include the following:

1. Reduce time pressures by alerting teachers early to upcoming deadlines and by providing directions and assistance to help teachers complete paperwork requirements.

2. Assist teachers in obtaining help for students with emotional and psychological problems; if district resources are not available, appeal to community service agencies and service clubs for help.

3. Provide training to help teachers deal with disruptive students and, when necessary, provide support for teachers who are experiencing problems with student behavior.

4. Remove the dread of performance evaluation by pointing out that everyone can improve in some area; give teachers the opportunity to evaluate the school administration.

5. Provide feedback to teachers on their classroom performance, including specific suggestions that will help them be more effective teachers.

6. Offer to participate in parent conferences when teachers request it; provide training in planning and carrying out parent conferences.

7. Make time for informal conversations with teachers and give them a chance to talk about whatever they wish to talk about, bearing in mind that the most conscientious teachers are most subject to burnout.

8. Plan faculty outings that provide a break from the routine and allow teachers to have a good time with colleagues.

9. Help discouraged teachers maintain perspective by reminding them of past successes. Invite former students who have done well back to the school to talk about their successes and how their teachers helped them succeed.

Teacher Absenteeism

One of the symptoms of excessive stress on the job is absenteeism. Although not all absences can be attributed to on-the-job stress, when chronic absenteeism is encountered, administrators should consider the possibility that teachers are under excessive stress.

Absenteeism is affected by the conditions in people's lives. Family responsibilities sometimes prevent a person from working, as when a teacher stays home because the babysitter fails to show up or a child is ill and unable to go to daycare. Personal illness and lack of transportation are other problems that contribute to absenteeism.

Working conditions also contribute to absenteeism. An individual's relationship with the work group influences attendance. A teacher who feels close to his or her colleagues hesitates to miss work out of concern that fellow workers will have to pick up the slack. One's work ethic, acquired in childhood, also factors into these decisions. A person with a strong work ethic may show up for work even on days when he or she does not feel well.

When it is necessary to hire a substitute to cover classes normally taught by an absent teacher, the district spends money that could be put to more productive use. School districts try to discourage excessive teacher absences in order to reduce costs and loss of student learning. When teachers are absent, student absenteeism also rises, and learning opportunities are lost. Some districts have succeeded in lowering teacher absenteeism by giving monetary bonuses to those who maintain perfect or near-perfect attendance records.

Loss of Learning

Does teacher absenteeism translate into loss of student learning? The research on this question shows mixed results. Some studies show that students of teachers who miss school frequently have lower achievement test scores than those whose teachers were regular in attendance, whereas other studies found no relationship between the variables. However, there are at least two good reasons why excessive teacher absences should be discouraged and efforts made to reduce them. First, absenteeism costs the district money. A district with 500 teachers and a 4 percent absenteeism rate that pays substitutes $90 a day incurs additional costs of $324,000 a year for substitutes. Second, teacher absenteeism is related to student absences. Students of teachers who miss school frequently tend to have poor attendance records, too, and because school funds are usually distributed on the basis of attendance, schools with poor attendance receive less money from the state (Steers & Rhodes, 1978).

Of course, some absenteeism is legitimate and necessary. No employee should be encouraged to go to work when he or she is ill. To do so puts other workers at risk and increases the chances that the employee's condition will worsen. There are also times when a "mental health" day is in order. Taking a day off to rest can help a teacher feel relaxed and improve his or her ability to concentrate.

Principals of schools in which teachers are absent frequently can work to change the culture that permits or encourages absenteeism. During World War II, workers were reminded that missing work hindered the American war effort. This appeal to patriotism reduced the amount of time lost to absences and improved the output of both military and civilian goods. In the same way, if teachers understand that their contributions to student learning are important, most will respond to appeals to maintain continuity of instruction by reducing unnecessary absences.

SUMMARY

Human beings seek psychological success from their jobs. Psychological success is more likely in a setting in which certain conditions are present. These include a clear mission and a professional culture, supportive administrative leadership, opportunity to use one's talents, comfortable and attractive physical space, time to do the job, and adequate supplies of materials and equipment. The focus on raising test scores has had the effect of narrowing the mission of schools and detracted from teachers' feelings of success. As the emphasis on testing has grown, schools have neglected other worthwhile outcomes, such as social and psychological development of students.

Professional cultures are those in which members share a culture, are committed to the group, care for colleagues, feel a sense of belonging, are interdependent, and are in regular contact. Some of these features are true of all schools, and a few are true of most schools. They are all true of schools with truly professional cultures. School cultures may also be described by a trichotomy (novice oriented, veteran oriented, or integrated).

All teachers experience job-related stress from four sources—time pressures, situational factors, encounter experiences, and anticipation. Many beginning teachers report they are inadequately prepared to teach and as a result experience increased stress. Prolonged, unrelieved stress leads to burnout, a condition in which an individual becomes alienated, depressed, and hostile. Principals can help reduce teachers' stress by such commonsense measures as providing training on how to deal with disruptive students and reassuring teachers who are nervous about upcoming evaluations.

SUGGESTED ACTIVITIES

1. Individuals vary in their tolerance for stress. Some people believe that stress makes life more interesting, whereas others think that all stress is unpleasant. Consider the following experiences and tell how much stress each produces for you (Some, A little, A lot) and whether it is pleasant or unpleasant.

    a. Riding a roller coaster

    b. Playing golf

    c. Watching a horror movie

    d. Rock climbing

    e. Witnessing a minor automobile accident

    f. Being involved in a minor automobile accident

    g. Watching a horse race

    h. Parachuting from an airplane

    i. Driving up a steep mountain road

    j. Being evaluated by your boss

    k. Evaluating an employee

2. Go to the website of the International Network on Personal Meaning (see Online Resources) and consider the seven dimensions of a positive workplace. Rate a school you are familiar with on each dimension, using a seven-point scale (1 = Not at all true; 7 = Very true). Are there other dimensions that you believe should be included? Should any be omitted?

3. The policies of some employers make it difficult for employees to meet their family responsibilities, whereas other employers make a concerted effort to support employees' families. Think about policies of a school district with which you are familiar. Tell what changes could be made in the district's policies that would make it more family friendly. Consider policies related to sick leave, family leave, medical insurance, moonlighting, and residence requirements.

4. Following are some voluntary organizations that solicit members. Identify one or two values that each organization seeks in its members, then list one or two values that the organization would not want its members to hold.

    a. College sorority or fraternity

    b. Bridge club

    c. Volunteer fire department

    d. Investment club

ONLINE RESOURCES

MERLOT (www.merlot.org)

> MERLOT is an acronym for Multimedia Educational Resource for Learning and Online Teaching. The site contains links to online learning materials in a variety of subjects. Many are interactive. The materials are designed for college level, but many are suitable for high school students and even gifted middle schoolers. Reviews are provided. Among the materials available are simulations, animations, tutorials, drills, tests, and references.

MathForum (www.mathforum.org)

> This site is a rich resource for teachers, students, and parents who are interested in learning mathematics or improving mathematics instruction in schools. It features puzzles and problems for students and identifies websites that link teachers who are seeking help with those who have ideas and suggestions to share.

International Network on Personal Meaning (www.meaning.ca/articles/presidents_column/climate_management.html)

> This article by Paul T. P. Wong describes the seven dimensions of a positive workplace. Three of the seven are controlling–empowering, secretive–open, and political–professional.

Environmental Protection Agency (www.epa.gov/iaq/schooldesign)

> This site has links to sites that provide information on improving air quality in schools.

Designshare (www.designshare.com/index.php/home)

Offers a wealth of information about the design and construction of schools. Includes articles on school facilities and links to organizations that advocate improved school building design and firms that offer design services.

CASE STUDIES

Case No. 1

Elliott Lander is principal of Aurora Middle School. The school has long had a stable faculty, many of whom are now retiring and will be replaced by younger teachers. The result is two distinct groups—an older, experienced group and a young, inexperienced set. About two-thirds of the teachers have been at Aurora for years. One-third arrived at the school within the past five years. Individuals within these groups are close, but there is little interaction across age lines. In fact, there is often friction between the groups. Older teachers sometimes reject ideas of the newcomers with such comments as "We tried that years ago and it didn't work." The younger teachers, meanwhile, consider the older teachers out of touch and irrelevant.

Lander believes that both groups could benefit from an honest exchange of views. He hopes to move the culture of the school toward a more professional orientation in which sharing would be common. However, because of the high level of distrust, he does not believe that one or two in-service programs featuring speakers from both groups would do much to change the culture of the school.

Lander himself is midway between the two groups in age, younger than the older teachers but older than the younger teachers. He arrived at the school three years ago, taking over for a principal who had been in the job for more than 20 years. The assistant principal, Joyce Butler, is in her late twenties. This is her first administrative position and her first year in this school.

Lander asked the director of instruction for advice on how to bring the two teacher cliques together. The director said, "Wait for the old teachers to retire. You'll never change them." Lander thanked the man but went away determined to make an effort to open lines of communication.

At present the faculty is considering a proposal to adopt block scheduling, which would increase the length of instructional periods from 45 minutes daily to 90 minutes. Some classes would meet daily, others twice a week. Older teachers generally oppose the change, although all science teachers and English teachers support it.

Question

1. Lander has asked you for advice on how to achieve these objectives: (a) to lead the faculty to a decision on the proposed block scheduling plan for the school and (b) to increase trust so that teachers are able to discuss ideas in an atmosphere of respect and acceptance. What advice would you give Lander?

Case No. 2

Marybeth Reynolds is beginning her second year as principal at Master Street Elementary School. She took over the school one year ago after budget cuts had resulted in layoffs of three teachers and increased class sizes. Adding to teachers' distress was an incident involving a veteran teacher who was charged (wrongly, most thought) with misuse of school funds and was dismissed. The case is still in court and the outcome is uncertain.

Ms. Reynolds tried to help teachers focus on the year ahead and put the bad news behind them, but she was only partly successful. The negative effects of the budget cuts and accusations against a respected teacher took a heavy toll. End-of-year test scores were flat or below the previous year's scores, and the pressure will be on this year to raise student achievement.

Ms. Reynolds met with the superintendent in July to ask for help. She explained that teachers were discouraged and needed a morale boost. The superintendent agreed to restore one of the lost teaching positions and gave Ms. Reynolds $4,000 to use for anything that she felt would raise teachers' spirits. But the superintendent also warned her that he expected to see results. "I want to see your test scores come up this year," he said. Ms. Reynolds has to decide how to spend the $4,000. Here are options she is considering:

  a. Give each of the 20 teachers $200 for instructional supplies

  b. Give half of the money to the school librarian to spend on instructional resources and put the rest in an emergency fund

  c. Invite teachers to submit a two-page request for up to $800 for instructional materials not available from other sources

  d. Use $500 for a party for teachers and aides and $3,500 to paint hallways and classrooms

  e. Spend half the money to create a school garden and reserve the other half for future upkeep of the garden

  f. Pay for travel and an honorarium for a speaker at an upcoming professional development session who will energize and entertain teachers

  g. Donate the money to the defense fund of the dismissed teacher

Questions
  1. Which of the options would you choose if you were Ms. Reynolds? Remember—the purpose is to help raise teacher morale.
  2. Which of these options would be most difficult to defend if the superintendent should question using the money for that purpose? If you had to defend the choice of that option, what would you say?

3. If you were Ms. Reynolds, would you make the decision about the use of the money without consultation, or would you ask for teachers' input? Explain.

REFERENCES

Albrecht, K. (1979). *Stress and the manager.* Englewood Cliffs, NJ: Prentice Hall.

Archer, J. (2005, April 13). R. I. downplays tests as route to diplomas. *Education Week,* pp. 1, 24–25.

Bailey, B. (2000). The impact of mandated change on teachers. In N. Bascia and A. Hargreaves (Eds.), *The sharp edge of educational change* (pp. 112–128). New York: Routledge Falmer.

Belenardo, S. J. (2001, October). Practices and conditions that lead to a sense of community in middle schools. *NASSP Bulletin, 85,* 33–45.

"Chat wrap-up." (2006, August 9). *Education Week,* p. 36.

Clover, M. W., Jones, E. B., Bailey, W., & Griffin, B. (2004, September). Budget priorities of selected principals: Reallocation of state funds. *NASSP Bulletin, 88,* 69–79.

Comer, J. P. (2006, January 5). It takes more than tests to prepare the young for success in life. *Education Week,* pp. 59–61.

Darling-Hammond, L. (2001, May). The challenge of staffing our schools. *Educational Leadership, 58,* 12–17.

Florian, J. (1999). *Teacher survey of standards-based instruction: Addressing time.* Aurora, CO: Mid-Continent Research for Education and Learning.

Fuller, B. (2006, August 9). Accountability plus. *Education Week,* pp. 32, 34.

Goldstein, L. (2003, May 28). Disabled by paperwork? *Education Week,* pp. 1, 23.

Hargreaves, A., & Fink, D. (2003, May). Sustaining leadership. *Phi Delta Kappan, 84,* 693–700.

Henderson, C. L., Buehler, A. E., Stein, W. L., Dalton, J. E., Robinson, T. R., & Anfara, V. A., Jr. (2005, September). Organizational health and student achievement in Tennessee middle schools. *NASSP Bulletin, 89,* 54–75.

Hoff, D. J. (2006, March 8). Georgia passes "65 percent" bill on classroom spending. *Education Week,* p. 18.

Huffman, J. B., & Hipp, K. K. (2003). *Reculturing schools as professional learning communities.* Lanham, MD: Scarecrow Press.

Ingersoll, R. M. (2001, May). The realities of out-of-field teaching. *Educational Leadership, 58,* 42–45.

Jacobson, L. (2005, March 30). States scrutinize teacher working conditions. *Education Week,* pp. 1, 16–17.

Kardos, S. M., Johnson, S. M., Peske, H. G., Kauffman, D., & Liu, E. (2001, April). Counting on colleagues: New teachers encounter the professional cultures of their schools. *Educational Administration Quarterly, 37,* 250–290.

Kennedy, M. (2006, March). From teacher quality to quality teaching. *Educational Leadership, 63,* 14–19.

Krajewski, B. (2005, March). In their own words. *Educational Leadership, 62,* 14–18.

Liu, E. (2003, April). *New teachers' experiences of hiring: Preliminary findings from a four state study.* Paper presented at the annual meeting of the American Educational Research Association, Chicago.

Louis, K., & Smith, B. (1990). Teacher working conditions. In P. Reyes (Ed.), *Teachers and their workplace: Commitment, performance, and productivity* (pp. 23–47). Newbury Park, CA: Sage.

National Center for Education Statistics. (2000). *Teacher preparation and professional development.* Washington DC: Department of Education, Office of Educational Research and Improvement.

Powers, S. M., & Barnes, F. M. (2001, November). Alternative routes for teacher professional development and resources: The MERLOT online community. *NASSP Bulletin, 85,* 58–63.

Provenzo, E., & McCloskey, G. (1996). *Schoolteachers and schooling: Ethoses in conflict.* Norwood, NJ: Ablex.

Rallis, S., & Goldring, E. (2000). *Principals of dynamic schools.* Thousand Oaks, CA: Corwin.

Stallings, J. (1984). *Effective use of classroom time.* Charleston, WV: Appalachia Educational Laboratory. (ERIC Document Reproduction Service, No. ED 252515.)

Steers, R., & Rhodes, S. (1978). Major influences on employee attendance: A process model. *Journal of Applied Psychology, 63*(4), 391–407.

Talbert, J., & McLaughlin, M. (1996). Teacher professionalism in local school contexts. In I. Goodson and A. Hargreaves (Eds.), *Teachers' professional lives* (pp. 127–153). London: Falmer.

CHAPTER

11 LEGAL ISSUES IN HUMAN RESOURCES

Legal authority to employ, assign, evaluate, transfer, suspend, and terminate teachers is assigned by the states to local school boards. The boards in turn delegate to administrative personnel the responsibility for recommending appropriate actions relating to personnel. For that reason it is important that principals and other administrators understand the legal foundation for such decisions and be aware of the legal ramifications of any actions they recommend.

PLAN OF THE CHAPTER

The following topics are examined in this chapter: (1) state legislation and school boards, (2) antidiscrimination legislation, (3) constitutional protections for employees, (4) defending personnel practices, (5) sexual harassment, and (6) affirmative action and reverse discrimination.

STATE LEGISLATION AND SCHOOL BOARDS

The states delegate to school boards the authority to hire and assign or reassign and terminate employees. The states also establish rules governing the preparation and certification of professional personnel, including teachers, counselors, school social workers, school psychologists, and administrators. State laws and regulations specify the course of study that the various personnel must complete and stipulate licensing procedures, including tests of general or professional knowledge. School boards may establish higher standards than those specified by the state, but they may not lower the standards.

Most states require school personnel to be free of communicable diseases, and school boards sometimes establish other policies dealing with employee health. Some states prohibit school boards from establishing a residency requirement, but where it is permitted, courts have usually upheld residency rules as long as the boards were able to establish a rational basis for the policy (*Wardwell* v. *Board of Education of the City School District of Cincinnati*, 1976).

School boards have authority to assign teachers to a school, grade level, or subject, and may transfer teachers at will, as long as the individual is qualified to hold the position to which he or she is assigned. In some states the law places limitations on the board's freedom to transfer a teacher from a higher-paying to a lower-paying job or from a position of more to a position of less responsibility. In Colorado and Wyoming, for example, state law allows transfers of teachers on the recommendation of the chief administrative officer of the district, provided the teacher's pay is not reduced from its current level for the remainder of that school year. Arizona, like many other states, permits governing boards to reduce salaries or eliminate positions in order to save money, but a board may not lower the salary of a certified teacher who has been employed by the district for three years, unless all salaries are reduced by a commensurate amount.

State laws also provide a number of safeguards and incentives for teachers, including the protection against a reduction in salary. Michigan law invalidates any contract or agreement between a teacher and a board under which the teacher would agree to waive any rights or privileges granted by state law. It also forbids school districts from assigning a teacher to more than one probationary period, thus denying districts the option of extending the probationary period for a teacher whose performance is not satisfactory. It is common for states to require that probationary teachers be notified by a certain date if their contracts will not be renewed for the following school year. If a district fails to notify a teacher that his or her contract will not be renewed, the contract is automatically extended for one year.

Alaska is one of the more generous states in providing incentives and protections for teachers. The law of that state requires school boards to provide information on the availability and cost of housing in rural areas and to assist teachers in finding places to live; school districts are even empowered to lease housing in order to rent living space to teachers. Alaska law also guarantees a 30-minute duty-free lunch period for teachers in schools with four or more teachers and requires districts to pay moving expenses for teachers who are involuntarily transferred to a school that is more than a 20-minute drive from their current location. In Arizona, a teacher who returns to teaching in public schools after a stint in charter schools is protected against loss of certification, retirement, salary status, or any other benefit provided under the law or school board policy.

Some state legislation also provides incentives for substitute teachers. In Michigan, a substitute who teaches for 60 days in one assignment is granted the same privileges as full-time teachers, including leave time and a salary equal to or higher than the minimum salary on the district salary scale.

ANTIDISCRIMINATION LEGISLATION

Antidiscrimination legislation is intended to protect identified groups from bias in selection, salary, and promotion decisions. The federal government, most states, and many localities have laws that prohibit discrimination on the basis of race, color, religion, gender, disability, or national origin. Discrimination based on age, marital status, and sexual preference is also prohibited under some state laws (Hauck, 1998).

These laws make it illegal to recruit employees in such a way that protected groups are discouraged or prevented from applying. Employers may decide to recruit new workers by asking current employees to tell friends and relatives about a vacancy, but they may not legally limit recruiting to that method because workers seldom recommend people of a different race. The employer is expected to advertise the vacancy widely so that all qualified prospects have a chance to learn about it (Sovereign, 1999). Discrimination occurs when decisions about selection, placement, promotion, compensation, discipline, or dismissal of individuals are made on the basis of characteristics other than qualifications, ability, and performance. A number of state and federal statutes, regulations, and executive orders forbid discrimination in recruiting, selecting, placing, promoting, and dismissing employees. In this section, some of the more important federal statutes relating to discrimination will be reviewed.

Civil Rights Act of 1964 and Pregnancy Discrimination Act of 1978

The most significant piece of legislation dealing with discrimination in employer/employee relations is the Civil Rights Act of 1964, as amended. Title VII of that act covers all employers with 15 or more employees, including state and local governments as well as schools and colleges. Religious institutions are exempt with respect to employment of persons of a specific religion.

The law prohibits discrimination with respect to compensation and terms, conditions, or privileges of employment on the basis of race, color, national origin, gender, or religion. The legislation also prohibits limiting, segregating, or classifying employees or applicants for employment in any way that deprives an individual of employment opportunities or otherwise adversely affects his or her status as an employee.

Title VII was amended by the Civil Rights Act of 1991 to end the practice of adjusting scores on employment tests to benefit particular groups of applicants. The amendments also prohibited setting lower cutoff scores on tests for certain groups in order to increase the number of people hired from those groups.

Title VII is administered by the Equal Employment Opportunity Commission (EEOC), which administers most federal legislation dealing with employment rights. Title VII requires that a charge of discrimination be investigated by a state or local agency if the employer is covered by a state or local fair employment practice law. Most states have such laws, which prohibit discrimination by employers on the basis of color, religion, gender, or national origin. Some also ban discrimination related to age, disability, marital status, physical appearance, sexual preference, and political affiliation (Hauck, 1998). The EEOC has no adjudicatory authority, but most claims of discrimination under Title VII must be reviewed by the EEOC before legal action is taken against an employer. If, following an investigation, the Commission concludes that the law has been violated, it attempts to persuade the employer to eliminate the illegal practice. If this approach does not work, the Commission will issue a finding confirming that a basis for legal action exists (www.rbpubs.com/ls/ls04.htm).

The Pregnancy Discrimination Act of 1978 extended the protections of Title VII of the Civil Rights Act to pregnant employees. This law requires employers to treat pregnancy the same as other temporary medical conditions. Except where state law establishes conditions that make separate policies necessary, school districts are advised to establish a single policy on medical leave, including maternity leave (www.eeoc.gov/types/pregnancy.html).

Types of Discrimination

Title VII prohibits both overt discrimination, also known as *disparate treatment,* and *adverse impact,* which occurs when employment practices that are neutral in intent have a discriminatory effect. Examples of disparate treatment include an employer who promotes only males into supervisor positions or one who pays African American employees less than whites. This is the most flagrant form of discrimination, but it is less common than adverse impact.

Among actions by an employer that can lead to charges of adverse impact are using a test for selection on which members of a protected group score lower than other groups or establishing educational or experience requirements that have an adverse effect on members of a protected group.

Once an adverse impact claim is established, the district must show that the practice is valid for the purpose intended. This is a "business necessity" defense. The Supreme Court accepted such a defense in allowing the use of the National Teachers Examination (NTE) for teacher certification and to determine employee salaries (*United States* v. *State of South Carolina,* 1978). However, in *Griggs* v. *Duke Power Company* (1971), the Supreme Court held that the use of a test of general intelligence for selection purposes was discriminatory because the test had an adverse impact on minority applicants and had not been validated for use in employee selection. The use of an arbitrary cutoff score as part of a selection process without prior investigation of the potentially harmful effects of such a decision is likely to be successfully challenged.

Even after overt discrimination ends, its effects may linger. Employers are required to take action to correct such hangovers from the past. Inaction by employers can result in *perpetuation of past discrimination*. In the South, after schools were integrated, segregated teaching staffs persisted. The lingering effects of years of discrimination in hiring eventually disappeared when districts began assigning newly hired teachers to schools with other-race staff members and, when necessary, transferring some teachers to schools with mostly other-race students.

Age Discrimination in Employment Act of 1967 and Older Workers Benefit Protection Act of 1990

The Age Discrimination in Employment Act (ADEA) of 1967, as amended by the Civil Rights Act of 1991 and the Older Workers Benefit Protection Act of 1990, forbids discrimination against individuals above the age of 40 in hiring, assignment, training, promotion, provision of fringe benefits, and the terms and conditions of employment. The law provides that employees who are discriminated against on the basis of their age may sue for monetary damages, although the Supreme Court has held that that right does not extend to employees of state and local governments (Twomey, 2002).

The legislation makes it unlawful to give preference to a younger person over an older one if the older person is within the protected range. For example, a district that promotes a 45-year-old employee rather than a 60-year-old because of the latter's age when the two are equally qualified would be guilty of age discrimination, just as it would be for promoting a 25-year-old employee over an equally qualified 40-year-old. The act offers no protection against discrimination based on age for individuals who are outside the protected range. Thus, refusing to hire a 21-year-old applicant on the basis of age is not unlawful.

An employer charged with violating the Age Discrimination in Employment Act may disprove the charge by showing bona fide occupational qualification (BFOQ). For example, a director hiring an actor to play the part of a 25-year-old man in a play could lawfully select a younger person over an applicant within the protected age range solely on the basis of age. An employer who uses age as a qualification for employment must be able to show a reasonable relationship between the requirement and job performance. This is usually done by citing a connection between employee age and safe performance.

The Third Circuit Court of Appeals upheld a lower court decision that a Pennsylvania district had violated the Age Discrimination in Employment Act by failing to hire a qualified applicant over the age of 40 to teach plumbing/HVAC (heating, ventilation, and air conditioning). The advertised qualifications for the position were possession of or eligibility for plumbing and HVAC certification and two years relevant experience. The applicant met those qualifications, but the job was offered to a person under the age of 40. The district claimed that the over-40 applicant lacked refrigerant recapturing certification, although that had not been listed as a qualification for the position. Comments by the district superintendent concerning the applicants' ages were cited as evidence of age bias. The over-40 applicant won $250,000 in damages, later reduced (*Potence* v. *Hazleton Area School District*, 2004).

Equal Pay Act of 1963

The Equal Pay Act of 1963 forbids employers from paying higher wages to employees of one gender if jobs performed by the other gender require equal skill, effort, and responsibility and are performed under similar conditions. Provisions of the act apply to federal, state, and local governments, as well as to private employers. The act is enforced by the Equal Employment Opportunity Commission, but more claims are brought under Title VII because a violation of one is also a violation of the other.

A question that frequently arises in litigation on equal pay is how similar two jobs must be in order for employees in those positions to receive equal pay. Male and female custodians perform many of the same duties in schools, but males may be required to perform duties from which females are exempt. For example, male custodians but not females, are required to shovel snow. In many districts male custodians climb ladders to change lightbulbs, install wiring, or repair air conditioning equipment, whereas female employees are exempt from those chores. In spite of these differences, however, courts have tended to hold that male and female custodians should receive equal pay. In general, courts are more likely to allow salary differences in cases in which the additional duties of the higher-paid gender take up a significant portion of employees' time.

Rehabilitation Act of 1973 and Americans with Disabilities Act of 1990

The Vocational Rehabilitation Act (VRA) of 1973 and the Americans with Disabilities Act (ADA) of 1990 prohibit discrimination in employment decisions against qualified individuals with disabilities. The VRA applies to federal contractors and agencies that receive financial assistance from the federal government, whereas the ADA applies to most employers with 15 or more employees. Both VRA and ADA provide that an individual with a disability who is able to perform the essential functions of a position with or without reasonable accommodation may not legally be refused employment solely because of the disability.

Courts have held that the inability to perform a particular job does not in itself constitute a disability under ADA. In *Thompson* v. *Holy Family Hospital* (1997), the Ninth Circuit Court of Appeals ruled that a nurse who was terminated because an on-the-job injury prevented her from performing her job was not protected by ADA. She had been injured in a fall and was not able to lift heavy weights, leaving her unable to perform the normal duties of her position without accommodation. Her employer, Holy Family Hospital, terminated her, and she filed suit, claiming discrimination. The court held that to be regarded as disabled under ADA, an individual must be substantially limited in one or more major life activities. Because the nurse's condition did not fit that definition, the court said, the hospital had not violated the law by firing her. Three questions are used to determine whether a particular task is an essential function of a position:

1. Does the position exist to perform this function?
2. Would removing this duty fundamentally alter the position?
3. What percentage of the employee's time is devoted to performing this function?

Consider the position of school crossing guard who halts traffic on streets near a school to allow students to safely cross the street. Stopping traffic and directing students are essential functions of the position. Crossing guards may also give safety talks at school assemblies to remind children about safety rules. However, that duty consumes a relatively small amount of time, and the job would not be drastically changed if that responsibility were taken away.

The EEOC defines *reasonable accommodation* as a modification or adjustment in the way a job is ordinarily performed that enables a qualified individual with a disability to perform the job without imposing an undue hardship on the employer. Examples of accommodations are providing entrance ramps to allow access to persons in wheelchairs, granting time off for medical treatments or physical therapy, and purchasing special equipment or adapting existing equipment to enable people with disabilities to perform a job.

The law does not require an employer to hire a person with disabilities who is less qualified than a person with no disabilities, but it forbids employers from refusing to employ individuals solely on the basis of a disability. Employers may legally refuse to hire an applicant with disabilities whose employment in a particular position would result in creation of a safety hazard for the employee or others when it is not possible through reasonable accommodation to eliminate the danger. However, the employer should be prepared to produce evidence that the claimed hazard is real and not simply a pretext.

Deciding whether to employ individuals with disabilities as teachers requires administrators to consider the safety and well-being of students as well as the rights of those who are disabled. Districts that are able to show that they have carefully weighed a disabled applicant's qualifications to perform the job with reasonable accommodation against the potential risk to students created by hiring the person stand a good chance of prevailing in court.

However, districts that refuse to consider a disabled applicant's qualifications are almost certain to lose a legal challenge. A district that declined to allow a blind applicant to take a qualifying examination for a teaching position on grounds that her blindness made her incompetent to teach sighted students lost its suit and was required by the court to hire the teacher and provide back pay and retroactive seniority (*Gurmankin* v. *Costanzo*, 1997).

Interviewers should ask applicants with disabilities to indicate how they will perform essential functions of the position for which they are applying and what accommodations they will need in order to carry out their duties. Requests for accommodation should be treated on an individual basis and decisions should take into account both the expected cost and the potential for creating hardships for other employees (Sovereign, 1999).

One question that is still largely unanswered is to what extent the law protects employees who contract contagious diseases. The Eleventh Circuit Court held that the legislation did not exclude persons with such conditions as long as their presence did not pose a risk to other people. The case involved a teacher who had been dismissed from her job because she had tuberculosis (*Arline* v. *School Board of Nassau County*, 1985).

Family and Medical Leave Act of 1993

The Family and Medical Leave Act (FMLA) was enacted to allow families to balance the demands of their jobs with the needs of their families. The act grants eligible employees up to 12 weeks of unpaid leave during a 12-month period to care for a newborn child, adopted child, or foster child; for personal illness; or to care for a parent, spouse, or child with a serious health problem. The legislation covers private employers with 50 or more employees and state and local government employers without regard to the number of people they employ. A *serious health condition* is defined by FMLA as a condition that requires in-patient care or continuing treatment by a health care professional. An individual may have a serious health condition under FMLA without qualifying for coverage under the Americans with Disabilities Act of 1990. To be eligible for leave under FMLA, an individual must have been employed for 12 months or more and must give advance notice if practicable.

Other Legislation

The Immigration Reform and Control Act of 1986 requires employers to verify that the people they employ are eligible to hold jobs in the United States. Only American citizens and foreign nationals with valid green cards are permitted legally to hold jobs in this country.

CONSTITUTIONAL PROTECTIONS FOR EMPLOYEES

All U.S. citizens have certain protections under the Constitution. Freedom of speech, association, and religion are guaranteed by the First Amendment, and the rights of due process and equal protection are secured by the Fifth and Fourteenth Amendments, respectively. Privacy rights also derive from the Constitution.

The Supreme Court has held in a series of decisions that public employees may express their views as citizens on matters of public concern but are subject to limitations on speech that relates to their official duties. In a recent decision (*Garcetti et al.* v. *Ceballos*, 2006) the Court held that the demotion and transfer of Ceballos, a Los Angeles deputy district attorney, for challenging the accuracy of an affidavit prepared by a deputy sheriff in a case involving theft of automobile parts did not infringe the employee's right of free speech. The Court said, "We hold that when public employees make statements pursuant to their official duties, the employees are not speaking as citizens for First Amendment purposes, and the Constitution does not insulate their communications from employer discipline."

As part of his official duties, Ceballos had written a memorandum informing the district attorney that he believed a deputy sheriff may have lied in an affidavit he prepared to request a search warrant. Ceballos recommended that the case be dropped, but the district attorney rejected the advice and proceeded to prosecute. Ceballos then informed a defense attorney of his doubts and gave him a copy of his memorandum. He was later called to testify in the case. When he was demoted and transferred, Ceballos sued.

In earlier rulings, the Supreme Court had held that a teacher who had been dismissed for writing a letter to a newspaper critical of the board and school administration was speaking as a citizen on an issue of public concern and that her speech was protected (*Pickering* v. *Board of Education,* 1968). The letter had faulted the board's and school administration's decisions regarding the allocation of school funds for academic and athletic programs. In two similar cases, the Court determined that teachers' criticisms of grouping practices in schools and their comments about school quality were matters of public concern and thus protected by the First Amendment (*Cox* v. *Dardanelle Public School District,* 1986; *Jett* v. *Dallas Independent School District,* 1986).

Protecting Privacy

Privacy is increasingly a concern of civil libertarians and ordinary citizens because of the widespread availability of information about individuals on the Internet and the enactment of legislation that allows the federal government extensive access to personal information. Most Americans regard the right to privacy as a fundamental freedom and resent what they regard as intrusions into their private affairs, whether by the government or others, yet when a person accepts a job, he or she surrenders the right of absolute privacy. Privacy on the job is limited, and employers can legally collect and act on information about their employees that many employees might prefer not to share (Hubbartt, 1998).

Disputes about employee privacy most often arise over second jobs; use of alcohol, tobacco, or illegal substances; criminal behavior; and, for teachers in particular, violation of community norms. An employee of a grocery store who is arrested for DUI arouses a legitimate concern for the employer, who is bothered by the potential damage to the company's image, but in the case of a teacher, the board is likely also to be concerned about the effect of the teacher's behavior on students.

One of the most contentious issues involving privacy concerns of employees has to do with lifestyles and off-duty activities. Most employees assume that what they do after working hours is their own business, but employers also have an interest in after-hours activities of their workers. Some school districts are reluctant to hire teachers with same-sex partners out of concern for the community's reaction and the fear that the teacher's presence might influence impressionable students to adopt a homosexual orientation, even though there is no evidence to support the latter fear.

School administrators should be well informed about the provisions of state laws dealing with employee privacy, and they would benefit also from knowledge of case law pertaining to the issue. Although there are no hard-and-fast rules for dealing with situations that involve employee privacy, knowledge of the law and previous court actions, combined with sound judgment, can help avoid legal entanglements.

Administrators who have access to personnel records have a responsibility to take precautions to prevent unauthorized persons from having access to the information contained in them. Failure to exercise care in maintaining records that contain personal information can result in liability for the district. An employee has a personal privacy interest if disclosure of information results in embarrassment, damage to his or her reputation, or loss of employment (National Center for Education Statistics, 2000).

All districts should have a policy on handling requests for information about employees. In general, districts are required to release information requested by law enforcement agencies but may refuse to honor requests for information from companies.

DEFENDING PERSONNEL PRACTICES

If a district is charged with discrimination in hiring practices, it may be able successfully to defend its actions by showing that the relevant characteristics of the applicant pool are comparable to the characteristics of the employees hired. Thus, for example, if 15 percent of applicants are members of a protected group and the district can show that an equal or greater percentage of persons hired were members of that group, that constitutes *prima facie* evidence of the absence of disparate treatment.

A more stringent test involves a comparison of the characteristics of those hired with the characteristics of members of the labor pool. This was the test used by the courts in the *Hazelwood* case. Hazelwood School District was charged by the Justice Department with violating Title VII of the Civil Rights Act by failing to recruit and employ African American teachers. The district's attorneys argued that, because the percentage of African American teachers employed by the district equaled or exceeded the percentage of African American students, the district was in compliance. The Supreme Court ultimately ruled that the relevant comparison was not the ratio of teachers to students but rather the ratio of minority teachers employed by the district to the number of qualified minority persons in the labor pool in the St. Louis metropolitan area. Hazelwood lost the suit and was required to hire and give back pay to minority applicants who had previously been rejected (*Hazelwood School District* v. *United States*, 1977).

Preventing discrimination before it happens is preferable to correcting it after it has occurred. School districts can help prevent discrimination by adopting an equal employment opportunity policy and publicizing it in advertisements and employee handbooks and by ensuring that personnel practices conform to the policy. Adopting practices that advance the goal of equal opportunity ensures that the policy will have its intended effect.

Human relations personnel should be reminded periodically that all records—including personnel files, correspondence, and computer files—are subject to subpoena when a suit is filed against the district. Even e-mail messages can be obtained by attorneys in the search for evidence that the district has performed actions that are illegal. A standard rule for human relations personnel should be: Never place anything in an employee's personnel file unless the individual has seen the document and signed a statement indicating that he or she is aware that it will be part of the personnel file. It is also recommended that employees have access to their personnel files periodically (Thome, 1996).

Establishing a Defense

Personnel practices that have disparate impact may nevertheless be allowed by the courts, provided that the district is able to show a BFOQ or business necessity. One school district was upheld by the courts after hiring a male applicant without a master's degree over a female with the degree by arguing the male could be hired at a lower salary and could also perform coaching duties.

Exclusion refers to the degree of pervasiveness of a particular practice. If personnel practices occasionally result in adverse impact to members of protected groups, there is a lower level of legal vulnerability than if the practices consistently result in adverse impact on those groups. Employers are most likely to win a legal challenge when a practice involves a low degree of exclusion and a high degree of business necessity. Employers are most vulnerable when exclusion is high and business necessity is low (Schlei & Grossman, 1976).

Other factors that are sometimes considered in discrimination cases are the degree of potential risk to human health and safety or the potential for economic loss resulting from employee performance. An airline company may be able to justify exclusionary selection practices in hiring pilots by showing that the practices are necessary to reduce the chance of injury or death to passengers resulting from performance of inadequately trained employees. A hospital might support exclusionary hiring practices by showing that they are necessary to protect the health of patients. Exclusionary practices may also be defended by showing that they reduce the amount of potential economic loss to the employer resulting from employees who lack essential skills. Employers whose work involves lower levels of risk would be held to a correspondingly lower level of exclusionary practice in hiring.

Accurate and detailed records are a necessity to a successful defense if a district is charged with discrimination in employment practices. It is recommended that the district human resources office maintain charts showing the age, race, color, sex, and national origin of all applicants and similar information about those hired. Because collecting such information on the application form itself may constitute *prima facie* evidence of discriminatory intent, it is advisable to use a preemployment inquiry form to collect that data. This is a form that all applicants are asked to complete and return separately from the application form itself. The applicant has the option of filling out the preemployment inquiry anonymously in order to avoid the possibility of being identified.

SEXUAL HARASSMENT

The Equal Employment Opportunity Commission defines sexual harassment as a form of sex discrimination that violates Title VII of the Civil Rights Act of 1964. The commission identifies two types of sexual harassment—quid pro quo and hostile environment.

Quid pro quo harassment occurs when an employer, supervisor, or co-worker makes an unwelcome request for a sexual favor as a term or condition of employment. The offer may be either explicit or implicit, and the two parties may be the same or different genders. The most direct form of quid pro quo harassment is in the form of an exchange offer: "If you want the promotion, you must do me a favor." However, sexual harassment may also appear as teasing, telling jokes, sharing lewd pictures, casual remarks, or suggestive questions.

The first response of many victims of sexual harassment is to ignore the offensive behavior. If that doesn't work, which many times it does not, then the victim asks the offender to stop. Sometimes the unwelcome remarks end at that point, but if they continue, the victim may endure the humiliation or resign from the job. A better option is to report the offender to the appropriate official.

Women are victims of sexual harassment more often than men, and the victimizers of women are usually male co-workers. Women in jobs that are thought of as men's jobs, such as firefighters, electricians, or machinists, are especially vulnerable to sexual harassment. Young people, those who are well educated, and minority persons also have greater odds of being sexually harassed than people who do not fit those categories. In determining whether quid pro quo harassment has occurred, the EEOC considers questions such as these:

- Did the victim make clear to the offender that the behavior was unwelcome?
- Did the victim do anything to solicit or encourage the actions or comments?
- Did the victim have a prior relationship with the person making the suggestive comments, and if so, what was the nature of the relationship?
- Were the remarks to which the victim objected derogatory or hostile?

Employees are sometimes afraid to challenge or report a supervisor who makes sexually suggestive remarks out of fear of retaliation. For that reason, an employee's failure to tell an offender that his or her behavior was offensive or to report it to the authorities is not an adequate defense against a charge of harassment.

A *hostile environment* exists when conditions in the workplace are intimidating, hostile, or offensive and interfere with an employee's being able to perform his or her job. Some questions that the EEOC considers to determine whether a hostile environment exists are these:

- Was the offensive behavior physical or verbal, or both?
- Did the offensive behavior occur more than one time? If yes, how often?
- Was the individual who behaved in an offensive manner a supervisor or co-worker?
- Did other people join in the offensive behavior?

In *Harris* v. *Forklift Systems, Inc.* (1993), the Supreme Court made the following statement regarding how to tell whether a hostile environment exists in a workplace:

> Whether an environment is "hostile" or "abusive" can be determined only by looking at all the circumstances, which may include the frequency of the discriminatory conduct, its severity, whether it is physically threatening or humiliating . . . , and whether it unreasonably interferes with an employee's work performance. The effect on the employee's psychological well-being is relevant in determining whether the plaintiff actually found the environment abusive. But while psychological harm, like any other relevant factor, may be taken into account, no single factor is required.

Employer Liability

When an employer knows about instances of sexual harassment and fails to take action to stop it, the employer may be held liable. Some courts have held that the fact that an employee did not object to a supervisor's remarks does not necessarily indicate that the employee welcomed them.

Harassment of Students

Although sexual harassment of students by school staff members has received little attention, the problem is more widespread than many people realize. One authority has estimated that about 15 percent of all students (more than one out of seven) are sexually abused by a school employee by the end of the twelfth grade (Hardy, 2002). Clearly this is a problem about which administrators need to be aware.

Under Title IX, students who have been victims of sexual harassment in school may be able to collect damages (*Franklin* v. *Gwinnett County Public Schools*, 1992). However, in *Gebser* v. *Lago Vista Independent School District* (1998), the Supreme Court held that a student who had been sexually harassed could recover damages under Title IX only if school officials knew about the harassment and failed to take steps to correct the problem (Dowling-Sendor, 2002). A single remark by a teacher or another student will not normally support a charge of sexual harassment. The behavior must have been severe or persistent.

Charges of sexual harassment made by students against school employees should be thoroughly investigated because students have been known to falsely charge a teacher or coach with harassment. Most children today have a pretty clear understanding of acceptable and unacceptable touching, but anyone investigating a child's charge of sexual harassment should check to be sure that the child correctly understands the concept.

Peer-to-Peer Harassment

Sexually suggestive questions and comments are not uncommon among middle and high school students, yet school officials occasionally ignore complaints about such remarks in the belief that such verbal banter is a form of flirting, even though flirting should not result in a child feeling embarrassed or humiliated. When school officials become aware that peer harassment is occurring, they need to take prompt action to end it. Knowing about such behavior without taking action can result in a school district being held liable.

A sixth-grade girl (EB) in South Kortright (New York) Central School District was subjected to verbal and physical sexual harassment for a seven-month period, during which she and other girls in her class were called various unflattering names by boys who also snapped the girls' bras; grabbed their breasts; and shoved, hit, and kicked them. EB and the other girls complained to the teacher and other school officials. When no corrective action was taken, EB and her parents met with school officials to ask that the treatment stop. The harassment continued, and the family initiated legal action under Title IX and Section 1983 of the Civil Rights Act (*Bruneau* v. *South Kortright Central School District*, 1999). The court held that the Civil Rights Act did not apply, and a jury found the defendants not guilty under Title IX. The decision was affirmed by the Appeals Court.

Sexual Harassment Policy

Schools should have in place a policy on sexual harassment, and employees and students should be informed about its contents. The Office for Civil Rights in the U.S. Department of Education recommends that the following features be included in sexual harassment policies:

1. A statement explaining that sexual harassment is forbidden by law and that anyone guilty of sexual harassment will be punished
2. A grievance procedure that details the steps employees and students should take if they have been victims of sexual harassment
3. An explanation of the actions the school will take in following up on complaints about sexual harassment
4. A statement requiring school officials who learn of possible sexual harassment to take immediate action to correct the problem, without waiting for the victim to file a complaint
5. A statement protecting teachers from limitations on academic freedom resulting from application of the sexual harassment policy

As they pertain to students, sexual harassment policies need to be administered with consideration for the ages of the persons involved and the nature of the situation. A school official who punished a six-year-old boy for kissing a girl in his class overreacted and used poor judgment. The policy as written made no allowance for the student's age, but after the parents of the boy complained, the policy was revised to say that students' actions would not be interpreted as sexual harassment unless it was clear that the student's actions or remarks were intended to humiliate or demean another student. Any discussion by teachers of sexual content must be appropriate for the age of the children in the class. As long as a class discussion is relevant and age appropriate, it does not constitute sexual harassment.

Sample Policy. Baltimore City Public Schools' policy on peer-to-peer sexual harassment is online at www.bcps.k12.md.us/school_board/policies/sexual_harassment_policy.asp. Among behaviors that the Baltimore policy classifies as sexual harassment are the following:

- Leering at someone's body
- Making comments, gestures, or jokes of a sexual nature
- Manipulating clothing in a sexually suggestive manner
- Displaying sexual pictures or objects
- Spreading rumors or commenting about sexual behavior
- Pressuring another person for a date or for unwanted sexual behavior
- Touching, grabbing, or pinching

Disciplinary actions for students in Baltimore schools who are guilty of sexual harassment range from counseling to suspension.

The Baltimore policy includes a list of actions to help students understand what sexual harassment is and whether they are guilty. Boys may not realize that girls are offended by words and actions they themselves regard as acceptable. A policy such as Baltimore's helps both boys and girls to understand what is acceptable.

Montgomery County (Maryland) public schools' policy on sexual harassment advises students who believe they are the subject of sexual harassment or "the focus of inappropriate behavior" to report the facts either verbally or in writing to their parents or to the principal, a guidance counselor, or a teacher. Students are also asked to provide supporting details, including the dates and times of any incidents, descriptions of the actions of the offending person, and names of witnesses. The policy defines sexual harassment and lists sexually suggestive actions that are prohibited (Montgomery County Public Schools, 1996).

AFFIRMATIVE ACTION AND REVERSE DISCRIMINATION

The purpose of affirmative action is to open job opportunities for groups that traditionally have been discriminated against. It is not intended to achieve proportional representation in the makeup of a workforce. The practice of giving preference to members of discriminated groups in personnel decisions is known as reverse discrimination. The Supreme Court has held that such practices are allowable only when they serve a compelling governmental interest and are narrowly tailored to correct specific instances of discrimination. In 1991, Congress made it illegal for employers to adjust scores on employment tests or use different cutoff scores for certain groups as a way of giving applicants from those groups an advantage in hiring decisions.

Actions by school districts to protect the jobs of minorities when layoffs occur were the subject of Supreme Court review in *Wygant* v. *Jackson Board of Education* (1986) and *Taxman* v. *Piscataway* (1996). In both of those cases, a white teacher was laid off while a minority teacher with less or equal seniority was retained in order to maintain or increase the proportion of minority teachers in the district. The action was justified as a means of correcting past societal discrimination. In both cases, courts rejected the board's actions. In the Piscataway (New Jersey) case, the Third Circuit Court stated (Moran, 2002):

> [T]he harm imposed upon a nonminority employee by the loss of his or her job is so substantial and the cost so severe that the Board's goal of racial diversity, even if legitimate under Title VII, may not be pursued in this particular fashion.

The Court added:

> [W]e recognize that the differences among us underlie the richness and strength of our Nation. . . . Although we applaud the goal of racial diversity, we cannot agree that Title VII permits an employer to advance that goal through nonremedial discriminatory measures.

SUMMARY

Local school boards are given authority by state legislative bodies to employ, assign, transfer, evaluate, suspend, and terminate teachers. For some of these actions, state laws spell out the procedures to be followed; in other cases, the state leaves those decisions to the local board. Title VII of the Civil Rights Act forbids discrimination against employees based on race, color, gender, religion, or national origin. Laws passed since that law went into effect have extended similar protections to pregnant women, people over 40 years of age, and people with disabilities. Two types of employment discrimination occur—disparate treatment, in which an employer discriminates against certain groups, and adverse impact, which occurs when a neutral action has an unintended discriminatory effect. Employers may defend against a claim of discrimination by showing its decision was based on a bona fide occupational qualification.

SUGGESTED ACTIVITIES

1. Ann Barber, a math teacher at Williway Middle School, had her larynx removed because of cancer and relies on an electromechanical device to speak. Her speech is labored, and students have difficulty understanding her. Jill Thompson teaches

English at Williway. She had a hip replacement operation and subsequently developed an infection; she now must use a wheelchair. Ms. Thompson's classroom is on the second floor of a building that has no elevator. What actions might the school board take to make accommodations for these teachers? If the board should decide to terminate one or both of these teachers for being unable to perform their jobs, is it your opinion that it will have violated the Americans with Disabilities Act? Explain.

2. Obtain a copy of a sexual harassment policy for a school district and answer these questions:

   a. What actions does the policy require a supervisor to take when he or she first learns about a charge of sexual harassment by a person whom he or she supervises?

   b. What procedures are recommended to ascertain the facts about a harassment charge?

   c. What corrective actions are suggested or required when a charge of sexual harassment is confirmed?

3. A teacher has asked for a one-month leave under the Family and Medical Leave Act of 1993 while she recuperates from cosmetic surgery. If you were director of human resources, what additional information would you need before recommending approval of the teacher's request? Suppose the teacher had asked for leave while her five-year-old son recuperates from surgery for strabismus. What would you recommend in that situation?

ONLINE RESOURCES

Equal Employment Opportunity Commission (www.eeoc.gov/types/ada.html)

This site provides information about the application of the Americans with Disabilities Act.

(www.eeoc.gov/types/sexual_harassment.html)

This site defines sexual harassment and has links to the text of Title VII, as well as current issues in sexual harassment, enforcement guidelines, and information about employer liability.

U.S. Department of Education Office of Civil Rights
(www.ed.gov/about/offices/list/ocr/docs/sexhar00.html)

The Office of Civil Rights provides information about sexual harassment of students, schools' responsibility to protect students against harassment, and the rights of students who feel they are being harassed.

Discovery Education Lesson Plan Library
(http://lessonplans/programs/sexualharassment/)

This site contains suggestions and materials for teaching students about identifying and preventing or stopping sexual harassment.

Human Resources Diversified Group (www.hrdgroupinc.com/links.htm)

This site has links to information about recruitment, selection, hiring, sexual harassment, equal employment opportunity, the National Labor Relations Board (NLRB), and privacy rights.

Cornell University Legal Information Institute (www.law.cornell.edu)

This site provides information on various aspects of employment law.

National Association of State Boards of Education
(www.nasbe.org/Educational_Issues/Policy_Updates/11_10.html)

This site addresses the problem of bullying in schools. In some cases bullying equates to sexual harassment and should be treated as such by school authorities.

CASE STUDIES

Case No. 1

Angela Minor, a sophomore, complains to her school counselor that two boys on her school bus make sexually suggestive remarks to her. She says they comment on her body and use crude, explicit language to propose certain sexual activities. She says that the boys deliberately brushed against her getting on or off the bus until she moved to a window seat. She tells the counselor she has tried to ignore the boys' behavior but that it hasn't helped. "They keep doing it," she says.

The counselor asks, "Did you tell the bus driver?"

"She hears them, she knows what's going on, but she doesn't do anything to stop it," Angela says.

The counselor asks how many times this has happened. Angela says, "It happens every time they're on the bus." The counselor asks if the boys make similar remarks to other girls. Angela says that they sometimes make remarks to two other girls but those girls just laugh and talk back. "I can't do that," she says. "It's too embarrassing." She continues, "I'm going to quit school if they don't stop." She does not know the names of the boys.

Questions
1. What do you think the counselor should tell Angela?
2. What action should the counselor take with regard to the boys' behavior?
3. Why is it important for the counselor to report this incident to the principal?

Case No. 2

Meredith Sanders is a junior at Park Place High School. Her history teacher, Mark Williams, makes comments about her appearance in front of other students. His words and the way he says them make Meredith feel uncomfortable. She is talking to her counselor about this problem.

COUNSELOR: What does he say to you?

MEREDITH: Well, sometimes he just says he likes the dress or the sweater I'm wearing. Or he says I look nice today.

COUNSELOR: What's wrong with that? I'd be flattered.

MEREDITH: He says it out loud in front of the whole class. But he doesn't say those things to anyone else. Then he'll ask Jeff Thurman, "Jeff, don't you think Meredith looks nice today?" Jeff blushes and nods. It embarrasses him and me too.

COUNSELOR: What really bothers you about this?

MEREDITH: It's the way he says it. It makes me feel icky. Like he'll say "You look really nice in that sweater, Meredith," and he'll smile and make a face.

COUNSELOR: What kind of face?

MEREDITH: Like he wants to reach over and touch my boob.

COUNSELOR: Has Mr. Williams ever touched you?

MEREDITH: No.

COUNSELOR: Have you said something to him about this?

MEREDITH: No. I'm too embarrassed. Besides, he would just say I've got a dirty mind.

COUNSELOR: I'll speak to Mr. Williams about it, but you need to tell him that this makes you feel uncomfortable and you'd like him to stop.

MEREDITH: What if he doesn't stop? What if it gets worse?

COUNSELOR: Come back and see me.

MEREDITH: I don't think he's going to stop.

Questions

1. Does the teacher's behavior amount to sexual harassment? Why or why not?
2. Do you agree with the counselor's suggestion that Meredith speak to the teacher? Explain.
3. What other action, if any, should the counselor take?

Case No. 3

Ken Oliver, principal of Olgart Middle School, was told by Margaret Eddings, an English teacher, that a male teacher (Gary Barnes) had been staying after school for an hour every afternoon this week with one of his students, an eighth-grade girl named Emily Robbins. Ms. Eddings said that she had also observed the girl in Barnes's classroom after school on several other occasions earlier in the year. "I don't want to be a tattletale, but I thought you might want to look into this," she said. "It's kind of strange. I've never known Gary to stay late before."

Questions

1. Do you think it is necessary for Oliver to investigate this situation considering that the only thing he has to go on is another teacher's suspicions?
2. If Oliver decides to investigate, should he talk first to Barnes or to the student?

3. Suppose you were Oliver and were meeting with Barnes. How would you approach the conversation?

4. Suppose you were meeting with Emily. How would you explain to her the reason for the meeting?

5. Do you think Oliver should make a statement at an upcoming faculty meeting regarding after-school meetings with students? If so, what should he say?

REFERENCES

Arline v. *School Board of Nassau County*, 772 F.2d 759 (1985).

Bruneau v. *South Kortright Central School District, cert. denied*, 526 U.S. 1145 (1999).

Cox v. *Dardanelle Public School District*, 790 F.2d 668 (1986).

Dowling-Sendor, B. (2002, August). School law. What did they know? *American School Board Journal, 189*, 40–42.

Franklin v. *Gwinnett County Public Schools*, 503 U.S. 60 (1992).

Garcetti et al. v. *Ceballos*, 126 S.Ct. 1951 (May 30, 2006).

Gebser v. *Lago Vista Independent School District*, 524 U.S. 274 (1998).

Griggs v. *Duke Power Company*, 401 U.S. 424 (1971).

Gurmankin v. *Costanzo*, 556 F.2d 184 (1977).

Hardy, L. (2002, June). Trust betrayed. *American School Board Journal, 189*, 14–18.

Harris v. *Forklift Systems, Inc.* 510 U.S. 17 (1993).

Hauck, V. (1998). *Arbitrating sex discrimination grievances.* Westport, CT: Quorum.

Hazelwood School District v. *United States*, 433 U.S. 299 (1977).

Hubbartt, W. S. (1998). *The new battle over workplace privacy.* New York: AMACOM.

Jett v. *Dallas Independent School District*, 798 F.2d 748 (1986).

Montgomery County Public Schools. (1996). *Board of Education of Montgomery County Policy: Sexual harassment.* Retrieved from www. mcps.k12.md.us/departments/policy/pdf/act.pdf.

Moran, J. J. (2002). *Employment law* (2nd ed.). Upper Saddle River, NJ: Prentice-Hall.

National Center for Education Statistics. (2000). *Privacy issues in education staff records: Guidelines for education agencies.* Washington DC: U.S. Department of Education.

Pickering v. *Board of Education*, 391 U.S. 563 (1968).

Potence v. *Hazleton Area School District*, 357 F.3d 366, 3rd Cir. (2004).

Schlei, B., & Grossman, P. (1976). *Employment discrimination law.* Washington, DC: Bureau of National Affairs.

Sovereign, K. (1999). *Personnel law.* Upper Saddle River, NJ: Prentice Hall.

Taxman v. *Board of Education of the Township of Piscataway*, 91 F.3d 1547 (3rd Cir. 1996).

Thome, J. (1996). *A concise guide to successful employment practices* (2nd ed.). Chicago: CCH Inc.

Thompson v. *Holy Family Hospital*, 121 F.3d 537 (1997).

Twomey, D. P. (2002). *Employment discrimination law: A manager's guide* (5th ed.). Cincinnati, OH: West.

United States v. *State of South Carolina*, 434 U.S. 1026 (1978).

Wardwell v. *Board of Education of the City School District of Cincinnati*, 529 F.2d 625 (1976).

Wygant v. *Jackson Board of Education*, 476 U.S. 267 (1986).

CHAPTER

12 COLLECTIVE BARGAINING IN SCHOOLS

The work of most teachers is governed by negotiated contracts between teachers' organizations and boards of education. The process by which the parties reach agreement on a contract is known as *collective bargaining*. The National Labor Relations Act, passed by Congress in 1935, explicitly granted to employees of firms engaged in interstate commerce the right to join trade unions and bargain with employers. The act also created the National Labor Relations Board, which oversees private sector collective bargaining in the United States.

PLAN OF THE CHAPTER

The following topics are covered in this chapter: (1) public sector bargaining, (2) scope of bargaining, (3) recent developments in collective bargaining, (4) new forms of collective bargaining, and (5) impact of collective bargaining on schools.

PUBLIC SECTOR BARGAINING

Public sector employees in the United States did not secure the right to bargain collectively with employers until long after employees in the private sector had secured that right. Wisconsin was the first state to authorize collective bargaining between teachers' unions and school boards. Only five states (Georgia, Missouri, North Carolina, Texas, and Virginia) now expressly prohibit public employees from bargaining collectively (Marczely & Marczely, 2002).

Laws governing collective bargaining for public employees vary in complexity. Some states, borrowing language from the National Labor Relations Act, provide simply for discussion of "wages, hours and other terms and conditions of employment." Others grant teachers' associations the right to "meet and confer" with school boards but leave to the discretion of the boards whether to accept or reject union requests. Still other states prescribe certain topics for discussion, while prohibiting others.

Public employees who provide essential services and those whose absence from the job would create a threat to public safety are generally forbidden by state law from striking. Although teachers are not regarded as essential employees, strikes by teachers are deplored because of the loss of learning that occurs when teachers desert the classroom for a picket line. Teachers are specifically prohibited from striking by legislative action in some states and by court order in others. Laws against teacher strikes provide for fines and/or jail terms for union leaders who authorize a work stoppage. However, strikes still occur. The number of teacher walkouts is small, but many people believe that even one strike is unacceptable if schools are forced to close.

Several states have adopted or are considering laws to eliminate teacher strikes altogether. Some of these laws require that boards and unions that reach an impasse submit their dispute to binding arbitration for settlement. Under Connecticut's revised Teacher Negotiations Act, for example, the two sides each submit their best offer to a three-member panel, which chooses one of the two proposals, which then becomes part of the official agreement. Lawmakers in Washington State and Pennsylvania are considering similar legislation.

In New Mexico, if the union and the local school board are unable to reach an agreement by October 1, either party may request mediation services from the board, which assigns a mediator from the Federal Mediation and Conciliation Service to assist the parties. After 30 days, if no agreement has been reached, either party may request a list of arbitrators from the Federal Mediation and Conciliation Service. The parties alternately strike names from that list until one remains. That arbitrator then has 30 days to reach a final decision on all unresolved issues.

SCOPE OF BARGAINING

State laws specify certain topics that boards and unions are required to discuss during negotiations, as well as some that may not be subject to bargaining. Michigan law states that the parties shall confer in good faith with respect to wages, hours, and other terms and conditions of employment but leaves decisions on certain other issues to the sole authority of the school board. Among the issues that are reserved to boards are the starting date for the school year, amount of pupil contact time, use of volunteers in schools, and decisions about the use of experimental or pilot programs and staffing of those programs.

Managerial Rights

The Illinois Educational Labor Relations Act states that employers are not required to bargain over "matters of inherent managerial policy," which include functions of the employer, standards of services, the budget, the organizational structure of the school district, selection of new employees, and direction of employees. The law requires boards to negotiate on wages, hours, and terms and conditions of employment.

If either party requests it, board and union negotiators in New Mexico are required by law to discuss deducting union dues from paychecks. That state also requires school boards to discuss the impact of their professional and instructional decisions with the union, when asked. Finally, New Mexico law requires that all agreements between boards and unions include a grievance procedure for settling disputes regarding terms and conditions of employment and related personnel matters.

Issues that are not mentioned in state law as being either required or prohibited are left to the discretion of the negotiating parties. In general, unions like to widen the scope of the negotiations to more issues, whereas boards seek to limit the range of topics, in the belief that subjects on which the contract is silent remain the prerogative of the board. Exhibit 12.1 shows a list of possible provisions in negotiated agreements between a union and a school board. Not all agreements are as comprehensive as the example, however. Some of the more common provisions of negotiated contracts are discussed in the sections that follow.

Some contract provisions have more impact on instruction than others. Examples of proposals that could have an effect on instruction are shown in Figure 12.1. The figure shows the positions taken by the union and the board of education on each issue. In the middle, a marker indicates the position that would be most likely to promote instructional quality. The nearer the mark appears to the position taken by one of the parties, the greater the likelihood that that party's position is instructionally responsible. The issues are discussed in the paragraphs that follow.

Teacher Evaluation

Teacher evaluation is an issue for which the opportunity exists for boards and unions to consider ways of improving student learning. Some boards and teachers' organizations recognize this fact and include provisions in their contract proposals to address student learning. The initial contract proposal prepared by San Juan (California) teachers included a list of specific standards on which teachers would be evaluated. They included

1. Progress of pupils toward mastering district and state achievement standards
2. Instructional techniques and strategies employed by teachers
3. Teachers' adherence to curriculum objectives
4. Teachers' establishment and maintenance of a suitable learning environment in the classrooms

These evaluation standards are not revolutionary. They have been used frequently by individual principals in evaluating teachers. What is unique is that the union proposed to make them mandatory for all teachers in San Juan schools. Including standards such as these in negotiated agreements helps make negotiators aware of the importance of considering the effects on student achievement of proposed contract terms.

EXHIBIT 12.1

TYPICAL PROVISIONS OF NEGOTIATED AGREEMENTS

    I. Recognition of the union and union rights

   II. Management rights

  III. Rules governing negotiations

  IV. Shared decision making

    V. Staffing
        Class size
        Placement of children with disabilities
        Common planning time
        Teaching load
        Duty-free lunch

  VI. Teacher assignments
        Transfers
        Layoffs and recall procedures

 VII. Professional development

VIII. Performance evaluation
        Teacher discipline and reprimands

  IX. Working conditions
        Class size
        Work day
        Academic freedom
        Books and supplies
        Teacher personnel files
        Parent conferences
        Telephones
        Parking
        Mail
        Classroom environmental control
        Student discipline

   X. Compensation and benefits
        Credit for previous work experience
        Salary schedule
        Advancement on the salary schedule
        Pay for extra duties
        Mileage
        Severance pay
        Retirement benefits
        Insurance

  XI. Leaves of absence and sick leave

(continued)

EXHIBIT 12.1   CONTINUED

> **XII.** Dispute resolution
> Grievance procedure
> Mediation
> Arbitration

FIGURE 12.1   Location of Most Instructionally Effective Position between Opposing Demands of Teacher Union and Board on Selected Issues

ISSUE	UNION POSITION
Teacher evaluation	Limited number of classroom observations with advance notice
Transfer and reassignment	More senior teachers have choice of teaching assignments; no involuntary transfers
Selection and hiring	Teacher committee interviews applicants and recommends person to be hired
Class size	Specified upper limit; class divided or aide provided if limit exceeded
Lesson preparation	Limit on number; additional planning time provided if exceeded
Extra-duty assignments	Duties required only if stated in agreement; pay for all extra duty
Reduction in force	Enrollment loss and program change only basis for reduction
	Reductions absorbed by attrition whenever possible; otherwise seniority governs
Working conditions	Require daily preparation period for elementary and secondary teachers
Employee leave	Sick leave allowed for illness of employee or family member; no proof of illness required; personal leave granted for any reason
Safety and security	District hires security guards for all schools and installs metal detectors in all schools

(continued)

FIGURE 12.1   CONTINUED

INSTRUCTIONALLY EFFECTIVE POSITION	BOARD POSITION
__ __ __ __ ✕ __	No limit, no advance notice
__ __ __ __ ✕ __	Administrators decide, considering teachers' expressed preferences
__ __ ✕ __ __ __	Principal interviews applicants and decides who to hire
__ __ __ ✕ __ __	Board adopts class size limits but may exceed the limit in special cases
__ __ ✕ __ __ __	Number of preparations kept as small as possible given available resources
__ __ __ ✕ __ __	Duties performed as needed on assignment by principal; pay only if contract requires
__ __ __ __ ✕ __	Enrollment loss, program change, budget cutbacks, and other factors allowed
__ __ __ __ ✕ __	Reductions absorbed by attrition if possible; otherwise seniority and other factors govern
✕ __ __ __ __ __	Provide preparation period for secondary teachers when practicable
__ ✕ __ __ __ __	Sick leave for illness of employee only; proof of illness required; personal leave for specified reasons only
__ __ __ __ ✕ __	District hires security guards for schools in neighborhoods with high rate of violence and provides metal detectors as needed

Many contracts contain provisions relating to teacher evaluation. They usually specify the number and length of classroom observations and the identity of the administrator or supervisor responsible for the evaluation but seldom identify instructional behaviors and practices teachers are expected to exhibit. Union negotiators press to include in contracts a requirement that evaluators must submit teacher evaluation reports in writing and share them with the individual being evaluated. They also ask for a provision to allow teachers to submit a written response to any statement by the evaluator that they regard as unfair or unfounded. Some agreements also specify content that may not be included in an evaluation summary. For example, a contract may say that an evaluator may not evaluate a teacher on any assignment that is not part of that person's regular duties.

Transfer and Reassignment

Teachers' unions generally oppose transferring teachers from one school to another unless the teachers themselves request the change. When involuntary reassignments are necessary because of enrollment declines or lack of funding, unions prefer to allow teachers with more seniority to have first choice of a new location. Boards recommend leaving decisions about transfers in the hands of administrators. From an instructional point of view, the ideal policy is to consider reassignments on a case-by-case basis, allowing the receiving principal to decide which teacher can contribute most to improving the quality of instruction in the receiving school.

The importance for teacher morale of contractual safeguards against arbitrary decisions on transfer and reassignment should not be underestimated, but neither should the potential negative consequences for the quality of instruction be overlooked. A principal who is prevented from selecting the most qualified teacher is hampered in trying to improve the quality of learning in the school.

Selection and Hiring

Union officials contend that involving teachers in the selection process improves the quality of hiring decisions. However, there is little evidence that negotiated agreements provide a formal role for unions. More than 85 percent of the respondents in a Pennsylvania study (www.andrew.emu.edu/user/rs9f/survey.pdf) said associations had no formal role, and 65 percent indicated that they lacked even an informal role. That did not mean that teachers were left out altogether. More than 20 percent of the respondents reported that teachers were represented on teams that interviewed applicants for teaching jobs.

Principals play a critical role in teacher selection. In a New York study, more than one-half of school principals surveyed said they had primary responsibility for hiring teachers, and more than 70 percent reported that they were responsible for deciding which applicants moved on to the next stage in the selection process, which in effect gave them veto power (www.emsc.nysed/gov/csl/resources/Hiring_Practices.htm). Principals may solicit the opinions of teachers when making these decisions, even though they are not required to do so. Unions would no doubt prefer a greater voice for teachers in teacher selection.

Class Size/Preparations

Class size is another contentious issue between boards and teachers' representatives. Teachers prefer smaller classes to larger ones, and they attempt to persuade boards of education of the benefits to student learning from reducing class size. Board members tend to be skeptical of these claims, and researchers who have studied the question are also divided about the possible benefits of small classes. There is agreement about the cost of reducing class sizes—it is expensive—but there is less agreement about the effects.

The best-designed study on class size was conducted in Tennessee in the mid-1980s. In this four-year study, students in the early grades were randomly assigned to one of three conditions (1 teacher to 20 students, 1 teacher to 20 students with an instructional aide, and 1 teacher to 15 students). Seventy-nine schools enrolling 6,300 students participated in the study. Students who were in small classes scored substantially better on standardized tests in reading, word-study skills, and mathematics than those in larger classes, including those in classrooms with an instructional aide. Moreover, the researchers found a strong relationship between the length of time children remained in small classes and their test scores. Each additional year that children were in small classes added to their learning advantage (Biddle & Berliner, 2002).

Limits on the number of different preparations a teacher may be assigned make sense from the point of view of instructional effectiveness. Again, however, such a policy is difficult to administer if expressed in absolute terms with no room allowed for administrative judgment.

Extra Duty

Unions prefer that the contract specify the extra duties teachers are required to perform and include rules to ensure fairness in the assignment of those duties. They also favor provisions for additional pay for noninstructional tasks.

Duties that have traditionally been a part of teachers' responsibilities, such as sponsoring clubs and meeting with parents, have become optional under most negotiated agreements. In districts that do not pay extra for them, these jobs are often not done. Even teachers who are willing to donate their time are discouraged from doing so by union officers anxious to preserve the principle of extra pay for extra work.

Some extra duties are necessary for the efficient operation of the school, but an excessive number can interfere with good instruction. It is not always possible to anticipate what duties may be necessary, so some flexibility is needed. Everything considered, the best solution seems to be to include in the contract a statement acknowledging the administration's responsibility for fair and judicious use of extra duty and providing extra pay for the more time-consuming tasks. The statement should also acknowledge teachers' responsibility to perform the duties.

Reduction in Force

Both sides have an interest in limiting the impact of reduction in force on employee morale. Usually both teacher and board negotiators are willing to discuss the order of release, but they sometimes disagree on the criteria to be used. Unions prefer that seniority be the only factor considered, whereas management argues for allowing considerations of performance and program needs in making reduction-in-force decisions.

Reduction in force can impact instruction by depleting the faculty of a school of persons qualified to teach certain subjects and by triggering bumping, which may lead to less qualified teachers taking over for those who are more qualified. Chapter 14 discusses this topic in more detail.

Working Conditions

Negotiations over working conditions are sometimes tedious because of the variety of issues covered. Working conditions include time for planning, use of telephones, delivery of mail, parking rules, parent conferences, and student discipline. The last two items on that list are the most likely to stir controversy. Teachers prefer to have scheduled times for parent conferences and do not like to be called on to confer with parents without advance notice. The administration, however, strives to address parents' concerns promptly, even when it means a teacher must remain after school on short notice to meet with a parent. The issue is usually resolved via compromise, with teachers agreeing to meet with parents on days reserved for that purpose and at other "mutually convenient times" as the need arises.

On matters pertaining to student discipline, teachers seek to establish rules that give them flexibility and support in dealing with student disruptions. Teachers want to be able to send a child out of the classroom when they believe it is necessary in order for instruction to proceed smoothly. Administrators argue that, because the school has no means of supervising students who are not in class, teachers should not be allowed to dispatch students at will.

Employee Leave

Employee leave is an area that requires careful thought and attention from human resources personnel if policies are to be administered equitably and at reasonable cost. Accurate record-keeping is important, and leave policies must be clear and detailed. There are many types of employee leave, and the rules vary from one type to another. Consider this list of some of the more common types of leave for which school employees are eligible:

> Bereavement leave
> Jury duty leave
> Medical leave
> Leaves of absence
> Military leave
> Maternity or paternity leave
> Sick leave
> Religious leave
> Educational leave

Some questions to be answered in developing leave policies include who is eligible for the leave, how often and for how long a leave may be taken, conditions that must be met in order for an employee to be eligible for leave, whether the leave is paid or unpaid, whether an employee continues to accrue seniority while on leave, and whether an individual retains the right to return to the previous position at the end of the leave period.

Teachers favor more and longer leaves, whereas school boards argue that leaves are expensive and not always in the interest of students. All agree that leaves can enhance employee morale, but they disagree on the number of days leave that are appropriate.

Safety and Security

Teachers who work in neighborhoods with a history of violence are understandably concerned about their safety in the building, as well in parking lots and on the street. Although the number of attacks on teachers is small, the possibility that an irate student will attack a teacher is always present. Teachers are also concerned about the safety of their students.

Safety has improved in urban schools since resource officers were added to school staffs and metal detectors were installed at entrances. Statistics reported by the National School Safety Center reflected this improvement. The NSSC data showed that fewer high school students had been in fights and fewer students were afraid of being attacked at school or on the way to and from school. However, some schools continued to have relatively high levels of violence. Twenty percent of all public schools experienced one or more serious violent crimes (rape, sexual assault, robbery, and aggravated assault), and 78 percent of school resource officers reported they had taken a weapon from a student on campus. The NSSC 2006 report is available online at www.schoolsafety.us/pubfiles/school_crime_and_ violence_statistics.pdf.

New Developments

Several new developments have occurred in recent years with regard to collective bargaining in schools. Watchdog groups have begun publicizing the contents of negotiated agreements in an effort to publicize the effects of contract terms on student achievement. The Rhode Island Education Partnership studied negotiated agreements in that state and concluded that they provided for teachers' pay and working conditions but had "little to do with students and improving their education" (Forti, 2005, p. 32). The partnership claimed that union negotiators advanced the economic interests of their members but ignored the need for improving children's learning.

Teachers' salaries have lagged in recent years, and because of the surge in the cost of health care, some boards have limited medical benefits for workers and retirees (Honawar, 2006). Workers' contributions cover only about 15 percent of the cost of their health care at present, compared to about 35 percent in 1970. Only about 40 percent of retired workers receive health insurance benefits from their former employers today, compared to about 66 percent in 1988.

Several other issues are also receiving attention in contract negotiations. Unions are pressing for more full-time nurses in schools. In schools that lack nurses or when a nurse is absent, teachers and other employees are expected to provide basic first aid for children's injuries. In most cases, these are minor scrapes and bruises and are easily treated, but in some cases riskier procedures are involved. Teachers hesitate to administer oral medications for fear, if the child should have an allergic reaction, they may be held liable. Teachers are equally uneasy about being asked to test blood glucose levels or administer medication to reverse the symptoms of a severe allergic reaction.

Unions are also asking boards to create health and safety committees to monitor hazardous conditions in schools and take action to remove threats to health and safety. Most high school science labs contain potentially dangerous chemicals that can cause injury if not properly handled. A teacher is usually given responsibility for storing and supervising the use of these materials. Teachers with this duty are generally knowledgeable and conscientious, but the additional oversight provided by a health and safety committee is helpful.

Unions are also asserting the right to be involved in restructuring decisions involving low-performing schools. Schools that are regarded as failing qualify for additional resources, and teachers feel they should be consulted about decisions on staffing and changes in the instructional programs in these schools.

Period of Calm

Recent years have been a period of relative calm in labor relations. According to the Bureau of Labor Statistics, the number of work stoppages in all industries in the United States declined from a high of 400 or more in the most strike-prone years between 1950 and 1980, to a low of only 19 in 2002. Similarly, the number of workers involved in stoppages declined from 2.7 million in 1952 to 46,000 in 2002 (www.bls.gov/cba/hwstable.pdf).

The number of teacher strikes has also dropped, partly as a result of legislation that provides other ways of settling impasses. Another reason for the decrease in the number of strikes has been the unions' decision to try to work with rather than oppose school boards. Although the National Education Association and the American Federation of Teachers have not merged, they are working together more closely than in the past and have granted to local affiliates the right to merge if they wish to do so. The acrimony that formerly characterized exchanges between the National Education Association and American Federation of Teachers is largely forgotten.

NEW FORMS OF COLLECTIVE BARGAINING

Traditional collective bargaining uses an adversarial format, in which management and employees compete to win concessions from the other side. Employees' representatives use the threat of work stoppages to win higher wages and better benefits. The adversarial model was developed in the industrial world at a time when corporations were extremely powerful and workers were weak. That model worked reasonably well and helped achieve a better balance between employers' prerogatives and employees' rights. The model was borrowed and applied directly to education, but it has some disadvantages in that setting. School boards do not have the freedom that managers in the private sector enjoy because school boards have limited control over resources.

In recent years school boards have begun to look into less adversarial models of collective bargaining. Several of these innovative approaches are discussed next.

Win/Win Bargaining

Developed by a sociology professor, Irving Goldaber, win/win bargaining is highly structured and includes detailed rules for negotiating. The success of this approach depends on the willingness of the parties to search for solutions that can be embraced by both sides. If both parties believe that the other party operates in good faith, the win/win approach can lead to better labor relations.

Expedited Bargaining

A problem with the industrial model of collective bargaining has been the substantial amount of time involved in reaching an agreement. It is not unusual for negotiations to continue for months, often past the expiration date of the current contract. In some cases, unions walk off the job when a contract expires, but in other cases they agree to continue working as long as progress is being made toward reaching a settlement.

Expedited bargaining is designed to speed up the process of reaching a settlement. The parties agree to limit the amount of time devoted to bargaining sessions and also pare down the list of issues to be discussed so that negotiations do not drag on. Some states have adopted expedited bargaining by setting a time limit for completion of a new agreement and providing for mediation if the parties are not able to settle within the allotted time. Oregon allows 150 calendar days. If the parties are unable to settle in that time, an impasse is declared and both sides submit their final offer to the mediator. At that point a 30-day cooling off period starts, and at the end of that time, several things may happen. The parties may reach a settlement, or they may agree to resume negotiations. The employer may decide to implement its own plan, or the union may give notice of an impending strike (www.osba.org/covered/bargain/regular.pdf).

Progressive Bargaining

Progressive bargaining works well when there is plenty of time available for reaching an agreement. In this model, negotiators take up more issues and devote more time to exploring them than in other forms of collective bargaining. Subcommittees are created to study specific issues and report their findings to the bargaining teams. The result is that more time is needed to reach an agreement. If an impasse occurs, the parties may resort to fact finding and/or mediation in order to arrive at a resolution.

Principled Negotiations

The principled negotiations approach to collective bargaining was developed by a team at Harvard University. It is intended for use in many settings, including negotiations between employers and employees. The goal of the model is to allow both parties to reach their objectives without having to compromise. Guidelines used in principled negotiations are intended to help negotiators get past hurdles that may lead to an impasse. Among the guidelines used in this approach are these:

1. Separate people from the problem. Participants are urged not to demonize members of the opposite team because that leads to heightened tension and dug-in positions.

2. Focus on interests, not positions. Participants are urged to try to understand the interest the other side seeks in advancing a particular idea. By gaining insight to the opposition's motivation, participants are able to move toward a mutually satisfactory solution.

3. Invent options for mutual gain. Participants are urged to think not only of their own interests but also those of the opposition and to suggest solutions that address both sets of interests.

4. Evaluate options, not power. Participants are urged to establish a set of criteria for judging proposals and adopting the proposals that come closest to meeting the criteria.

Bargaining Stages

Successful negotiations ultimately depend on the development of trust between the parties. Establishing trust takes time, particularly when the participants have not previously faced one another. Members of both teams want to learn more about their counterparts on the other team and find out what their strengths and vulnerabilities are. If the school board has received criticism from the public for increasing class sizes to save money, the teachers' team may try to use that issue to extract concessions. Similarly, if the union received a black eye in the press for refusing to meet with the superintendent to discuss ways of improving instruction, the board's team may try to exploit that for its own purposes.

Negotiations between employees and employer tend to advance in stages, as shown in Figure 12.2. Early in the negotiations, the two sides stake out their positions. They make demands and counterdemands and are often quite far apart at the outset. Union representatives may say, "We must have decent raises so that we don't fall further behind other school districts," to be answered by the board's representative explaining how tight budgets are and how many other demands there are on limited resources. Thus, the stage is set for confrontation.

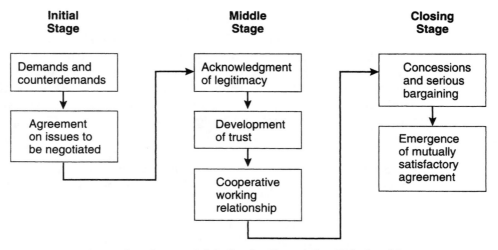

FIGURE 12.2   **Stages in a Successful Collective Bargaining Relationship**

However, if the parties are patient and bargain in good faith, trust begins to develop, and a cooperative working relationship emerges. In the final stage of bargaining, the parties reach a point at which they are willing to seriously consider proposals put forth by the other side and to scale back their own demands in the interest of reaching an agreement.

The two sides learn that they cannot win on every issue. Teachers realize early on that it is to their advantage to set priorities. By yielding on issues that are not vital, they hope to prevail on issues that they consider to be more important. Teams may float proposals that have no chance of being accepted by the other side so that they can appear to make a concession by ditching the proposal at a critical moment. The teams plot strategies to help them advance their vital interests. The board, for example, might propose to wait until near the end of negotiations to discuss salaries, thinking that teachers may be more willing to compromise at that point in order to reach an agreement. The teachers' team, however, may ask to take up the salary issue early, in order to demonstrate the importance they attach to it.

As the distance between the parties narrows, bargaining becomes more difficult because the negotiators are nearing their final positions. Impasses are not uncommon at this point and are more likely to occur when one or both sides is poorly informed about the other's true position.

When the board signals that it is making its final salary offer, for example, union negotiators must decide whether the board is bluffing and will, under pressure, agree to a higher amount. Teachers' representatives may propose a figure they believe is slightly above the board's predetermined limit in hopes that board negotiators will yield in order to reach a settlement, but this strategy has some risks. If the teachers miscalculate, they may provoke a strike that neither side wants.

If the differences are resolved and an impasse avoided, an agreement is finally reached. The work is now finished unless the teachers or board members reject the settlement. If negotiators have stayed in close touch with their constituencies throughout the process, however, that should not happen.

Resolving Impasses

The climate of negotiations is affected by several factors, including the personalities of the participants, the pressure each side feels from its constituencies, and the nature of the situation. When trust breaks down and union and management representatives find themselves at an impasse, outside intervention may be needed.

Mediation, fact-finding, and arbitration are tools for resolving differences between two parties. The mediator's role is to clarify the issues that prevent the parties from reaching an agreement and help the parties arrive at a mutually acceptable solution. A fact-finder gathers information about the issues on which the contending parties disagree and proposes a solution to resolve their differences. In some states the law defines criteria for settling impasses. These may include availability of funds, the interest and welfare of the public, and comparisons of salaries and working conditions in the same or similar positions in the region (Marczely & Marczely, 2002).

Neither mediation nor fact-finding imposes a solution on negotiators. However, in *compulsory* or *binding arbitration,* the arbitrator hears both sides and makes a decision which is binding on both parties. An approach that is becoming more popular is *final offer arbitration,* in which the two sides each submit a final, best offer. The arbitrator then chooses one of the two to be implemented.

In preparing for final offer arbitration, each side must consider how the other side is likely to respond. Teacher representatives making a final offer on salaries are aware that if they are unreasonably demanding the arbitrator will be likely to adopt the board's position. Similarly, board representatives must try to anticipate the position the teachers are likely to take in order to present an offer that has a reasonable chance of being accepted. Thus, both parties are prevented by self-interest from making offers that are unreasonable or nonresponsive.

IMPACT OF COLLECTIVE BARGAINING ON SCHOOLS

Collective bargaining has had a major impact on the operation of schools in the United States, but observers disagree on the question of whether, on balance, the effect has been positive, negative, or neutral. Three questions that are often asked about the impact of collective bargaining are: (1) What has been its effect on teachers' salaries? (2) How much and in what ways does collective bargaining affect the quality of instruction in schools? and (3) What effect has it had on principals' power? The following paragraphs try to answer those questions.

Teachers' Salaries

Stone (2000) recently reviewed research on the effect of collective bargaining on teachers' salaries and found that teachers employed by districts with collective bargaining received salaries that ranged from 5 to 12 percent greater than those of teachers in districts without collective bargaining. The research also showed that teachers from districts with collective bargaining enjoyed an even greater advantage over nonunionized teachers in size and number of fringe benefits paid to them by their employers. Teachers in collective bargaining districts also received advantages in nonmonetary benefits such as more planning time and fewer students.

Student Learning

If quality of instruction is measured by student academic achievement, then the research evidence suggests that the effect of collective bargaining on student learning is, for the most part, positive. Stone (2000) cited studies that showed slightly higher scores on standardized mathematics tests for students from districts with collective bargaining teacher contracts and a difference of between 6 and 8 percent in scores on SAT and ACT tests favoring students from districts with collective bargaining. However, the studies cited by Stone also found that average students in districts with collective bargaining for teachers benefited most, whereas students who were either above or below average actually learned less on average than similar students in districts without collective bargaining. The research also suggested that the dropout rate was higher in districts with negotiated contracts.

Potentially, the most damage to student learning occurs when negotiators reach an impasse and a work stoppage results. Strikes are traumatic events for school personnel. Everyone loses, and it may take years to repair the damage. Student learning is affected both by the length of a strike and by whether or not striking teachers are replaced by substitutes.

There has been relatively little research on the subject, but the available studies show, as one would expect, that shorter strikes are less harmful than longer ones. Mathematics achievement seems to be more sensitive to loss of instruction than reading. Mathematics is negatively affected both by the length of a strike and by the presence of substitute teachers, whereas reading achievement appears to be affected more by the length of a strike than by the presence of substitute teachers (Crisci & Lulow, 1985). That may be because substitute teachers are less likely to be proficient in teaching mathematics.

For principals and human resources managers, the obvious lessons from this research are, first, to take actions that will prevent or limit the length of teacher strikes and, second, if strikes occur, to seek to maintain normal instructional routines to the extent possible.

Work of Principals

Some authorities charge that collective bargaining has imposed limits on principals' abilities to lead their schools. They point out that principals believe that unions protect incompetent teachers by making it so difficult to terminate one that administrators abandon hope of weeding out those who are not performing effectively. Unions deny that charge and insist that the problem is not overzealous unions but weak-kneed and ineffective administrators.

Principals who are accustomed to a free-wheeling style of management may have difficulty adjusting to life under a negotiated agreement. Being successful in such a situation requires an individual with considerable flexibility—one who is careful to abide by the provisions of the master contract, yet able to inspire teachers to give more than the minimum effort in order to increase learning.

Most administrators will admit that collective bargaining has some positive features. Among these are the increased security that teachers feel and the increased clarity of teachers' work responsibilities. Principals who work in districts with contracts that detail duties teachers are expected to perform report that they have no problems in getting those duties carried out (Jessup, 1981).

All in all, administering a school that operates under a negotiated agreement probably requires skills that are no different from those required in schools in which there is no agreement in effect. In both cases, the administrator must attend to details and provide leadership to move the faculty toward a goal of improved instruction.

SUMMARY

Employees of companies engaged in interstate commerce won the right to bargain with their employers over wages and working conditions with the passage of the National Labor Relations Act in 1935. Bargaining rights for public sector employees came much later, and a few states still do not allow public employees to bargain collectively. Negotiated agreements between teachers and school boards address teacher pay and fringe benefits but are usually silent on instructional matters. However, under pressure, unions and boards are beginning to include provisions in contracts designed to help improve instruction and student learning. Negotiations proceed through three stages—staking out positions, emerging trust and cooperation, and granting concessions. School boards are looking for less adversarial models of negotiation. These include win/win bargaining, expedited bargaining, progressive bargaining, and principled negotiations. When the sides reach an impasse, outside assistance is called for. Mediation, fact-finding, and arbitration are tools that help resolve impasses.

SUGGESTED ACTIVITIES

1. The contract between the union and the board contains this provision:

   "Any time a principal has knowledge of a problem that may have a negative impact on an employee's performance evaluation, the principal shall provide the employee that information in writing and shall allow the employee to have a union representative present when the information is discussed."

A fourth-grade teacher, Mary Ramsey, was told by her principal informally that a parent had complained that Ms. Ramsey was partial toward girls in her class and punitive toward the boys. "I'm telling you this so you'll be aware how this parent feels," the principal said. "I wouldn't worry about it, but if the parent continues to complain, I'll set up a meeting between the two of you." The principal declined to tell her the parent's name but said, "I think you can guess who it is." Ms. Ramsey contacted the union representative, who then met with the principal and told him that he was out of order. "If you have anything further to say to Ms. Ramsey about this matter," the representative said, "invite me to the meeting and come with the complaint in writing." The principal responded, "I wanted Ms. Ramsey to know what the parent said. She had already told Ms. Ramsey that she was unhappy, so this shouldn't have been a surprise. I offered to move the child to another classroom, but the parent declined. I don't think there is any basis for the parent's complaint, but I thought Ms. Ramsey ought to know."

Did the principal's action violate the contract provision? How should the principal proceed if the parent should call again to complain that her son is being treated unfairly? Explain your reasoning.

2. Following is a statement on class size proposed by the teachers' union. Take and defend a position for or against the proposal as written. (You are not allowed to rewrite it.)

"We believe instruction is most effective when class sizes are kept small enough to permit teachers to diagnose students' needs and plan instruction to meet them. To permit the level of teacher attention needed for learning to occur, we ask the board to agree to place a limit of 20 students in classes in reading and English in grades 1–12 and to limit all other classes in grades 1–12 (except special education) to no more than 24 students. Each special education student assigned to a regular class will count as two students for purposes of calculating size limits."

3. Principals are sometimes excluded from joining the board's negotiating team because board members believe they might be inclined to side with teachers. Principals argue that they could help the board's representatives understand how proposed contract provisions might affect instruction, and thus avoid language likely to harm learning. Take and defend a position on this proposition:

"Principals should be represented on the board's negotiating team."

4. Locate contract provisions from two master contracts relating to one of the following topics. Read the provisions from each contract and compare and contrast them. Tell which provision is more favorable to teachers and which is more favorable to the board. (You may wish to use one of the online master contracts listed under Online Resources.)

   a. Evaluation of teachers
   b. Teacher safety and security
   c. Teacher transfer and promotion
   d. Extracurricular duties of teachers

5. Negotiation occurs in many activities of life other than collective bargaining. Give three examples of situations in which you negotiated with another individual or group on a matter of importance to you. How did the negotiations turn out? Did you feel successful or unsuccessful? If unsuccessful, what might you have done differently?

ONLINE RESOURCES

Boston Teachers Union (www.btu.org/leftnavbar/contractdownload.html)

Agreement between the School Committee of the City of Boston and the Boston Teachers Union Local 66 AFT.

Cornell Law School Legal Information Institute
(www.law.cornell.edu/topics/collective_bargaining.html)

This site has links to federal statutes, federal agency regulations, and U.S. Supreme Court and Appeals Courts decisions pertaining to collective bargaining.

Education Commission of the States (www.ecs.org/clearinghouse/37/48/3748.htm)

Information about state policies on collective bargaining for teachers is available here. The site covers the scope of bargaining, procedures for resolving impasses, and policies on teacher strikes for all 50 states.

Lawrence Teachers Union
(www.lawrence.k12.ma.us/lps/educators/educator%20contract.pdf)

Agreement between the Lawrence Massachusetts School Committee and the Lawrence Teachers Union Local 1019 AFT.

Nova Scotia Teachers Union
(www.nssba.ednet.ns..ca/labor/Pdfs/scap_nstu_agreement.pdf)

Agreement between the Conseil Scolaire Acadien Provincial and the Nova Scotia Teachers Union.

Portland Association of Teachers (www.patpdx.org/agreement.htm)

Agreement between School District No. 1 Multomah County Oregon and the Portland Association of Teachers.

Providence Teachers Union (www.proteun.org/agreement.htm)

Agreement between the Providence Teachers Union AFT Local 958 and the Providence School Board.

CASE STUDIES

Case No. 1

Superintendent Okie Sellers glanced around the table at the members of his central staff. "Sick leave is eating us up," he said. "Harvey just gave me the numbers from the past school year. Teachers took one-third more sick leave than the year before. What's going on?"

Harvey Banks, head of human resources, nodded. "That was teachers," he said. "The noninstructional people were up about one-fourth."

Sellers looked at Delores Hall, associate superintendent for instruction. "So . . . I repeat. What's going on?"

"There was a lot of flu last winter," Ms. Hall said. "That accounts for some of the increase."

"Maybe," Sellers said. "Tell you what I'm thinking. I'm considering recommending to the board negotiator that he propose limiting teachers to eight days sick leave and cut back personal leave to two days. Right now they get ten days sick leave and three days personal leave. We say that personal leave has to be approved in advance, but we really don't enforce that."

"I think you'll have a problem." Joseph Brittain was associate superintendent for administration. "The union will never agree to cutting sick leave. They always tell you about the teacher who has to stay home with sick kids."

"We want that teacher to take care of his or her kids," Sellers said. "The problem is the person who decides to take a mental health day and calls in sick."

"We could require a doctor's statement after so many absences," Ms. Hall said. "I know several districts that do that. Teachers don't like it but it works."

Sellers was making notes. "What if we offered a trade-off?" he said. "Increase salaries by maybe 3 or 4 percent and cut back on sick leave or give 2 percent salary increases and keep 10 days sick leave?"

"Maybe," Brittain said. "Teachers don't like to have to make decisions like that, though."

"I think they might agree," Ms. Hall said. "If you look at who uses sick leave, you'll find a fairly small number of teachers use a lot of sick leave. The majority only miss one or two days."

"Or none," Banks said.

"Give certificates to those who don't use sick leave," Brittain said.

Sellers laughed. "I'm sure that would solve the problem."

"Some districts have had pretty good luck with sick leave banks," Banks said. "Teachers are allowed maybe five days and they can borrow from the bank if they need more. No one is left without leave."

"How does that save money?" Sellers asked.

"Teachers know there's a limit and if they use all of their leave, they'll have to borrow from the bank. They're more careful."

"We don't want people coming to work when they're sick," Ms. Hall said.

Sellers nodded. "No, of course not. But we've got to control our costs."

Questions

1. Discuss the merits of Sellers' proposal to offer a larger salary increase if teachers agree to cut back on sick leave. Is it a sound proposal? Suggest a counterproposal the union might offer.

2. Discuss the other ideas proposed by the participants. Which of the suggestions do you think deserve further consideration?
3. What other actions might the district take to reduce its costs?

Case No. 2

Okie Sellers was meeting with his staff to discuss upcoming contract negotiations with the teachers' union. "The board negotiator asked for our thoughts on health and safety committees in the schools. He's expecting the union to push that idea. What do you think, Harvey?"

Harvey Banks was head of human resources. "It's something we need," he said. "But I would recommend one districtwide committee instead of a committee in every school."

"That makes sense to me," Sellers said.

"What does a health and safety committee do?" Delores Hall, associate superintendent for instruction, asked.

Banks responded, "They check buildings for pollutants and safety hazards and fire hazards—that sort of thing."

"Do they have anything to do with security, like installing metal detectors?" Ms. Hall asked.

"Not usually."

"Joe, this is your area. What do you think?" Sellers asked.

Joseph Brittain was associate superintendent for administration. "I really don't see a need," he said. "If there's a problem, our work crews can handle it. When you create a committee like that, you get a lot of gripes about overheated classrooms and potholes in the parking lot."

"That pothole could be a safety issue," Sellers said. "If someone steps in it and breaks an ankle, we could be liable."

"But how does having a health and safety committee help?" Brittain asked. "I can send someone out to fill a pothole without a committee debating it."

"I think teachers feel that their concerns are ignored at times," Banks said. "They want someone they can go to who'll get something done."

"Maybe we need an omsbudsman," Ms. Hall said.

"Not a bad idea," Banks said.

"An omsbudsman is different," Sellers said. "They try to improve communication. A safety committee tries to prevent injuries and health problems."

"Right now we need to check our chemistry labs," Brittain said. "Some of these labs have stuff that's been there for years. We need to clean them up and throw away the outdated chemicals. I don't have enough people to do the job, but sooner or later it's got to be done."

"Couldn't a health and safety committee help with that?" Banks asked.

Brittain shook his head. "You need trained technicians to handle chemicals."

"Should we reject the Association's proposal?" Sellers asked.

"Not necessarily," Brittain said. "It probably won't cost much. I simply don't think it'll do much good. It may actually slow things down. Instead of picking up the phone and calling my office, principals will have to refer a problem to a committee. That'll take a month or two."

"Harvey?"

"I think Joe makes a good point, but I'd be inclined to go with the union on this. If we reject it, we'll create hard feelings that we don't need. Besides, we'll get bad press. Everyone's in favor of health and safety."

"Delores?"

"I would agree to establish committees, but I'd give them a broader mission. I'd make security part of their charge."

"Thanks for your input." Sellers checked the item off his agenda and prepared to move on to the next topic.

Questions

1. Of the three ideas—reject the union's request, accept it in the interest of harmony, or make a counteroffer—which one seems to you to make the most sense? Explain.
2. Banks thinks that teachers' concerns are ignored by the administration, yet when he pointed that out to the group, he was ignored. Is there some way he can get the group to focus on that problem? Aside from agreeing to create health and safety committees, what might the district do to deal with teachers' feelings of being ignored?
3. What additional information would help you decide what position the district should take on the union proposal?

REFERENCES

Biddle, B. J., & Berliner, D.C. (2002, February). Small class size and its effects. *Educational Leadership, 59,* 12–23.

Crisci, P. E., & Lulow, R. J. (1985). The effect of school employee strikes on student achievement in nine Ohio school districts. *Journal of Collective Negotiations, 14,* 197–212.

Forti, V. (2005, November 16). Directing funding away from student needs. *Education Week,* pp. 44, 32.

Honawar, V. (2006, April 5). Labor disputes heating up in urban districts after respite. *Education Week,* p. 7.

Jessup, D. (1981). *Teacher unionism and its impact: A study of change over time.* Washington, DC: National Institute of Education.

Marczely, B., & Marczely, D. W. (2002). *Human resource and contract management in the public sector.* Lanham, MD: Scarecrow Press.

Stone, J. (2000). Collective bargaining and public schools. In T. Loveless (Ed.), *Conflicting missions?* (pp. 47–68). Washington, DC: Brookings Institution.

13 MANAGING CONFLICT IN SCHOOLS

Conflict is a common occurrence in public schools, but it is not inevitable, and when it occurs, it is possible to manage it without it causing lasting damage to teacher morale or productivity. In a diverse democracy people hold strongly to views that are often divergent. In such a system it is not hard to see why conflict is so common.

Conflict takes place between individuals or groups, or between an individual and a group and arises from disagreements regarding values, responsibilities, and ways of doing things, as well as from competition for scarce resources. The focus of this chapter is on conflict that involves school personnel and, in particular, that which takes place between and among teachers or between teachers and administrators. Conflict involving students and parents is not discussed in this chapter.

PLAN OF THE CHAPTER

The following topics are examined in this chapter: (1) the nature of conflict in organizations, (2) methods of resolving conflict, (3) managing conflict through the grievance process, (4) arbitration of work rules, and (5) other issues in arbitration.

NATURE OF CONFLICT IN ORGANIZATIONS

In any human activity, disagreements and conflict are inevitable. In the workplace, much conflict centers on one of four issues: disputes regarding the allocation of resources and privileges; disagreements about the application of laws, rules, and policies; confusion about duties and responsibilities of employees; and disagreements about performance evaluation. Examples of these types of conflict are shown in Exhibit 13.1.

EXHIBIT 13.1

EXAMPLES OF FOUR TYPES OF CONFLICT IN SCHOOLS

DISPUTES OVER ALLOCATION OF RESOURCES AND PRIVILEGES

Example 1. A teacher in the mathematics department and the department head both request permission to attend a regional conference sponsored by the math teachers' association. There is not enough money in the budget for both to attend. The principal approves the department head's request and denies the teacher's application. The teacher protests this action and accuses the principal of favoritism.

Example 2. Department heads were asked to limit requests for instructional materials for the next school year to essential items because of the tight budget. The foreign language department's request is the largest of any department, although its enrollment is small. The department head justifies the materials as essential for good instruction and says that language materials are more expensive than materials for other subjects. The head of the science department states that, although the biology laboratory needs new equipment, he did not include the equipment in his request and suggests that, because the school's accreditation is based in part on students' performance in biology and chemistry, his department should receive more support than foreign language.

DISPUTES OVER APPLICATION OF LAWS, RULES, AND POLICIES

Example 3. Board policy states that high school teachers may not leave school until 15 minutes after students have been excused "except in case of emergency." A teacher who left school early argued that she needed to have a prescription filled and that that should qualify as an "emergency."

Example 4. Members of the marching band held a car wash and collected $170 for new uniforms. Board policy requires that clubs obtain advance approval for fund-raising activities, and, because the band members did not have approval for the car wash, the principal told the band instructor that he would cancel a second fund-raiser for the band scheduled for the spring. The instructor objected and pointed out that the band had sponsored car washes for at least seven years and that, under the previous principal, he never had to obtain permission because it was understood that car washes were part of the band's fund-raising activities.

CONFUSION ABOUT DUTIES AND RESPONSIBILITIES

Example 5. A teacher's aide complains that the teacher asked her to help two students with a reading assignment. The aide says she is not qualified to teach and that her job description does not mention instruction. The teacher says the aide was asked to help two students with difficult words, which she argues is tutoring, a duty aides are expected to perform.

Example 6. District budget cuts have forced the elimination of drivers for vans to carry students to away football and basketball games. Coaches of other sports have been told they must drive the vans to transport their teams to games. The district has agreed to pay for liability insurance to cover the coaches. The coaches argue they should be paid extra for driving their teams to games, especially because basketball and football coaches are exempt from the added duty.

(continued)

EXHIBIT 13.1 CONTINUED

DISPUTES OVER PERFORMANCE EVALUATION

Example 7. A biology teacher has been absent from school 21 days during the year, most of the absences resulting from an infection contracted during a summer trip to Latin America. The teacher's evaluation is downgraded from "Excellent" to "Average" as a result of his absences. The teacher protests that he should not be penalized for illness.

Example 8. An English teacher is rated "Average" by the principal. The teacher points out that the principal's only visit to her classroom was very brief and that she therefore cannot possibly evaluate her fairly. The principal responds that she had input from other sources, including a district supervisor who observed the class one time, as well as parents and students.

Disputes over Resources

Resources are scarce, and differences of opinion about how they should be used are inevitable. These decisions should be guided by the school's mission and priorities. Principals sometimes try to avoid conflict among teachers by dividing resources evenly among all departments. However, that approach ignores the organizational mission and gives equal support to the most and least important activities. A more effective plan is to try to reach a consensus about which activities are most important and allocate resources accordingly. However, because of differences in the cost of different programs, it may be necessary to give a larger share of resources to more expensive programs. As the department head in Example 2 in Exhibit 13.1 points out, foreign language programs require expensive equipment, without which the program is less effective.

Application of Rules

Rules and policies are defined by how they are administered. In Example 3 in Exhibit 13.1, a question has arisen about what constitutes an "emergency" that would justify a teacher's leaving school early. When the policy was adopted, it was assumed that the meaning was clear. Most people think of an emergency as sudden illness or injury, but the teacher in the example thinks filling a routine prescription should qualify as an emergency. Before agreeing to the teacher's request, the principal should keep in mind that whatever decision is made will set a precedent. If the teacher is allowed to leave school early, other teachers will expect to be granted the same privilege in the future.

Confusion over Duties

Questions about duties and responsibilities arise most often with newly added positions or in situations in which a change is made from a previous practice.

Fewer questions arise when the human resources department prepares a description of duties and responsibilities for the new position. In Example 5 in Exhibit 13.1, for example, tutoring is listed as a responsibility of teacher aides but teaching is not. What is the difference between tutoring and teaching? Some would say that working with one or two students at a time is tutoring, whereas working with a group of 15 or 20 is teaching. What about five or six students? There are other ways of defining the two activities as well. If advance planning and preparation are required, does that mean the act should be regarded as teaching? What about reviewing students' work and giving grades? Are those actions of a tutor? Thinking ahead to anticipate questions that are likely to arise when terms such as *emergency* and *tutoring* are used can help prevent problems. However, not all questions can be anticipated. Even a detailed list of duties is unlikely to answer every question that might arise. There is always a need to interpret and clarify policy.

Evaluation Questions

Performance evaluations lead to conflict because the evaluator is making judgments, often subjective, about others' performance. The person being evaluated has much at stake, including personal pride, salary, and perhaps even job security, and that person probably believes he or she is an effective, even an outstanding, performer. It is rare that an employee who receives a poor performance rating agrees with the evaluator's judgment. More often than not, the employee challenges the evaluator's knowledge, fairness, or judgment. It is difficult to avoid disagreements about performance evaluation, but there are ways to make the process somewhat more objective and less subject to disputes.

Discussing evaluation procedures in advance is helpful. Going over the evaluation criteria in advance helps teachers understand how they will be evaluated and helps the evaluator focus his or her attention on the most relevant aspects of the performance. Using an evaluation tool that involves tabulating instances of specific behaviors may help reduce disagreements. Teachers are more willing to accept evaluation as fair and unbiased when the evaluator takes into account the context in which the evaluation occurs. A teacher of a class of mostly below-average performers has a more difficult job than someone who teaches high achievers. If the evaluator recognizes the difficulties such a teacher faces and makes allowances for them, the teacher will be more inclined to feel that she has been treated fairly.

METHODS OF RESOLVING CONFLICT

Negotiation is the most widely used means for settling conflict in organizations and is the least costly in terms of time and money. Exhibit 13.2 presents the steps involved in negotiating a resolution to a dispute. The first step (defining the problem

---

EXHIBIT 13.2

STEPS IN SETTLING A DISPUTE BY NEGOTIATION

1. Define the problem using language that all parties agree to and identify fundamental issues
2. Select the issue ranked most important by the people involved
3. Identify alternative solutions for that issue
4. Evaluate the alternatives one at a time, seeking input from all parties to the dispute
5. Identify the most acceptable (least objectionable) alternative and ask for consensus
6. Move to the next issue and repeat Steps 3–5

---

in language that the parties accept) is important. Sometimes simply clarifying the terms used to describe a disagreement can lead to a solution.

An example of how disputes arise from differences in definitions held by the parties is found in Example 5 in Exhibit 13.1, where the instructional aide objects to helping two students with reading, which she considers to be an instructional task, whereas the teacher regards it as tutoring. Resolving this disagreement requires clarifying the meanings of the terms *instruction* and *tutoring*, as applied in this setting. Example 8 from Exhibit 13.1 illustrates that unverified assumptions can lead to disagreements.

Step 2 in the negotiation process is to rank the issues and begin discussing the most important one (Isenhart & Spangle, 2000). Example 2 in Exhibit 13.1 describes a situation in which several issues are involved. The department heads in this example were instructed to keep their budget requests modest, but that was insufficient guidance to avoid disagreements over priorities. The question that the participants must now tackle is how to decide which values will prevail in the distribution of scarce resources. The foreign language chair believes that cost of materials should be considered in formulating instructional requests, whereas the science department chair stresses the need to base requests for materials on their potential contribution to accreditation. Size of enrollments is suggested as still another criterion by which funds might be allocated. Identifying alternative solutions to the problem is Step 3 in the negotiation process, and evaluating potential solutions is Step 4 (Isenhart & Spangle, 2000). These steps are often combined. All reasonable solutions should be examined, with both advantages and disadvantages explored. Participants should be asked to withhold committing to a solution until all the possible solutions have been evaluated. This may not be easy to accomplish, but if the participants can reserve judgment, it will make it easier for the parties to eventually arrive at a solution that is acceptable to all.

Mediation

The problems mediators deal with are fairly complex because simple problems are usually resolved by negotiation. The mediator has no power to impose a solution and must depend on his or her skill to bring the parties together. Mediators are trained to help parties consider all of the issues involved in a dispute and to work to identify common interests that may be used as the basis for a settlement. The mediator must be impartial but frank and must seek to help each of the parties understand the other's position.

When emotions run high, the mediator usually meets separately with each side in order to gain a better understanding of their fears and concerns. During these early meetings, the mediator is often able to identify issues on which the parties are reluctant to compromise for fear of being seen as weak, either by adversaries or constituents.

By listening at length to the parties, the mediator gains an understanding of the issues involved in the dispute and the positions held by each side. He or she probes to identify areas in which compromise may be possible, all the while stressing the importance of reaching an agreement. After exploring the dispute in detail with each side, the mediator will suggest a solution that has features attractive to each party. If the parties respond favorably, the mediator may then bring them together to discuss the proposed solution in an atmosphere free of hostility and recrimination. By insisting on civility, the mediator allows calm, rational discussions to take place. It is through a respectful discussion of differences that the parties begin to understand and trust one another. In such an atmosphere, the parties are inclined to accept a solution that meets at least some of their requirements (Masters & Albright, 2002).

Arbitration

An arbitrator acts as a mediator in some respects, but arbitrators have power that mediators lack: They can impose a settlement that the disputing parties are obligated to accept. A party to a dispute will be likely to avoid arbitration if he or she believes that the arbitrator's decision will go against his or her interests. For this reason, arbitration is usually reserved for disputes in which the lines are firmly drawn and neither party has shown a willingness to make concessions. Arbitration is a more formal process than mediation, usually involving hearings at which witnesses may be heard and the parties represented by counsel. The arbitrator may also refer to documents that provide background information on the dispute.

The advantages of arbitration are that it leads to a resolution of a dispute rather quickly and at a lower cost than legal action. A disadvantage is that neither party may be happy with the solution that the arbitrator announces. A method that helps avoid this problem is final-offer arbitration, in which each side presents its final offer and the arbitrator must choose one of the offers. Each side is inclined to present an offer that it believes the arbitrator will find responsive to the other side's demands in order to increase the odds of its being accepted.

Ombudsmen

Some districts now have ombudsmen to help parents and others negotiate the district bureaucracy and work with employees to resolve disputes. The role of the ombudsman originated in Sweden 200 years ago and has been adopted by many companies in the United States. As organizations have grown in size and bureaucracies have become more complex, the need has arisen for an insider to assist those from outside who are confused about what department handles particular questions or which official to contact in order to register a complaint.

In schools, the process of special education placements has become more adversarial, and school personnel sometimes have conflicts of interest as they try to balance the competing interests of a child and the district. It is estimated that about 20 school districts now have ombudsmen (Ombusdman Soothes . . . , 2006). Ombudsmen try to remain neutral, but because they are employees of the district, parents assume they will side with the district in a dispute. However, most ombudsmen are more interested in clarifying the law and board policies for parents and helping them get fair hearings before appropriate administrators.

Achieving Cooperation

Most efforts at dealing with conflict seek ways to solve disputes after they arise. Some school districts are beginning to investigate ways of avoiding conflict by emphasizing cooperation. They reason that the best way to avoid the harmful effects of conflict is to work to improve cooperation and collaboration among and between units and individuals. This is accomplished by creating a climate that places a high value on cooperation and developing supporting structures to achieve it.

Creating a climate favorable to cooperation requires that the board commit itself to maintaining a harmonious relationship with employees and their representatives. A statement by the board, such as the following, commits the board to work for cooperation and avoid unnecessary conflict:

> The board agrees to establish and support a harmonious working environment for staff and students. The board and representatives of employees agree to avoid the use of language or actions that convey disrespect, harassment, or verbal or physical abuse of other members of the school community.

Of course, adopting such a statement does not guarantee that some administrators and teachers won't use disparaging language toward others or take actions that show lack of respect for those who disagree with them. However, a written declaration does serve as a reminder to individuals to monitor their words and actions.

Administrators who take a stand in support of cooperation and who show by their actions that they are committed to cooperation have a positive effect on the school climate. Once a climate of cooperation is established, individuals are more easily persuaded to work together to achieve the school's mission.

School boards and employee unions have long taken part in adversarial contract negotiations in which each party seeks to advance its own interests at the expense of the other. This attitude carries over into the day-to-day work that goes on in schools and often results in unnecessary acrimony between employees and managers. Some school districts have begun to move away from the adversarial model of collective bargaining. Chapter 12 describes alternative models of collective bargaining that rely on cooperation.

Montgomery County (Maryland) schools have established two programs that help promote cooperation between the board and its employees. The first is the Labor-Management Collaboration Committee, a district-level committee composed of representatives of the board and of each of the various employee groups, which discusses issues of mutual interest. The committee interprets negotiated agreements between the board and employee unions and establishes guidelines for collaboration. It also serves as a resource for the schools and arranges for collaborative training for members of school leadership teams.

The second innovation, though hardly unique, is school leadership teams. Each school has such a team. The purpose of these teams is to provide a way for employees to participate in decisions at the school level. Some of the decisions in which leadership teams have a voice include the following:

- Curriculum, instruction, and assessment
- Professional development
- Student discipline
- School improvement plans
- Grading and reporting on students' work
- Parent communication

MANAGING CONFLICT THROUGH THE GRIEVANCE PROCESS

Negotiated contracts between school boards and teachers' unions normally include a grievance procedure by which employees can seek to resolve complaints about the actions of a principal, supervisor, or district administrator whom they believe has violated the terms of the collective bargaining agreement. Grievances protect employee morale and help maintain good working relationships. They also help to deter managers who might be inclined to take arbitrary or punitive actions against employees. They serve management by providing a safety valve for employees and by helping to prevent the cost of settling disputes in the courts.

A grievance clause in a master contract usually includes a definition of a grievance, tells who may initiate a grievance, establishes a deadline for filing a grievance, and sets a time limit for an administrative response.

Steps Involved

Most grievance procedures consist of three or four steps. An informal step occurs when the employee brings the grievance to the attention of a supervisor. If that does not result in a satisfactory outcome, the employee may appeal the decision by filing a written complaint describing the action that led to the grievance and naming the article of the agreement that the grievant believes has been violated or misinterpreted. The written grievance may be submitted on a form such as that shown in Figure 13.1. This is Step 1.

The administrator who is designated to hear the grievance meets with the grievant to discuss the complaint and later announces a decision. The grievant may appeal the designated administrator's decision to Step 2, where the grievance is heard by the director of human resources or, in smaller districts, the superintendent or assistant superintendent. Again the administrator meets with the grievant to hear the complaint and renders a judgment. If the grievant is still not pleased, he or she may appeal to Step 3. At that time the grievance is referred for arbitration or mediation. The parties obtain lists of qualified arbitrators or mediators from the American Arbitration Association or the Federal Mediation and Conciliation Service. They alternate removing names, one at a time, until one person is left. That person conducts the hearing and announces a decision. The board may then review and approve or disapprove the decision. In some districts the board hears the complaint at Step 3.

FIGURE 13.1   Form for Submitting Grievance

Date _____

Name of grievant _____

School _____

Identify contract provision allegedly violated or misinterpreted _____

Describe incident, decision or practice that led to grievance _____

_____

Date of occurrence _____

Describe relief sought _____

Signatures

_____   _____
            Grievant   Person receiving grievance

                                          Date _____

Kansas City (Missouri) schools allow either party to a grievance to request mediation or advisory arbitration for certain disputes that have not been resolved prior to Step 3. The disputes that may be submitted to mediation or advisory arbitration include involuntary demotion, involuntary transfer, involuntary reduction in pay, unpaid suspension, and termination.

Some states do not allow the use of arbitration in public schools because they believe doing so constitutes unlawful delegation of the board's decision-making power. Advisory arbitration was intended to circumvent that restriction and give school boards access to the skills of arbitrators.

Unions favor grievance plans that include binding arbitration as the final step because they feel that it guarantees employees a fair hearing for their complaints. However, most school boards prefer advisory arbitration, which leaves the final decision on a dispute in the hands of the board. The grievance clause also specifies which parties may file grievances. In some districts, teacher associations and unions are allowed to file, whereas in others only individuals are permitted to grieve the employer's actions.

Contract Interpretation

Arbitrators must interpret the language of the contract in order to determine whether a provision has been violated. They follow several rules of interpretation in carrying out that task. One of these rules states that they should consider only the contract itself and disregard proposals or discussions during negotiations except those that were given explicit expression in the final agreement. Another rule states that words should be given their generally accepted meanings, and if the meaning of a term is unclear, the arbitrator may ask for clarification from the parties themselves.

ARBITRATION OF WORK RULES

Many grievances have to do with application of work rules. It has been noted that principals are expected to discuss disagreements concerning work rules with the involved parties and that doing so increases the chances that the principal will be successful in mediating future disputes. Disagreements over work rules usually involve these three questions:

1. What action or activity is covered by the rule?
2. Under what conditions is the activity appropriate?
3. To whom does the rule apply?

Consider a policy that states, "Teachers will confer with parents on request and at a mutually convenient time regarding students' academic performance." What actions are covered by the rule? If a teacher discusses a child's work with a parent by telephone, does that constitute conferring? What about an exchange of notes? If the request for a conference originates with the principal rather than a parent, does that constitute a "request" within the meaning of the policy?

Under what conditions is the activity appropriate? Suppose a teacher tells an inquiring parent that there is no need for a conference because the child in question is doing well. Has the teacher violated the rule? Suppose the teacher has a second job and cannot arrange a mutually satisfactory time for a conference. Is she exempt from the rule?

To whom does the rule apply? Are both part-time and full-time teachers obligated by the rule? Is a teacher who has a child for one period a day under a mainstreaming arrangement equally as bound by the rule as the child's base teacher? Is an itinerant teacher who spends only three or four hours per week in a school required to meet with parents who request it?

Deciding Which Rule Applies

In some disputes, a question arises regarding which of two or more rules governs. In one such case, the contract between teachers and the board of the Anoka-Hennepin District in Minnesota contained a provision stating that "teachers shall not be disciplined, reduced in rank or compensation without just cause." Teachers who missed school because of snow requested they be granted personal leave for the half-day they missed. The request was denied and the teachers lost one-half day's pay. They filed a grievance that ultimately went to arbitration. The teachers cited the "just cause" clause, but the district argued that its action was justified by a clause governing emergency leave. That provision held that absence from school because of the effects of weather on transportation would not be approved for emergency leave purposes. The arbitrator supported the district in this case (Coulson, 1986).

Grievances on Evaluation

A good many grievances filed by teachers concern evaluation procedures. In handling these disputes, administrators must be guided by the language of the contract. When contract language is specific with regard to evaluation procedures, any departure from the provisions will probably be rejected in arbitration. If the language is permissive, then an administrative decision is more likely to be upheld.

Teachers sometimes complain that principals use information for evaluation purposes that was not obtained by means of classroom observations. Arbitrators have held that the use of such information is acceptable unless it is specifically prohibited by the contract.

Negative Norm Setters

A reprimand of a teacher who has accumulated "excessive" absences is unlikely to be sustained if other teachers in the district with equal or greater numbers of absences were not reprimanded. Employees with the most checkered record set the standard by which all other employees are judged. Individuals who break rules or violate district policies are sometimes called "negative norm setters" because they establish the behavioral standard for all employees.

Noncompliance with work directives is a charge that most often arises in connection with noninstructional duties. Teachers are expected to monitor hallways, cafeterias, and restrooms in most schools. In some schools they also supervise the playground and bus-loading ramps. If the contract defines particular duties as voluntary, teachers may refuse to perform them without being subject to penalty. A question arises, however, when a teacher has agreed to perform a duty and later discontinues the activity before the task is complete. Consider a teacher who agrees to serve as sponsor of a cheerleading squad and resigns at midyear because of an increased workload related to a part-time job just taken on. Would a reprimand issued to a teacher in such a situation be sustained?

There is no way to predict what an arbitrator will decide in a given case, but if the contract is silent on the issue in question, then the arbitrator will use other information, including past practice, in making a decision. In this case, several factors must weigh on the decision. The arbitrator might consider whether the teacher understood that the assignment was for the full year, whether the teacher received supplemental pay for sponsoring the cheerleaders, and whether the teacher gave advance notice of her impending resignation and offered to help train a successor.

OTHER ISSUES IN ARBITRATION

Arbitrability

One of the issues that frequently confronts arbitrators is the question of arbitrability. *Arbitrability* refers to whether a grievance is subject to arbitration. Grievances that deal with powers granted to the board by statute are not arbitrable, and those that are not timely are also likely to be judged nonarbitrable. Most grievance policies limit the number of days that may elapse after the occurrence of an event before a grievance is filed. If the allowable number of days for filing a grievance is exceeded, it may be declared nonarbitrable unless the teacher failed to learn of the precipitating event until after it occurred.

Timeliness

Just as teachers must file a grievance within a specified number of days after the occurrence of the event they are grieving, administrators are required to respond to formal grievances within a few days of receiving them. Even though a grievance may arrive at a time when a principal is overwhelmed with other responsibilities, an answer must be given within the required time or the administration faces the possibility of losing in arbitration because of delay.

Questions of Law

Because grievances frequently touch on questions of law, arbitrators must be familiar with and guided by relevant court decisions. An example of one such grievance was *Twinsburg (Ohio) Board of Education and Twinsburg Support Staff, Ohio Education Association/National Education Association (OEA/NEA)* (2003). The grievant in this case was an instructional aide who had asked to be reassigned because a back injury had impaired her ability to perform her job. She presented a doctor's statement saying that she could lift no more than 20 pounds. Because she worked with students who required assistance with toileting, her injury prevented her from performing some aspects of her job. When the district denied her request, she grieved the decision, claiming it violated the Americans with Disabilities Act. The arbitrator concluded that the aide was not disabled within the meaning of ADA, citing *Thompson* v. *Holy Family Hospital* (1997). The grievance was denied. (For a discussion of *Thompson* v. *Holy Family Hospital,* see Chapter 11.)

Past Practice

Arbitrators are instructed to refer to past practice in deciding grievances when the contract is silent on an issue or if the language of the contract is ambiguous. If a particular practice has been consistently followed over time and there is nothing in the contract to indicate that the negotiators intended to change it, arbitrators will usually hold that the practice should continue.

A grievance in which the issue of past practice arose was *Stryker (Ohio) Board of Education and Stryker Education Association* (2003). The teachers' association filed a grievance after the superintendent made schedule changes that reduced teachers' planning time. The collective bargaining agreement promised elementary teachers 200 minutes planning time each week. Teachers had been planning while students were out of the classroom for instruction in music, art, and physical education or in the library.

To allow more time for teaching core subjects, the superintendent shortened the length of supplemental classes, thus reducing teachers' planning time. The board contended that teachers could use before- and after-school duty time to make up the difference, but the association argued that by depriving teachers of a continuous block of planning time, the superintendent had violated the contract and past practice. The board insisted that past practice was not relevant because the contract was clear about the planning requirement. The arbitrator agreed with the board and rejected the grievance.

Sometimes contract language seems to sanction a departure from past practice when it is not clear that the negotiators actually meant to make a change. In one district, principals met with teachers after each classroom observation to discuss the lesson. When a new contract was adopted, the language was changed to read, "The principal shall meet with the teacher to discuss the results of classroom observations," which principals took to mean that they no longer had to meet after every observation.

When a teacher complained that the principal had not scheduled a follow-up conference, the principal explained that he was no longer required to confer following every observation. The arbitrator had to decide whether the negotiators had meant to change the existing practice. Representatives of the board and the teachers' association disagreed on whether such a change was intended, so the arbitrator ruled that past practice would prevail and that meetings should continue after each observation.

Effects of Arbitration on the District

Arbitrators' decisions can have considerable impact on district personnel policies. For that reason, most district administrators attempt to include in the contract language that narrowly defines which disputes may be taken to arbitration. Some administrators make it a practice never to go to arbitration unless they are certain of winning (Salmon, 1983). There is some wisdom in that position. Although the contract language may appear to be straightforward and clear to district administrators, there is no guarantee that the arbitrator will agree with their interpretation, and once an arbitrator's decision has been announced, it establishes a precedent that may be difficult to change (*Contract Administration*, 1983).

SUMMARY

Conflict is common in all organizations, including schools. Several methods of dispute resolution are in use in organizations, including negotiation, mediation, and arbitration. The position of ombudsman has been adopted by some districts to ensure that people who have complaints are able to get fair hearings. Most negotiated contracts include a grievance procedure that provides a chance for employees who feel that the contract has been violated to receive a hearing. Arbitrators who hear complaints that involve interpretation of work rules generally seek answers to three questions: what action or activity is covered by the rule? Under what conditions is the activity appropriate? To whom does the rule apply?

SUGGESTED ACTIVITIES

1. Suppose you are representing one of the parties in a dispute with the administration over whether coaches should be required to drive team buses to away games without extra pay. Work in teams of four, two representing the board and two representing the association. With your partner, write a final offer. The other pair writes a final offer for their side. Both offers are submitted to the arbitrator, who chooses one. Bear in mind that the side that submits the offer that the arbitrator regards as most fair and most responsive will have its offer accepted. Designate a member of the class to serve as arbitrator.

2. What are the main differences among a mediator, an arbitrator, and an ombudsman? In what ways are they similar?

3. Interview a principal or director of human resources to learn more about the types of conflict situations that arise with regard to interpretation and application of work rules and how they are usually resolved.

4. Read the following rule and answer the questions that follow.

   Rule: "The school day begins at 7:30 A.M. and ends at 2:45 P.M. Employees should sign the register at the beginning of the day and again at the end of the day. Failing to sign in or out or signing in or out for another person may result in disciplinary action. A person who needs to leave school early should request approval from the principal."

Questions
1. If an employee leaves school at 1:30, is she required to sign out?
2. If a teacher arrives at school at 7:45 A.M. but indicates an arrival time of 7:30, is that a violation of the rule? What is the penalty?
3. To which of the following groups does this rule apply (teachers, student teachers, substitutes, central office personnel, custodial personnel, secretaries, administrators)?
4. Read Example 4 in Exhibit 13.1 and tell how you would respond to the teacher's complaint if you were the principal.

ONLINE RESOURCES

A number of sites with information on dispute resolution are listed below.
American Arbitration Association (http://www.adr.org/publications.html)

   This site shares a list of AAA periodicals that address the latest developments in alternate dispute resolution.

CPR-Institute for Dispute Resolution (http://www.cpradr.ord/welcome.htm)

   This site provides information about a nonprofit alliance of corporations and firms using alternate dispute resolution.

Equal Employment Opportunity Commission (http://www.eeoc.gov)

   This site lists discriminatory practices forbidden by federal law and explains such concepts as "qualified individual with a disability," "reasonable accommodation," "undue hardship," and "prohibited inquiries and examinations." It also explains how to file a charge of discrimination on the job.

Federal Mediation and Conciliation Service (FMCS) (www.fmcs.gov/about fmcs.htm)

   FMCS is a federal agency that provides mediators free of charge to parties at an impasse in contract negotiations. It also provides parties with lists of grievance arbitrators.

Mediate.com (www.mediate.com)

   This site contains a number of articles on topics of interest to human resources professionals and others. Among the titles are these: "Best Practices in ADA Conflict

Management," "Negotiation: The Tension Between Doubt and Certainty," "We Have to Talk: A Step-by-Step Checklist for Difficult Conversations," "Mediation and Culture: How Different Cultural Backgrounds Can Affect the Way People Negotiate." The site also provides lists of mediators by state.

Office of Personnel Management (www.opm.gov/er)

This site offers information on federal classification, job-grading standards, and information on compensation administration.

U.S. Ombudsman Association (www.usombudsman.org)

This site is sponsored by the USOA, which represents professional ombudsmen in public sector organizations. The site has information about the history of the ombudsman movement and the work they do to protect individuals against unresponsive bureaucratic organizations.

CASE STUDIES

Case No. 1

Katherine Sparrow, chair of the social studies department at Norris Able High School, was meeting with the principal, Dan Grace, to discuss a problem with a teacher. "It's Melody Ramirez," he said. "She doesn't show up for department meetings, and when she does come, she leaves early. Other teachers complain about it. They ask why they should come when Melody doesn't bother to show up."

"Have you talked to her about it?" Grace asked.

"Sure. She says she had babysitting problems or a dental appointment. She always has an excuse."

"What did you tell her?"

Ms. Sparrow answered, "I told her it was important to attend. She came once but then missed again last week. Said she forgot."

"Does she understand this will affect her end-of-year performance review?"

"I haven't told her that. I assume she knows. I really need her to be at these meetings. She doesn't attend and then she complains that I don't keep her informed. Can you talk to her?"

The phone rang and Grace reached to shut it off. "Melody's new this year," he said, "and she may not fully understand her responsibilities. It's your job to clarify your expectations. I know you're reluctant to confront her. No one likes confrontation, but sometimes it's necessary. You're doing a great job as department head, and this problem is manageable. I'll be glad to go over some strategies that you might use if you like. You just need to take the bull by the horns, so to speak."

"Yes, I would like to talk about some strategies." Ms. Sparrow frowned. "I'm not very optimistic that she's going to change though."

"Let's get together in the next couple of days."

Questions

1. Grace ignored Ms. Sparrow's request that he talk to the teacher. Do you think he should have agreed to meet with Ramirez? Explain.

2. What do you think about Grace's insistence that Ms. Sparrow "take the bull by the horns"?

3. Ms. Sparrow doesn't have much confidence in her ability to solve the problem. Do you think that Grace's offer to suggest ideas for dealing with the teacher will be helpful? What strategies would you have suggested if you were the principal?

Case No. 2

Josh Hanger is chair of the social studies department at Great Harbor High School. He is meeting with the principal, Barbara Thompson, to discuss a problem. "We're reviewing history texts," Hanger said. "The book we're using is out of date, and there won't be a new edition out for a year or two. I've suggested we wait for the new edition, but about half the group wants to pick a book now."

"What's the problem with adopting a book that's available now?" Ms. Thompson asked.

"All of the books we've reviewed have problems. One of them is pretty good, but Alice Parsnip objected because it barely mentions minority groups and their contributions."

"Does it ignore all minorities?"

"Not all. There's some information on prominent African Americans such as Martin Luther King, Jr., and Rosa Parks but almost nothing on Hispanics and Asians."

"What about the other books?"

"They all have problems. One has a very difficult vocabulary. Delcie Snow said her students wouldn't be able to read it. Another book we looked at had factual errors. Marvin Bell objected to that. He thinks history books ought to be absolutely accurate. It seems there's no really good book available."

Ms. Thompson thought a minute. "It sounds like someone finds something wrong with every book you consider," she said. "If you're looking for a book that no one will object to, you may be out of luck."

"I know. They're very picky, but I don't want to force a book on them."

Ms. Thompson said, "It's not a matter of forcing something. The group has a problem and they have to find a way to solve it. They can stick with the book you've been using until a new edition is ready, or they can adopt a different title. But they have to agree. There is no perfect textbook, as I'm sure you know."

"So we'll keep talking. What if they can't agree?"

Ms. Thompson smiled. "Then it's your responsibility to make a decision."

Hanger winced and shook his head. "I hope it doesn't come to that."

"It won't if you're able to provide the leadership they need."

"I'll try."

"Good. Keep me posted."

Questions

1. Could Hanger use some of the techniques for resolving conflict described in this chapter to reach a decision about a history text? What strategies from negotiation, mediation, and arbitration might be adapted to help the group solve its problem?
2. What approach did Hanger use to select a text? How might he have structured the problem differently to avoid the stalemate that has occurred?
3. What is your opinion of Ms. Thompson's response to Hanger's request for help? Do you think she was helpful? If you were the principal, would you have handled the situation differently? Explain.

Case No. 3

Two teachers share a classroom at Grapevine High School. Alex Drummond teaches a first-year class in music appreciation, and Bonnie Deavers teaches second-year French. Ms. Deavers complained that Drummond left books out on the table she uses for recording equipment. When she spoke to Drummond about it, he promised to put his materials away but soon started leaving them out again. Ms. Deavers again spoke to him about it, and he told her that he doesn't have time to put the books back on the shelves. "We use those materials every day," he said, "and it doesn't make sense to put them away after every class. Can't you put your equipment on your desk?"

Ms. Deavers ultimately complained to the principal, Howard Jeffers. She claimed that she loses 5 to 10 minutes from every class period moving Drummond's materials. "The room has to be shared, and he ought to clean up so that the next person to use it won't have to take time to put his stuff away." Jeffers spoke to Drummond and asked him to start putting his things on the shelf after his class. "Just stop a little earlier so you'll have time to do it," he said. "It's not an unreasonable demand."

A week later Ms. Deavers was back in the principal's office. "He's leaving his things lying around again," she said. Jeffers inspected the room. The table was large. He thought it would hold both the recording equipment and three stacks of music books.

"What about sharing the table?" he asked.

Ms. Deavers was adamant. "I want him to move his books out of my way. If you can't see to it that he does that, then find me another room."

"She just wants control," Drummond said. "She can easily teach her class without having to move my books, but she insists on making a big deal out of nothing."

"I want to see both of you in my office after school on Thursday," Jeffers said. "We'll work this thing out."

Questions

1. If you were the principal, how would you proceed in the meeting on Thursday?

2. Is there an ideal solution to a dispute such as this one? If so, what is it?
3. This argument has the appearance of a power struggle. In a power struggle the goal is to win. Even though a compromise might be possible, one or both parties are determined to emerge victorious. Power struggles are difficult to resolve because the parties view a compromise as a defeat. How would you proceed in working with two teachers who are engaged in a power struggle? How would your approach differ from a situation in which the parties are receptive to reasonable suggestions for a solution?

REFERENCES

Contract administration: Understanding limitations on management rights. (1983). Eugene: University of Oregon, Center for Educational Policy and Management. (ERIC Document Reproduction Service No. ED 271842).

Coulson, R. (1986). *Arbitration in the schools: An analysis of fifty-nine grievance arbitration cases.* New York: American Arbitration Association.

Isenhart, M. W., & Spangle, M. (2000). *Collaborative approaches to resolving conflict.* Thousand Oaks, CA: Sage.

Masters, M. F., & Albright, R. R. (2002). *The complete guide to conflict resolution in the workplace.* New York: AMACOM.

Ombudsman Soothes Disputes. (2006, July 26). *Education Week,* p. 5.

Salmon, H. (1983, April). *A superintendent's perspective of the grievance process.* Paper presented at the annual meeting of the National School Boards Association, San Francisco. (ERIC Document Reproduction Service No. ED 251927).

Stryker (Ohio) Board of Education and Stryker Education Association, 119 LA 794 (2003).

Thompson v. Holy Family Hospital, 121 F.3d 537 (1997).

Twinsburg (Ohio) Board of Education and Twinsburg Support Staff, OEA/NEA, 119 LA 54 (2003).

14 TERMINATION AND REDUCTION IN FORCE

The emphasis in this book has been on how to improve teacher quality and performance through the application of sound principles of human resources leadership. This positive approach, when carried out consistently over time, will produce significant gains in the quality of instruction in schools.

However, there are times when less pleasant actions must be taken. When enrollments decline or funds are lost, reductions in force may be necessary, and when a teacher who appeared promising proves to be unable to manage a classroom successfully, termination must be considered. These actions are the subject of this chapter.

PLAN OF THE CHAPTER

The following topics are discussed in this chapter: (1) carrying out a reduction in force, (2) reduction in force and employees' rights, (3) dealing with employee misconduct, (4) dismissal and nonrenewal, (5) documenting unsatisfactory performance, and (6) rights of dismissed teachers.

CARRYING OUT A REDUCTION IN FORCE

The purpose of a reduction-in-force (RIF) policy is to permit the district to achieve necessary cutbacks in the number of employees on the payroll without disrupting services. That outcome is most likely to be achieved if a policy providing fair, efficient, and consistent procedures for carrying out cutbacks has been developed in advance of the need.

The need for a reduction in force usually arises as the result of loss of funding, dropping enrollment, or cancellation of a program. The steps involved in carrying out a reduction in force are illustrated in Figure 14.1. The process begins

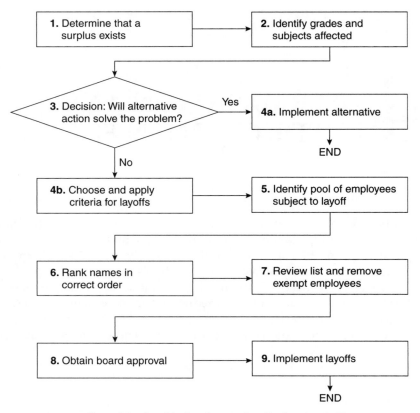

FIGURE 14.1   Steps Involved in Implementing Reduction in Force

when it is determined that the district has surplus personnel. The next step is to identify the programs, subjects, or grade levels with excess personnel. Personnel needs are calculated by grade level or program. A typical pattern might include these categories: elementary grades, secondary grades (by subject areas), special programs, support programs, other districtwide programs, an individual school, and administrative positions.

Suppose that enrollments have dropped in grades 9 and 10. It is necessary to determine which subjects have more teachers than needed. The chart in Table 14.1 summarizes (hypothetical) data on district enrollments and teacher supply for grades 9 and 10 in selected subjects.

According to the table, the district has five more teachers in grades 9 and 10 than are justified by the enrollments. Three departments have more teachers than the enrollment will support, but biology qualifies for one additional teacher. Mathematics stands to lose three teachers, and English will lose two. The approved teacher–pupil ratio for all departments is 1:20.

TABLE 14.1   Total Teachers and Excess Teachers in Grades 9
and 10 by Subject (Hypothetical District)

SUBJECT	NUMBER OF TEACHERS IN GRADES 9 AND 10	NINTH- AND TENTH-GRADE STUDENT ENROLLMENT	EXCESS TEACHERS
English	12	1,000	2
Mathematics	12	900	3
Biology	10	1,100	−1
French	4	300	1
Total	38	3,900	5

The next step in carrying out a reduction in force is to decide which individuals are subject to being laid off. In making those decisions, criteria chosen for this purpose are applied. The usual order of layoffs is as follows: (1) teachers without valid teaching certificates, (2) nontenured teachers with performance deficiencies, (3) nontenured teachers with the least seniority and, if necessary, (4) tenured teachers with the least seniority. A ranked list is prepared with names of teachers who are subject to layoff. These teachers are referred to as the "pool."

Once this list is prepared, human resources personnel examine it to determine whether any individual should be removed from the list. The coach of an athletic team or the sponsor of a student organization might be exempt from the reduction in force. Some teachers are exempt because they teach more than one subject and are needed in the second subject area. The completed list is submitted to the school board for approval, after which individuals subject to the layoff are notified. When the emergency is past, employees may be recalled in the reverse order of their release. For example, the teacher who was laid off last will be recalled first. In general, tenured teachers have the right of recall but probationary teachers do not. Probationary teachers may reapply for their jobs when the district begins hiring again, but they are not automatically reinstated.

Some flexibility in class sizes is necessary because enrollments don't always occur in convenient multiples of 20 or whatever number is preferred as the desirable class size. Some classes will end up with more students than the target figure, and some with less, but the average should come close to the target.

Reviewing Alternatives

Layoffs are a traumatic experience for the individuals involved. When layoffs occur, even employees who are not directly affected may experience feelings of depression and anxiety out of empathy for colleagues who are being laid off and feelings of concern for their own future security. It is sometimes possible to avoid the stress of layoffs by taking action to postpone or avoid the need to carry out a reduction in force. Among the actions to be considered are early retirement, unpaid leaves of absence, part-time employment, assistance in finding alternative employment, and retraining.

Early Retirement.   Early retirement is one of the most widely used methods for avoiding reductions in force because it solves the problem of surplus personnel without the trauma of layoffs. However, early retirement is expensive and is not always a satisfactory solution. It works best when enrollments are declining at an equal rate in all grade levels and programs and when the district has a relatively large number of employees nearing retirement age. If personnel surpluses are concentrated in a few programs or grade levels or if few individuals are close to retiring, early retirement is less likely to be a viable solution.

Leaves of Absence.   Unpaid leaves of absence have the advantage of allowing employees to continue in-force insurance policies that are provided by the district. An employee is thus able to secure health insurance for self and family at rates below those that are available to individuals. Normally, the individual must pay the premium for the policy, but in some instances that cost is borne by the district. Employees on unpaid leave will be reinstated if a position is available at the expiration of the leave. Unpaid leaves offer psychological support at a crucial time by letting employees know that the district still values their contributions and wishes to continue the employer/employee relationship.

Part-Time Employment.   Half-time or substitute positions are sometimes offered to employees who otherwise would be laid off in the belief that most people would rather work part time than not work at all. If one position is assigned to two half-time employees, both have some income, whereas an employee who is laid off receives no income. As a temporary measure to give employees time to find alternative employment, half-time work helps.

Job Hunting Assistance.   Providing assistance to help individuals who are laid off find new jobs is a psychologically sound strategy because it motivates these employees to take action and move forward. Employees who receive layoff notices are sometimes immobilized by the hope that they will quickly be recalled. Rather than trying to find another job, they sometimes waste months waiting for a recall notice. Beginning a systematic and wide-ranging job search can help them cope more realistically with their situation by assessing their strengths and examining their options.

Retraining Teachers.   Retraining teachers who are about to be laid off is a viable strategy if enrollments in the subjects in which they are retrained are expected to remain stable. Teachers who are near being certified in critical subjects are sometimes allowed to begin teaching classes in those subjects on temporary teaching certificates while they continue taking courses to qualify for full certification. However, teachers who lack the necessary subject matter competence should not be permitted to teach until they acquire it.

Staffing Adjustments Required

When a reduction in force takes place, principals are required to make adjustments in staffing by redistributing instructional and noninstructional assignments among the remaining staff members. In the case of elementary schools, this may involve nothing more than reducing the number of classes in the affected grade levels and reassigning students, but it often involves much more. In middle and high schools, principals are faced with making adjustments in the master schedule to reflect shifting enrollment patterns brought about by the elimination of some course offerings. For example, if fewer classes are offered in the business education department because of staff reductions, existing classes in that department as well as in other departments may increase in size, as a result of the reduced number of elective options available to students.

These changes in enrollment patterns also have implications for the purchase of equipment, materials, and supplies. If business education classes increase in size, it may be necessary to purchase additional computers to accommodate the increased enrollment.

If teachers who were laid off were sponsors of student clubs or activities, it will be necessary for the principal to arrange to recruit other teachers to take over those duties rather than let the programs languish. If the layoffs involved non-teaching personnel, such as guidance counselors, the principal must see to it that the workload is redistributed equitably among remaining staff members.

The decision to carry out a reduction in force is not an easy one, but it is simple compared to the difficulty and distress that faces an administrator who attempts to terminate a teacher. A subsequent section addresses the topic of teacher discipline and termination.

REDUCTION IN FORCE AND EMPLOYEES' RIGHTS

Collective bargaining agreements and state statutes grant certain rights to employees who are subject to being laid off. These rights include privileges earned through seniority, the opportunity to continue health insurance in effect at the employee's expense, and future reinstatement when funding permits.

When a reduction in force is necessary, teachers with less seniority are generally laid off before more senior teachers. If the district decides to lay off a more senior level teacher while keeping one with less seniority, it should be prepared to defend the decision.

Under collective bargaining agreements in many school districts, employees who are threatened with layoffs may replace or "bump" an employee with less seniority. However, this right has limitations. The bumping teacher must possess a valid certificate to teach the subject taught by the teacher being bumped and must have more seniority than the bumped teacher. It is common to require teachers who bump other teachers to have had recent and successful experience teaching the subject to which they are requesting to transfer. In some districts, the bargaining agreement gives the principal of the school receiving a replacement teacher the prerogative of reviewing the transferring teacher's credentials to determine whether that individual's qualifications are sufficient to maintain program quality. In districts with such a policy, a teacher who received certification to teach a subject many years earlier but has never taught in that field and has taken no recent coursework would not be permitted to replace a teacher with more up-to-date credentials and experience.

Minority employees who have been hired under affirmative action programs often have the least seniority in their districts and, therefore, are most vulnerable to reductions in force. Bargaining agreements sometimes provide protection from layoffs for these individuals. In one case involving such a policy, the Supreme Court held that the board failed to show a "compelling purpose" in arguing that past societal discrimination justified the plan and so rejected it. The Court stated

> Societal discrimination alone is [not] sufficient to justify a racial classification. Rather, the Court has insisted upon some showing of prior discrimination by the governmental unit involved before allowing limited use of racial classifications in order to remedy such discrimination (*Wygant* v. *Jackson (MI) Board of Education*, 1986).

However, in a case tried under Title VII of the Civil Rights Act, the Supreme Court upheld a plan that benefited individuals who had not been identified as actual victims of discrimination (*Geier* v. *Alexander*, 1986).

DEALING WITH EMPLOYEE MISCONDUCT

School employees on the whole abide by the law and carry out their responsibilities conscientiously and with relatively few errors in judgment. However, when a staff member breaks the law or exercises poor judgment, the individual's supervisor has the duty to initiate corrective action. Minor infractions by staff members usually are handled informally at the school level, but more serious offenses are referred to central administration or to law enforcement authorities. Whether the resolution of the problem involves district administrators or law enforcement officials depends on the nature and seriousness of the offense and provisions of the law, board policy, and the master contract. Needless to say, administrators who have responsibility for human resources leadership need to be familiar with all provisions of the contract and board policies that deal with employee conduct.

The purpose of employee discipline is to educate employees and prevent future violations of school policies. The goal is not to punish the rule breaker. Nothing is gained if an employee believes that the disciplinary action was unfair, unduly harsh, or carried out for the purpose of retribution. If the episode results in an employee who feels alienated, the disciplinary action will not have been successful.

Types of Offenses

Actions of staff members that require disciplinary action fall under one of three levels of severity. The least severe type of offense includes actions that are inappropriate or reflect poor judgment but that require no action by the administration other than a reminder. Occasional absence from work and tardiness fall into this category. Failure to turn in information on student attendance, failure to issue receipts for money brought by students, and missing meetings are examples of offenses that belong in the least severe category. However, these offenses can escalate into actionable charges if repeated often enough.

More serious offenses include the use of inappropriate language with students, parents, or colleagues; leaving the school during the school day without signing out or notifying the office; carrying a concealed weapon in school; conducting fund-raising activities without securing advance approval; abusing drugs or alcohol; leaving students unsupervised; and using excessive force with a student. For these offenses, teachers would receive a written reprimand to be placed in the personnel file. The Montana Code identifies eight offenses for which teachers may receive a written reprimand (www.data.opi.state.mt.us/bills/mca/20/4/20-4-110.htm). Among these are incompetency, neglect of duty, conviction of or a guilty plea to a crime of moral turpitude, nonperformance of the employment contract, and making a false statement.

The most serious offenses are those for which a staff member may be suspended (with or without pay) or terminated. Among the offenses in this category are committing a felony or morals offense, taking money from school funds for personal use, misrepresenting one's professional credentials, and being drunk on the job. Repeated offenses of a less serious type may also result in suspension.

Levels of Discipline

Disciplinary actions start with a conference between the staff member and his or her immediate supervisor. The conference serves three purposes: (1) to collect information about the precipitating incident and hear the staff member's explanation, (2) to explain to the staff member the reasons that the behavior is unacceptable, and (3) to inform the staff member of disciplinary actions to be taken and warn of more severe consequences in the future should the behavior be repeated.

Verbal Reprimand.   The mildest disciplinary action for a staff member who has violated a school board policy or a provision of the master contract is a verbal reprimand. When issuing a verbal reprimand, the supervisor identifies the action that violated the policy or contract and informs the staff member that this is a verbal reprimand. The supervisor then warns the staff member to avoid repeating the behavior and suggests the possibility of more severe consequences if the behavior recurs.

Written Reprimand.   Above the verbal reprimand is a written reprimand, which consists of a letter addressed to the employee that identifies the action that is in violation of the law, policy, or contract. Typically the letter presents a detailed description of the action or actions for which the employee is being reprimanded, including dates and times, and identifying any other persons who were involved. The letter also cites the specific provision or provisions of board policy or the master contract that the employee violated. Finally, the staff member is urged not to repeat the behavior and is warned of more serious consequences should that happen. A written reprimand is placed in the staff member's personnel file but may be removed after a period of time if the behavior has not been repeated. Exhibit 14.1 shows a sample format for a written reprimand.

EXHIBIT 14.1

SAMPLE OF A WRITTEN REPRIMAND

Date: February 15, 2007

TO: MaryAnn Witcher, fifth-grade teacher

FROM: Helen Maness, Principal

SUBJECT: Written Reprimand

This is an official reprimand issued to you for leaving your class unattended on February 13 for approximately 15 minutes while you made a telephone call from the teachers' workroom. Another teacher went into your classroom while you were out to ask your students to be quiet and return to their seats. This is the second time you have left your class. After the first time, you were counseled about the importance of remaining in your classroom at all times when students are present.

I remind you that leaving your class unattended results in a loss of instructional time for your students and causes disruptions for other classes. It also creates a risk of injury for your students. In the event that in the future an emergency arises that requires you to leave the classroom for any reason, you are to notify the office and wait in the room until someone is able to relieve you.

Leaving your class unattended in the future may result in more severe disciplinary action, including the possibility of a suspension.

_____ Date _____
Signature of Supervisor

_____ Date _____
Employee's Signature

(By signing, you acknowledge having received a copy of this written reprimand; your signature does not indicate that you agree with the contents. You may submit a response to this memorandum, which will be attached, and both placed in your personnel file.)

Involuntary Leave. Employees who are accused of or charged with breaking the law may be placed on leave until the case is resolved. The leave may be with or without pay, depending on the seriousness of the offense. When an employee is suspended without pay, the individual's salary is held in escrow until he or she is cleared or found guilty. If found guilty of a moral offense, abuse, or misuse of public funds, the employee will be terminated and may have his or her professional license revoked.

DISMISSAL AND NONRENEWAL

Many employers operate under an employment-at-will doctrine that allows the employer to terminate an employee at any time for any cause or no cause. The employer who is protected by the doctrine incurs no legal liability for terminating an employee. The exception to employment-at-will occurs when an employee is under contract or is protected by statute (Sovereign, 1999). Nontenured teachers are usually employed under contract, and if a district determines that the teacher's performance is not satisfactory and acts to terminate the individual before the contract expires, the district generally must be prepared to defend its action. The exception occurs if a teacher is hired without a written or implied contract.

Nonrenewal occurs when a nontenured teacher's contract expires and the district chooses not to renew it. No reason need be given, and the teacher generally has no recourse. Administrators should exercise care not to imply to an employee that his or her contract will be renewed. Suggesting that a contract will be renewed is referred to as an *implied contract* and may require that the district furnish reasons for its decision not to renew the individual's contract (Sovereign, 1999).

An administrator who initiates action to terminate a tenured teacher should be familiar with the applicable policies, contract provisions, and statutes and should be prepared to follow the procedures prescribed in those documents without deviation, including strict adherence to timelines. The district superintendent must recommend termination and the board must approve. Acceptable reasons for terminating a teacher are specified in most state codes. If a teacher is dismissed for a reason that does not appear in the code, a persuasive rationale will be needed to avoid a reversal of the decision in court.

State statutes identify specific causes for which teachers may be dismissed. Arizona law states that a teacher who is charged with unprofessional conduct, conduct in violation of laws or rules, or inadequate classroom performance must be given specific examples of the actions or omissions that led to the charge and a list of the rules or laws that the teacher is alleged to have violated. The purpose of this provision is to allow the teacher to prepare a defense. Arizona also grants any teacher receiving such a notice the right to a hearing (Dismissal of Certificated Teacher, 2000).

According to the American Federation of Teachers, the five most common reasons for dismissing teachers reported by union officers for the years 1993–1996 (from more to less frequent) were incompetence, physical or mental incapacity, insubordination, professional misconduct, and conviction of a crime. Abuse of drugs or alcohol was also frequently cited as cause for dismissal. These reasons are discussed below.

Incompetence refers to lack of ability, knowledge, or fitness. An inexperienced person may lack skill but is likely to improve over time, whereas someone who is an incompetent performer seldom improves noticeably unless remediation is available. In evaluating competence, we normally consider what are called the "essential tasks" of a position. For a computer programmer, these tasks include the ability to use programming language to produce desired results, and for a baseball player, essential tasks include hitting and fielding the ball. Essential tasks for a bus driver are collecting fares, operating the bus safely, and adhering to a schedule.

The essential tasks of teaching are preparing lesson plans, presenting information, and producing learning in the students. However, there are other expectations of teachers that are equally as important as these tasks. Teachers are professionals, and, as such, they are expected to place the well-being of their clients (the students) above other considerations. Teachers are guided in their work by a statement of ethics that defines their responsibilities as professionals. The Code of Ethics published by the National Education Association holds teachers responsible for protecting students from conditions that are harmful to their health and safety and for allowing students access to varying points of view. Codes of ethics issued by the National Education Association and enacted by the states of Texas and Minnesota are available online. (See the Online Resources section at the end of this chapter.)

Teacher Dismissal

Some administrators claim that the protections enacted to safeguard teachers' academic freedom make it difficult or impossible to dismiss those few who are incompetent. They say that the elaborate procedures involved in documenting poor performance are so time consuming and the chances of success so small that they have given up trying. However, in spite of such claims, it is possible to remove incompetent teachers when administrators take the time to prepare documentation and adhere closely to the procedural details. In hopes of making it easier to remove poor teachers, some legislatures have eliminated tenure for teachers, substituting in its place a renewable two- or three-year contract.

If sound selection and evaluation procedures are in place and working well, there should rarely be a need to dismiss teachers. Yet, even when care and thought are exercised in selecting and placing teachers, and when opportunities for professional growth are provided, there will still be a few who do not perform the job satisfactorily or who lapse into substandard performance after a time. Districts should monitor the performance of all teachers and be prepared to take action against those few who fail to meet their standards of performance.

School boards review recommendations for dismissal of school employees and decide whether the action is warranted. Traditionally, boards have also heard appeals of a decision to dismiss an employee. Teachers believe that school boards have a conflict of interest that lessens the chance that a person who is terminated will receive a fair hearing. As a result of these concerns, legislatures in more than half of the states have in recent years enacted laws to change the procedures by which termination decisions are made and appeals heard (Lopez & Sperry, 1994).

A variety of alternative practices for ensuring due process to teachers who have been terminated have emerged to replace the practice of lodging all authority with school boards. In most of the states that have revised their procedures, hearing officers or panels, usually individuals with legal training who are not employees of the board, serve as objective fact-finders, and school boards determine whether the facts justify dismissal of an employee. In a small number of states, school boards have been removed from the process of teacher termination altogether (Lopez & Sperry, 1994).

Immoral or Unprofessional Behavior

Dismissing a teacher on grounds of immoral or unprofessional conduct places on the board the burden of showing that the teacher's behavior had an adverse impact on students or other teachers. There is no absolute standard against which such behavior is judged. Rather, the courts take into account such factors as age and maturity of the students, degree of adverse impact, motive for the behavior, and the likelihood that it will be repeated.

Teachers have been discharged on grounds of immoral behavior for engaging in sexual misconduct with students. Some courts have held that when sexual involvement occurs between teacher and student, a presumption of adverse impact is justified without additional proof (McCarthy & Cambron-McCabe, 1987). Other examples of immoral behavior for which teachers have been discharged are physical abuse of students, use of profanity, misconduct involving drugs or alcohol, and misappropriation of funds.

A homosexual lifestyle has been allowed as grounds for dismissal of teachers in some cases but not in others. As a general rule, private sexual behavior, whether homosexual or heterosexual, is allowable as grounds for dismissal only to the extent that it affects the individual's effectiveness as a teacher.

Insubordination

Insubordination is a lawful cause for dismissal of teachers in many states. Actions that may be construed as insubordinate include failing to follow rules and regulations pertaining to use of corporal punishment, absenteeism, tardiness, and failing to complete required reports.

Insubordination also includes a teacher's refusal to perform properly assigned duties. Administrators may assign duties that are not specified in a bargaining agreement as long as they are reasonably related to the instructional program and are not unduly time consuming or burdensome. However, a teacher may not lawfully be dismissed for refusing to perform duties for which he or she lacks competence or that are unrelated to the school program.

Some courts have held that a single incident of insubordination is sufficient to justify dismissal. A teacher in Kansas was dismissed after he had his wife call the school to report that he was ill while he was actually in Texas interviewing for another job. The teacher had earlier requested and been denied leave. The principal of the school at which the teacher taught learned of the deception when the principal of the Texas school in which he interviewed called for a recommendation. The Kansas Court of Appeals upheld the decision to terminate the teacher's contract, noting that a single incident of insubordination could be sufficient to justify termination (*Gaylord v. Board of Education*, 1990). A similar conclusion was reached by the Colorado Supreme Court, which held that a district was justified in dismissing a teacher who had used profanity in front of several students after having been ordered by the superintendent to refrain from doing so (*Ware v. Morgan County School District*, 1988).

A board is most likely to win a legal test of a decision to dismiss a teacher for insubordination if it can show that the teacher knew about but repeatedly violated a rule, regulation, or directive, thereby causing harm to the school. The board's case will be further buttressed if the teacher's behavior is considered irremediable.

DOCUMENTING UNSATISFACTORY PERFORMANCE

Most teachers occasionally violate school rules, but most of those violations are minor and many of them are ignored by principals. When serious or repeated violations occur, however, the principal is obligated to take action. Reports of classroom observations and disciplinary conferences with a teacher should be shared with the teacher and a copy placed in the teacher's personnel file. The teacher's signature on the report indicates that he or she has read it. In any notes written after a conference with a teacher, it is wise to describe suggestions made to help the teacher avoid future rule violations or to improve his or her performance. Placing comments in a teacher's file without a signature is risky. When a dismissal action reaches court, the teacher's attorneys routinely check personnel files looking for notes the teacher may not have seen. If they find any, they are often successful in having the case dismissed.

When a parent registers a complaint about a teacher, it is advisable to keep a record describing the complaint and noting any follow-up action taken by the principal. Follow-up actions might include a conference with the teacher or a joint conference with both teacher and parent. Agreements reached in such meetings should be documented in a memorandum with a copy for the teacher. The principal should also send a note to the parent explaining the action taken.

Surprisingly, principals have been known to recommend a teacher for termination even though the same principal had previously rated the teacher's performance as satisfactory or better. It's difficult to convince a judge that a teacher whose performance was rated satisfactory for several years suddenly became incompetent. To build a sustainable case for termination, a principal should be able to show that the teacher's evaluations were always low or had declined steadily over time.

RIGHTS OF DISMISSED TEACHERS

A district may refuse to renew the contract of a nontenured teacher without stating reasons for the decision, except in states with statutes that require notification. Tenured teachers, however, are entitled to certain protections prior to dismissal. Successful dismissal of a tenured teacher requires that the district strictly observe these procedural requirements.

The following list enumerates the due process protections that are provided tenured teachers by various state statutes (Cambron-McCabe, 1983):

1. A statement of charges
2. Access to evidence and names of witnesses
3. A choice of an open or closed hearing
4. Opportunity to be represented by counsel
5. Opportunity to introduce evidence, call witnesses, and cross-examine those witnesses
6. A transcript of the hearing on request
7. A written decision
8. Right of appeal

A teacher may be suspended without a hearing if his or her presence in the school represents a potential threat to students or other persons, or if the individual is charged with a crime involving moral turpitude.

The Constitution grants certain rights to all American citizens, and employees are protected from employers' actions that infringe on those rights. The Fourteenth Amendment provides that government shall not "deprive any person of life, liberty, or property without due process of law." Tenured teachers and nontenured teachers under contract have potential property and liberty interests that are jeopardized by termination, and thus they are entitled to procedural due process before being terminated. Due process involves, at a minimum, notice of charges and an opportunity for a pretermination hearing at which evidence must be presented to show that the charges are true and support the proposed action.

Teachers who are threatened with dismissal are often given the option of resigning in order to avoid embarrassing and damaging publicity. Administrators should use care in attempting to persuade a teacher to resign because courts may view the resignation as coerced and order the teacher reinstated. Courts have held that when an employer makes working conditions so unpleasant that an employee resigns rather than continue to work under such adverse conditions, the employer's action is unfair. Employers can avoid such an outcome by counseling and, if necessary, disciplining employees for cause rather than trying to force them to resign. If an employee can demonstrate that an employer's actions were taken for the purpose of forcing the employee to resign and conditions were so bad that the employee had no choice, then the employer may be held liable (Thorne, 1996).

If the behavior that leads a board to consider dismissing a tenured teacher is considered remediable, the board has an obligation to postpone taking action to allow the teacher to correct the problem. The board's decision on the question of remediability is subject to judicial review. Administrators are advised to assume that problem behavior is remediable and to allow the teacher an opportunity to correct it. The teacher should also be offered assistance to make the needed changes. There is no absolute standard for deciding how much time a teacher should be allowed to correct a problem. Five weeks was found by a court to be insufficient in one case, and eight weeks was judged adequate in another case.

SUMMARY

Reduction in force is a management tool districts may use to achieve cost reductions while maintaining services. The steps involved include determining that a personnel surplus exists and identifying the departments or programs to be targeted for cutbacks. Nontenured teachers are released before tenured teachers, and those with less seniority before those with more seniority. Employees who violate district policies or state law are subject to discipline using a graduated series of actions ranging from the least serious (verbal reprimand) to the most severe (suspension or termination). Nontenured teachers who work under contract may not have their contracts renewed without cause when the contracts expire. Tenured teachers who are terminated have certain due process rights that must be observed. Nontenured teachers released while their contracts are in effect have similar rights. State laws specify the offenses for which a district may terminate tenured teacher, which include immoral or unprofessional conduct and insubordination.

SUGGESTED ACTIVITIES

1. Select a state and locate that state's code on the Internet and determine what due process rights are guaranteed to tenured teachers who are dismissed from their jobs in that state. Compare your findings to those of others in your class who chose different states.

2. In which of the following situations is a written reprimand of the employee appropriate? Select one of these situations and prepare a written reprimand to be issued to that employee.

a. A teacher was absent from school for the third time this year without notifying the school office.

b. A teacher called a student a "little terrorist" after the student cursed the teacher for insisting that he stay after school for misbehaving in class.

c. A school bus driver ran a red light and collided with a van while on his way to the school to pick up students. The bus driver said that his brakes had failed. A police officer at the scene said that the bus driver appeared to be intoxicated. He was charged with reckless driving. No children were in the bus at the time of the accident.

d. A physical education teacher collected money for gym outfits. Six students complained that they had given the teacher money but had not received their outfits. The teacher disputed their claims and said none had given her money. The students were not able to produce receipts. Other students in the class said that the teacher did not always give receipts.

3. Mark Willett is principal of Grove Avenue School. Ronnie Bowen, a teacher at the school, asked for educational leave to attend a one-day workshop on teaching about the Holocaust. Willett denied the request, explaining that the only paid leave offered by the district is for personal illness. On the day of the workshop, Bowen called in sick. Willett suspects that Bowen used the day to attend the workshop, but he can't prove it. However, another teacher, Deborah Matthews, attended the workshop on her own time (no pay). Willett is considering asking Ms. Matthews whether Bowen was present at the workshop. Do you believe he should or should not do that? What ethical questions are raised by this case?

4. Explain how dismissal under a reduction-in-force policy differs from termination of a teacher for cause.

5. Examine Table 14.1 and answer this question: The district employs four French teachers, one more than is justified by enrollment. However, the district may have to keep all four of these teachers on the payroll. Why might it not be possible to release a French teacher?

ONLINE RESOURCES

Minnesota Code of Ethics for Teachers and Code of Ethics for Administrators (www.mnstate.edu/howell/310/310rcs/ethics.pdf)

The Minnesota Code of Ethics for Teachers is a concise set of 10 ethical principles governing teachers' relationships with students, parents, and others. Among the issues addressed in this code are misrepresenting one's qualifications, disclosing confidential information about individuals, and using relationships for personal advantage.

National Education Association Code of Ethics (http://www.nea.org/code/html)

The code describes the responsibility of professional educators for students' health, safety, and learning.

Texas Educators' Code of Ethics (www.tcta.org/capital/sbec/codeapproved.htm)

The code is organized in three sections: (1) ethical conduct practices and performance, (2) ethical conduct toward professional colleagues, and (3) ethical conduct toward students.

CASE STUDIES

Case No. 1

Jeff Pritchard is a first-year principal at Brady Road Middle School. He asked for a conference with you, the director of human resources, to discuss a teacher whose performance he describes as "unsatisfactory."

The teacher in question is Roberta Mellon, who teaches history to fifth- and sixth-grade students. Ms. Mellon has 20 years experience in the classroom. Pritchard explained that Ms. Mellon's classroom management techniques are poor. He said that students are rowdy and inattentive in her class. He explained that he had met with Ms. Mellon on several occasions to discuss this problem and that her response was to send students out of the class, either to the office or simply to stand in the hall. "I told her that's not a solution," he said, "but she still does it. I want to initiate action to have her terminated. She is totally ineffective, and her problems are not remediable."

Questions

1. As director of human resources, you must decide whether to proceed with action to terminate this teacher. What additional information do you need in order to make that decision?
2. What is your opinion of the way Pritchard has handled this problem? Is there anything Pritchard might have done differently? Anything he didn't do that he might have done?
3. Do you agree with Pritchard that Ms. Mellon's problem is nonremediable?
4. What answer will you give Pritchard regarding his request?

Case No. 2

Sam Gray is associate superintendent for administration of Preston School District. He is meeting with central office staff members and school principals to discuss a problem. The district has 3,000 students and 170 teachers in five schools. Because of funding cutbacks, it is necessary to reduce expenditures for the coming fiscal year by $600,000. Gray must develop a plan to achieve the necessary savings. He is asking the group for suggestions.

GRAY: We have to implement a reduction in force because I can't think of any other way to save so much money. We're losing about 3 percent of our budget. If we lay off 12 teachers at an average salary of $52,500 each, including fringe, we'll save $630,000. Letting 10 go will save $525,000.

HAL CROCKETT (HIGH SCHOOL PRINCIPAL): Where will the 10 or 12 positions come from?

GRAY: That's what we have to decide. I've talked with Thomasina about going back to half-day kindergarten to save five positions, and if we eliminate drivers ed in the high school we can eliminate one more.

GEORGIA PRATT (DIRECTOR OF INSTRUCTION): We can increase class sizes in physical education at the high school from 30 to 35 students and make one of the assistant coaches part time. Those two things will save almost a full position. Eliminating one counselor at the high school will save another position.

THOMASINA WALTERS (ELEMENTARY SCHOOL PRINCIPAL): I think Hal should be able to get along nicely with two secretaries. I don't have a secretary and Hal has three. Also it might be possible to lay off one teacher at my school depending on how the enrollment falls.

CROCKETT: It looks like the high school is taking a beating here. I need those secretaries, Thomasina.

MS. WALTERS: I need a secretary too, Hal, but I manage to get along without one. You ought to try it.

CROCKETT: Not a chance.

MS. WALTERS: Seriously, I hate to see us give up full-day kindergarten. It helps my students get ready for first grade. Frankly, I'd rather see us eliminate foreign languages at the high school. That would cause less harm to students.

GRAY: That's a possibility. There are three foreign language teachers.

CROCKETT: Maybe one language, but not all three. I don't want to see the high school suffer all the pain. There should be cuts at all levels. How about getting rid of the school nurse at the elementary school and reducing the librarian to half time? Do you really need a full-time nurse and librarian?

MS. WALTERS: The nurse is already part time, Hal. And, yes, we do need a full-time librarian. How about shortening the school day by one-half hour and reducing teachers' pay? That way everyone shares in the pain.

MS. PRATT: We can't do that unless the board declares a financial emergency. I don't think they'll do that.

CROCKETT: We need to think long term. Increasing phys ed class sizes is manageable, and when the crisis is over, we can go back to smaller classes. But eliminating whole programs creates problems. If we do away with a foreign language, what about students who are going into the second year? What do they do—start over with a new language?

MS. PRATT: Eliminating whole programs is not the best way to go. Let's look for ways to make reductions that we can recover from without too much difficulty.

MS. WALTERS: What about the administrators? Are we going to make teachers carry the whole burden?

GRAY: What about that? We have two assistant principals on 11-month contracts. Could we cut them back to 10 months?

Questions

1. There are advantages and disadvantages to all of the reductions being considered. What is your opinion of the ideas discussed? Which cuts would you favor? Which would you oppose? Explain.
2. Ms. Walters and Crockett playfully suggest ways the other one can make cuts. But behind the joking they raise serious questions related to staffing and program priorities. What are your thoughts about the issues they raise?
3. What do you think of Gray's style in conducting this meeting? Suppose he had offered a plan to manage the budget reduction and asked for comments from the group. Would the results have been different? In what ways?
4. Gray now has a number of suggestions to work with in preparing a plan to manage the budget shortfall. Which of the proposals do you think he is most likely to include in his plan? Which will he probably veto?

REFERENCES

Cambron-McCabe, N. (1983). Procedural due process. In J. Beckham and P. Zirkel (Eds.), *Legal issues in public school employment* (pp. 78–97). Bloomington, IN: *Phi Delta Kappan*.

Dismissal of Certificated Teacher, Ariz. Rev. Stat. *ss* 5-15-539-E (2000). Retrieved from www.azleg.state.az.us.

Gaylord v. *Board of Education, School District 218*, 794 P.2d 307 (Kan. App. 1990).

Geier v. *Alexander*, 801 F.2d 799 (1986).

Lopez, C., & Sperry, D. (1994). *The use of hearing officers in public educator termination actions.* Salt Lake City: University of Utah, Utah Education Policy Center.

McCarthy, M., & Cambron-McCabe, N. (1987). *Public school law: Teachers' and students' rights* (2nd ed.). Boston: Allyn and Bacon.

Sovereign, K. (1999). *Personnel law.* Upper Saddle River, NJ: Prentice Hall.

Thorne, J. (1996). *A concise guide to successful employment practices* (2nd ed.). Chicago: CCH, Inc.

Ware v. *Morgan County School District*, 748 P.2d 1295 (Colo. 1988).

Wygant v. *Jackson Board of Education*, 476 U.S. 267 (1986).

INDEX